MARGERY KEMPE OF LYNN AND MEDIEVAL ENGLAND

By the same author:

The Early Church in Eastern England (1973)
The Early Church in Northumberland (1977)
The Early Church in Wessex and Mercia (1980)

Margery Kempe of Lynn
and Medieval England

MARGARET GALLYON

The Canterbury Press
Norwich

First published 1995 by The Canterbury Press Norwich
(a publishing imprint of Hymns Ancient & Modern Limited,
a registered charity)
St Mary's Works, St Mary's Plain,
Norwich, Norfolk, NR3 3BH

British Library Cataloguing in Publication Data

A catalogue record for this book is available
from the British Library

ISBN 1–85311–111–2

*Typeset by David Gregson Associates
Beccles, Suffolk
and printed in Great Britain by
St Edmundsbury Press Limited
Bury St Edmunds, Suffolk*

Preface

King's Lynn is an attractive and historic town in which to work. My journey to school would often take me past one or other of its historic buildings: St Margaret's Church, the Greyfriars Tower, the Guildhall of the Holy Trinity, the Guildhall of St George. It was always a delight too to teach in one of the upper-floor classrooms which overlooked the river, and, when the tide was high, to watch the ships sailing into the port, some of them brightly painted and coming from northern Europe or Scandinavia.

While teaching at the High School an unexpected parcel arrived one day from my brother, who was then teaching at Gordon College in Rawlpindi, in West Pakistan. The parcel contained a small book in the World's Classics series, *THE BOOK OF MARGERY KEMPE*, which he had purchased at a bookstore in Lahore. I read it with great enjoyment and interest, but was too occupied at the time teaching, preparing lessons and marking books, to give it my wholehearted attention. Some years later, however, with more time at my disposal, I reread it, and went on to obtain a copy of the Middle English version in the Early English Text Society edition, the study of which stimulated an interest in the medieval Christian mystics in general, both English and continental, and led eventually to this study of Margery Kempe and medieval England.

All the time I was writing this book and sifting through the mass of material available, I was conscious that what I was writing about so briefly and sketchily, could be expanded in much greater detail by scholars more knowledgable and competent than myself. This book, therefore does not pretend to be more than an introduction to Margery Kempe and medieval England, and it is to be hoped that others will follow it with further studies on the subject.

Various scholars and critics have read random chapters of my book and in particular I should like to thank Dr Paul Richards, an expert on King's Lynn, for his comments on all the material which relates to the town of King's Lynn.

Contents

St Margaret of Antioch, West Window, Mileham, Norfolk, c1350.

List of Illustrations

FULL-COLOUR

MONOCHROME

Acknowledgements

The author and publisher are grateful to the following for use of illustrations listed:
Colour photographs: © The Rickitt Encyclopedia of Slides, Nos. 1, 3 (top), 5; © Julia Hedgecoe, No. 4 (lower); Educational Productions, No. 7; Margaret Gallyon, front cover, Nos. 2 (two), 3 (lower), 4 (top), 6, 8.
Monochrome: by kind permission of the Syndics of Cambridge University Library, pp. 40, 65, 100, 204, 205, and (from *Parish Life in Medieval England* by Abbot F. A. Gaquet 1906) 184, 192, 198, 203; Cambridge City Library p. 16; The British Library, p. 8; Northallerton Library, p. 15; The Priest in Charge and Churchwardens, St Margaret's, King's Lynn, p. 73; Norfolk Library and Information Service, pp. 65, 80 (two), 82, 104; The Revd Martin Adams, Vicar of Sedgeford Church, p. 88; Longmans Group Ltd (from *The Medieval Monastery* by Marjorie Reeves) pp. 106, 111, 118, 126, 130; Dean and Chapter Library, Norwich Cathedral, p. 155; Mark Butler-Stoney, p. viii.

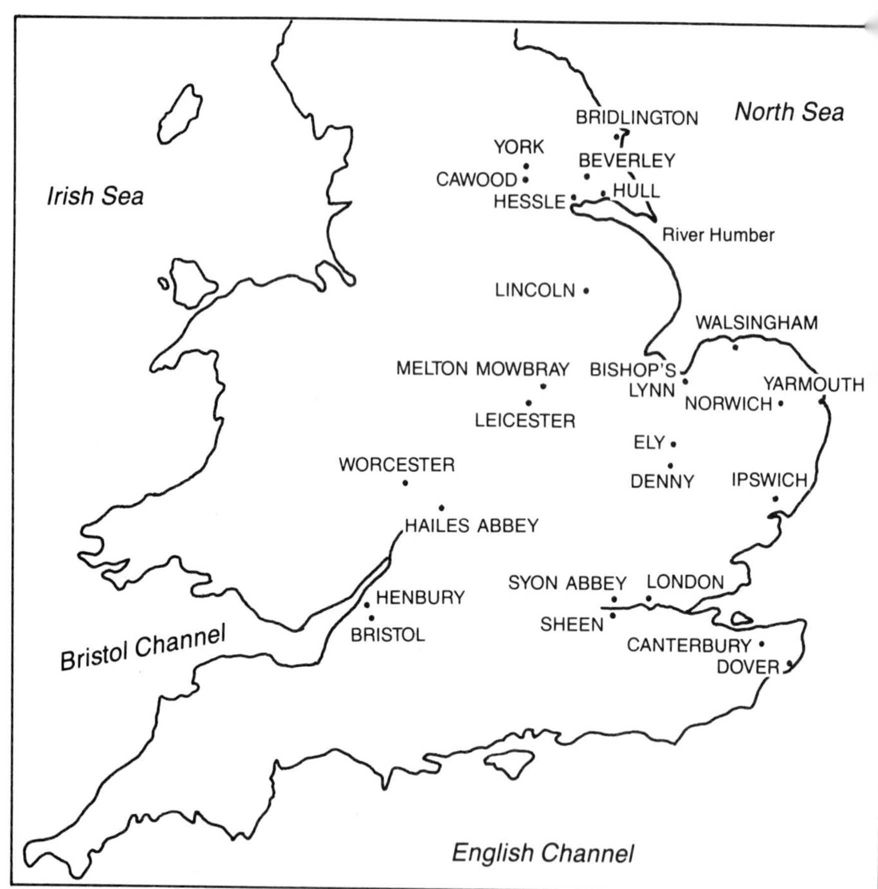

Places in England to which Margery Kempe travelled.

Introduction

In December 1934 a letter appeared in *The Times* from the American scholar, Miss Hope Emily Allen, announcing the discovery in the library of Colonel Butler-Bowden of Pleasington Old Hall, in Lancashire, of a complete manuscript of *THE BOOK OF MARGERY KEMPE*. This fascinating document had, in the words of Colonel Butler-Bowden, 'been in the possession of the present owner's family from time immemorial.' An entry, however, on the binding leaf, indicated that it had once belonged to the Carthusian priory of Mount Grace, near Northallerton in Yorkshire, where it was supplied with marginal notes. The Carthusian Order was a contemplative one, the brethren being devoted to prayer, austerity and silence and cherishing a profound interest in, and enthusiasm for works of devotional and mystical literature, into which category Margery Kempe's *BOOK* is to be assigned. Handwriting experts fixed the manuscript to a date around the middle of the fifteenth century, and believed it to be an early copy of the original manuscript penned by Margery's amanuensis between 1436 and 1438.[1]

The manuscript, now in the British Library, consists of a detailed account of the life, religious experiences and pilgrimages of this daughter of a wealthy and prominent citizen and burgess of King's Lynn – then Bishop's Lynn – in Norfolk. As a religious treatise Margery Kempe's *BOOK* stands in a class of its own, for in addition to furnishing us with some lofty spiritual teaching, she embeds that teaching into an autobiographical framework. This the other medieval writers of devotional treatises do not do. They give us systematic guides to the spiritual life and describe the stages by which the soul may attain to union with God through contemplative prayer, but they tell us little, if anything about themselves and their own spiritual journey. Not so Margery Kempe. She makes no attempt to emulate these masters of the spiritual life: Richard Rolle, Walter Hilton and others, but instead she tells her own personal story, 'how mercifully, kindly and lovingly our Lord Jesus Christ moved and stirred a sinful creature to his love.' [Proem]

Unlike the majority of medieval mystics and authors of spiritual guides, who were espoused to a celibate existence, Margery was a married woman and mother of a large family, and displayed a wonderful ability to combine her domestic and maternal duties with a life of prayer and religious devotion. Contemplatives of the English tradition were invariably monks, nuns, hermits or anchorites, their writings intended for, and dedicated to, men and women of similar style of life. But Margery's concern is with ordinary people living in the world and for these she has written her *BOOK* 'to bring them comfort and solace, and to help them to understand the indescribable love and mercy of our sovereign saviour, Jesus Christ.' [Proem] By her life of prayer and religious devotion she utterly refutes the notion that religion and mystical encounter with the Divine Being are for clergy and cloistered celibates only. Her approach to God is through Christ, and Christ, she believes, is for all people everywhere at all time. Though she may lack the profound spiritual insight and intellectual vitality of her contemporary mystic, Mother Julian of Norwich, who was her friend and counsellor, yet she writes with a freshness, sincerity and candour which goes straight to the heart. The very absence of artistry in her narrative contributes to its charm and authenticity.

The discovery of this long-lost manuscript was one of those happy finds which has delighted scholars in a variety of academic disciplines: English literature, social and ecclesiastical history, medieval theology and Christian mysticism. As Edmund Colledge comments, 'There is nothing about Margery Kempe which is not sensational: the very circumstances of her *BOOK*'s discovery startled the academic world.'[2] As well as being packed with amusing anecdotes, vignettes of real life and gems of spiritual wisdom, her *BOOK* contains numerous incidental references to the customs, conditions, fashions, beliefs and personalities of her day. She writes of crafts and trades and merchant guilds, of the brewing of ale and the milling of corn, of fashions in dress and hair-style, of pilgrimage and pilgrim ships, of religious festivals, ceremonies and processions, and of famous churchmen like Thomas Arundel, Archbishop of Canterbury, and Henry Bowet of York.

THE BOOK OF MARGERY KEMPE wonderfully epitomises the spirit of the Middle Ages, which was one of sharp contrasts and opposites. On the one hand it was an age of coarseness and brutality, of battle, murder, drunkenness and debauchery, while on the other it was an age of chivalry, of profound religious sentiment and delicacy of feeling, of tender devotion to our Lady and the Christ-Child, of compassion for the suffering Saviour, and an age of exquisite art and lovely lyric poetry. As Johan Huizinga states, 'it bore the mixed smell of blood and roses. The men of that time always oscillate between the fear of hell and the most naive joy, between cruelness and tenderness, between harsh asceticism and insane attachment to the delights of this world, always running to extremes.'[3]

A quaint and freakish figure Margery Kempe may sometimes appear to be, yet one cannot read her *BOOK* without forming the opinion that she was entirely sincere, an ardent lover of God and a genuine recipient of visions and divine locutions. As Edmund Colledge observes, 'When all the evidence has been taken into account, which she herself furnishes, of her many physical and mental disorders, still we have in her *BOOK* the autobiography of a soul who loved God, after its own extraordinary fashion, with a rare and pure single-mindedness.'[4]

Literary and Religious Influences

It would be impossible in this short survey of literary and religious influences to do adequate justice to the numerous mystics and contemplatives, theologians and authors of spiritual guides who contributed towards the shaping and development of Margery Kempe's religious life and thought. Indeed an entire book could be devoted to the subject. All that can be attempted here is a brief reference to those particular writings which she herself specifically mentions as having been read to her by her confessors and clergy friends, and in addition a selection of those others works, which because of their relevance and popularity, must certainly have been brought to her attention.

As a citizen of the flourishing seaport of Bishop's Lynn with its overseas contacts, its merchants and traders, its learned friars and clergy and its monastic establishments, Margery was at the heart of a culture which was both native and foreign. Although almost certainly unable to read herself, or only very little, the *BOOK* which she dictated to her scribe and secretary, provides abundant evidence that she moved among an élite company of scholarly and well-read clerics both in her home-town of Lynn and in Norwich and other religious centres to which she travelled. It was through these men who read to her that she had access to many important theological, devotional and mystical works of English and continental origin.

Margery Kempe herself belongs in the wake of the English school of medieval mysticism, which flourished in the fourteenth and fifteenth centuries, and which profoundly influenced her. Among this notable company of mystics and contemplatives were Richard Rolle, hermit of Hampole (1300–1349); Walter Hilton, an Augustinian canon of the priory of Thurgarton in Nottinghamshire, and author of the famous *Ladder of Perfection* (*c*1340–1396); the anonymous author of the *Cloud of Unknowing*, written in about 1370; and Dame Julian of Norwich (1342–*c*1416) author of the very fine work, *Revelations of Divine Love*.

Margery makes special mention of Richard Rolle's immensely popular Latin work *Incendium Amoris*, written in 1343, which she would have heard read to her either in an English translation, or translated direct from the Latin as the reader proceeded, her clergy friends being competent Latin scholars. To souls ablaze with love for God, like Richard Rolle, mystical signs and sensory phenomena, accompanied their prayers and contemplations, such as those of supernatural warmth which suffused their whole being, feelings of great sweetness and divine love, and the hearing of heavenly music, wholly other than any earthly music. There is much in Rolle's *Incendium* which finds an echo in Margery's mysticism as described in her *BOOK*, for she too was granted the same ineffable manifestations of the Divine Being.

Margery speaks of 'Hilton's book' by which she no doubt means his most influential work *The Scale (or Ladder) of Perfection*, a book of spiritual direction, written for a solitary nun, an anchoress and contemplative, though probably with a wider audience in mind. *The Scale* is a beautiful work of elegant English prose, humane in tone, sober and cautious in respect of emotional excesses, which may be said to characterise Rolle's *Incendium*.

Although the *Scale* displays wide learning and draws on many sources such a Sts Augustine, Bonaventure, Bernard, Aquinas and the Parisian School of St Victor, there is nothing pretentious and obscure about it, nor anything that an ordinary Christian layperson could not understand or benefit from reading. There are echoes of *The Scale* in Margery's *BOOK*; for example Hilton writes, 'turn your thoughts into your own soul where He is hidden, and seek Him there. For as the prophet says ... Truly, Lord, Thou are a hidden God' (Is 45.15).[5] Margery writes, 'Therefore, daughter, I am like a hidden God in your soul'. [Ch 84] Hilton's emphasis on the Blessed Manhood of Christ would have struck a special chord in Margery's heart, and so also the need for charity and humility. 'Try to learn humility and keep it, for it is the first and last of all virtues.'[6]

Margery refers to a further Latin work which enjoyed great popularity in the Middle Ages, *Stimulus Amoris* (The Prick of Love), which was read to her by a priest, newly arrived in Lynn, who lodged in the town with his mother. The book consists chiefly of a series of meditations on Christ's Passion, intended to stir the heart with love. Margery, in defence of her propensity to shed tears of compassion at the thought of Christ's suffering, quotes from the second chapter of this work. 'Why should I call upon you and cry anymore, for you delay and do not come to me, and I am weary of yearning and seem like a fool, since I am ruled by love and not by reason. I run eagerly wherever my love leads me, and those who see me deride me because ... they do not understand that a longing for Jesus burns in my heart.'[7]

Although Margery mistakenly attributes the *Stimulus Amoris* to St Bonaventure, as was commonly done, the very fact that she twice refers to this great scholar and Christian mystic, suggests that she may well have been familiar with some of his compositions, most notable among them the *Journey of the Mind into God*. Bonaventure, (1221–1274), a Franciscan friar, who studied, taught and preached at the University of Paris, was a man of brilliant intellect and author of many philosophical, theological and mystical works. Elected Minister General of the Order of St Francis in 1257, he was commissioned to write a biography of Francis, for whom he had great admiration. We may be sure that this popular biography of one of the best loved saints in the medieval world, would have been read to Margery Kempe in Lynn where the Franciscan friars would have been eager to promote their beloved Founder. Indeed in certain aspects of her devotional life it is clear that Margery is attempting to shape her conduct according to the pattern set by St Francis, especially when in Rome, in an extravagant gesture of generosity, she gives away all her money in order to become, like Francis 'bare for the love of Christ' or when she visits a leper-house and shows compassion for the inmates.

Margery makes no reference to the English devotional classic, *The Cloud, of Unknowing*, though it is unlikely that she was unfamiliar with this well-known spiritual work. There is one particular passage in her *BOOK* which is reminiscent of *The Cloud*. She writes of Christ's words to her, 'I take no heed to what you have been, but what you would be.' [Ch 36] The author of *The Cloud* writes, 'It is not what you are or have been that God looks at with his merciful eyes, but what you would be.'[8] The similarity between these passages suggests that Margery may have been drawing on the *Cloud* as a source of inspiration.

Neither does Margery make any mention of the popular little devotional tract *Remedies Against Temptation* by William Flete, of whom we shall hear more in chapter six. Yet there is much in Margery's *BOOK*, on the subject of temptation, which reminds us of Flete's *Remedies*, indicating that she was acquainted with the work. Written originally for a nun, this fourteenth century Austin friar, William Flete, is careful to impress upon the lady that, what may seem to her to be an excessive use of masculine language, is not really so. 'Sister, when I speak of man in this writing, take it for both man and woman, for so it is meant in all such writing, for all is mankind.'[9]

Apart from the books named by Margery as having been read to her, she speaks of 'other books such as these'. Among them we may be sure that the widely popular and influential devotional manual, *The Ancrene Riwle* (The Anchoresse's Rule) figured. An erudite work of the early thirteenth century, the RULE was addressed to three well-born ladies, embarking on an enclosed life as anchoresses, and is full of biblical references with allegorical interpretations. The work contains little on the subject of contemplation, which was of special interest to Margery, but emphasises instead the ascetic element of religion, dwelling much on the themes of confession and penance, mortification, sin and temptation. Margery could well have derived benefit from this book, though her mode of life as a married woman with children, living in the world would have been very different from that of the anchoress ladies and she certainly would not have been attracted to its markedly male chauvinist tone. The sisters are instructed not to speak to men, nor to preach to them, nor to advise them, nor to blame them, all of which Margery does not hesitate to do when she considers that their behaviour warrants it.[10]

Female saints and mystics who had been married were particularly appealing to Margery, since they, like her, had experienced the difficulties of sustaining a deep and strong spiritual life while at the same time fulfilling the duties and responsibilities of marriage. By far the most influential of these women was the Swedish saint, Bridget, whose book, *Liber Revelationum Celestium S. Birgitta*, was read to her, though not, we may imagine, in its entirety, since, Bridget's prolific writings cover eight volumes.[11]

Born in 1303, Bridget, at the age of thirteen was married to a nobleman, Ulf Gudmasson, and bore him eight children. Widowed at the age of forty one, she then spent a large part of her life in the city of Rome, devoting much of her time to prayer and meditation, caring for the sick and needy, intervening in ecclesiastical affairs, dispensing advice to popes and prelates and dictating her revelations to her confessors. Bridget is also notable for the founding of a religious order at Vadstena in Sweden, which provided the impetus for the establishment of further Brigittine houses in different parts of Europe, the most renowned of which was Henry V's foundation at Sheen on the bank of the Thames at Twickenham Park, eventually one of the wealthiest abbeys in England.

Those female visionaries, who, like Margery, had received the gift of tears, were of special interest and importance to her, one of whom was Marie of Oignies (1177–1213), born at Nivelles, in the diocese of Liège. Marie was married at the age of fourteen, dutifully complying with the wishes of her parents, though she had privately resolved to live a celibate life of religious devotion. She

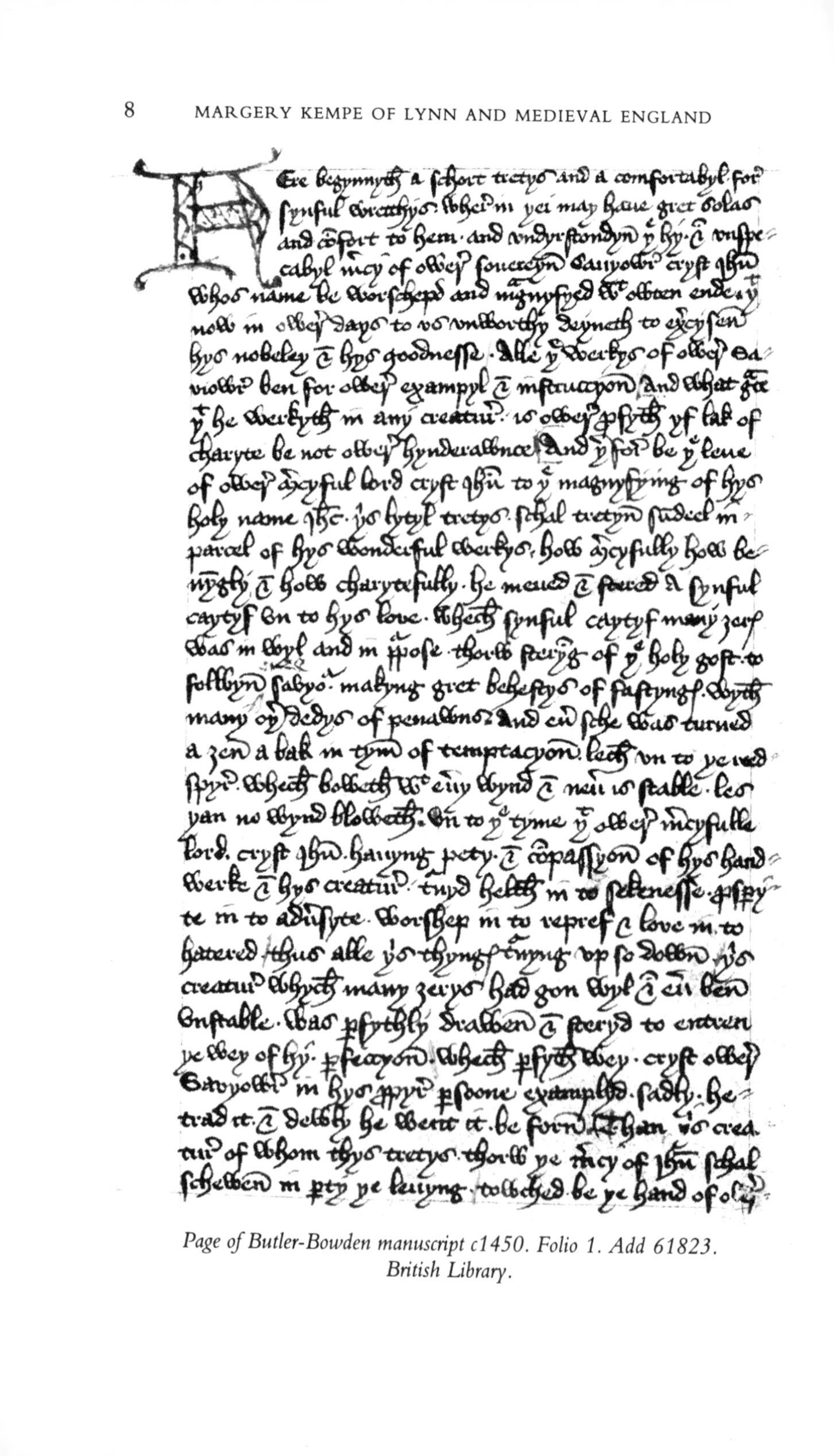

Page of Butler-Bowden manuscript c1450. Folio 1. Add 61823. British Library.

Here beginneth a short treatise and a comfortable, for
sinful wretches, wherein they may have great solace
and comfort to them and understand the high & unspe-
ekable mercy of our sovereign Saviour Christ Jesus,
whose name be worshipped and magnified without end,
that now in our days to us unworthy deigneth to exercise
his nobility and his goodness. All the works of our Saviour be for our example and instruction, and what grace that he worketh in any creature is our profit, if lack of
charity be not our hindrance. And therefore, by the leave
of our merciful Lord Christ Jesus, to the magnifying of his
holy name, Jesus, this little treatise shall treat somewhat in
part of his wonderful works, how mercifully, how be-
nignly & how charitably he moved and stirred a sinful
caitiff unto his love, which sinful caitiff many years
was in will and in purpose, through stirring of the Holy Ghost to
follow our Saviour, making great behests of fastings with
many other deeds of penance. And ever she was turned
again aback in time of temptation, like unto the reed-
spear which boweth with every wind and never is stable less
that no wind bloweth, unto the time that our merciful
Lord Christ Jesus, having pity & compassion of his hand-
iwork & his creature, turned health into sickness, prosperity into adversity, worship into reproof, & love into
hatred. Thus all these things turning upside down, this
creature, which many years had gone astray and ever been
unstable, was perfectly drawn and stirred to enter
the way of high perfection, which perfect way Christ our
Saviour in his proper person exampled. Sadly he
trod it and duly he went it before. Then this creature, of whom this treatise through the mercy of Jesus shall
show in part the living, touched by the hand of our Lord

Transcript in Modern Spelling (by author) of page reproduced opposite.

therefore persuaded her husband to take an oath of chastity, and together they occupied themselves tending the sick at a leper colony at Williambroux. With her husband's consent, Marie finally retired to a cell near to the church at Oignes, near Namour, where she lived in great austerity and virtue, and so intense was her love for Christ that she was unable to gaze at the crucifix or to hear Christ's Passion being recounted without dissolving into tears of pity and compassion.[12]

Another saint and visionary mentioned by Margery Kempe as possessing the gift of tears was Elizabeth of Hungary (1207–1231), the daughter of King Andrew II, and youthful bride of Ludwig IV, Count of Thuringia. Following six years of happy marriage and the birth of three children, Elizabeth's husband died while on Crusade, leaving his wife grief-stricken. She found consolation, however, in religion, renounced the world, made provision for her children, joined the Third Order of St Francis and devoted herself to serving the sick and the poor at Marburg, Hesse, placing herself under the stern and insensitive direction of her confessor, Master Conrad. 'But his methods did not break her spirit: she was humble and obedient, and bowed before every storm; and after it had passed she straightened up, strong and unhurt, like grass after heavy rain.'[13] Her death at the early age of twenty four and her noble character greatly endeared her to the German people, her canonisation taking place in 1235.

The book of visions and divine consolations of the great Italian mystic, Angela of Foligno (1248–1309) was almost certainly known to Margery, thought she makes no direct reference to it. Particular passages in Margery's *BOOK* are powerfully reminiscent of Angela's writings, often displaying striking verbal similarities, indicating a familiarity with her work. Converted from a life of worldliness and self-indulgence, Angela joined the Third Order of St Francis, embraced a life of poverty, discipline and prayer, and became the recipient of some remarkable visions and revelations which she dictated to her confessor, friar Arnaldo, who, in turn, translated them into Latin, thus extending their accessibility to various countries in Europe, including England. Like Margery, Angela was subject to loud and uncontrollable outbursts of crying whenever she looked upon a crucifix.[14]

Miss Hope Emily Allen has drawn our attention to yet another married female visionary, Blessed Dorothea of Prussia, born at Montau in Pomerania in 1347 and surviving until 1394, when Margery was about twenty one years old. Dorothea, Miss Allen believes, was a formative influence on Margery Kempe, and certainly there are strong resemblances between Margery's type of spirituality and Dorothea's. Dorothea was married at the age of sixteen to a Danzig burgess, produced nine children, only one of whom survived. She and her husband then too a vow of chastity, and Dorothea, like Margery, was permitted to receive weekly Communion. The death of her husband in 1390 freed her to follow her religious inclinations and to become a recluse at Marienwerder cathedral, where her learned confessor, John of Marienwerder, wrote an account of her life and visions. Vigorous trade links existed between Lynn and Germany, with the attendant exchange, not only of merchandise, but of literary works, cultural and religious ideas. Margery's travels and pilgrimages brought her to Danzig where she stayed for about six weeks, during which time local knowledge of Dorothea, whose cult was strongly in evidence at the time, would have reached her. Dorothea too was granted the gift of holy tears.

Margery's association with the Dominican friars in Lynn, especially with the anchorite who was her counsellor, confessor and supporter, would have ensured that she possessed some knowledge of the great Dominican mystics, female and male. It is unlikely that she was ignorant of the life and writings of the German mystic, Mechthild of Magdeburg in Lower Saxony (1212–1282), who for forty years lived as a beguine, the beguines being a loosely organised community of religious women, founded in the Netherlands in the twelfth century, spreading to Germany, France, Italy and Spain, whose members were celibate, though bound by no vows and free to marry if they wished. They devoted themselves to prayer and charitable works, were supported by gifts and endowments but also earned their living by manual work, spinning, weaving and so forth. While at the beguinage Mechthild imposed a strict regime of prayer and austerity upon herself, during which time she wrote her visions down in her native dialect, Low German, her Dominican confessor, Heinrich of Halle, organising her scattered sheets of writing into a book, *The Flowing Light of the Godhead*, which as well as containing her strange and wonderful visions, denounced the laxity of the clergy and the abuses of the Church, which attracted a great deal of opposition. 'No soul can be pierced by God's love without suffering' she declares. 'Christ did not say he would take away sorrow, but "I will turn your sorrow into joy".' Similarly Margery Kempe writes:

> **Our gracious Lady spoke to her in her soul ... 'Daughter, all these sorrows that you endure for me and for my Blessed Son shall be turned to great joy and bliss in heaven'.** [Ch 73]

Mechthild grieves for sinners and has a profound zeal to win souls, and by her prayers, hopes to save them from the power of Lucifer, and to constrain God himself in saving them.[15] So also Margery Kempe, on a Good Friday, prays long and earnestly for man's salvation.

> **'I ask nothing, Lord, except that which I know you may well give me, and that is to have mercy on the sins of the people ... for you are all love, Lord, and love brought you into this wretched world and caused you to suffer grievous pains for our sins ... I wish I had a well of tears to constrain you with, so that you would not take utter vengeance on man's soul and separate him from yourself for ever, for it is fearful thing to think that anyone on earth could ever sin so grievously that he could be parted from your glorious face for ever.'** [Ch 57]

Of the host of male mystics and visionaries, other than those she mentions, who influenced the spiritual life of Europe in the Middle Ages, we cannot say with any certainty which ones exerted an influence on Margery Kempe, except of course, St Francis of Assisi. But we may conjecture that the writings of the dominant figure of the twelfth century, St Bernard of Clairvaux, (1090–1153) were read to her by her teachers and confessors, his book *On the Love of God*, for instance, his *Sermons on the Song of Songs*, and his *Homily in Praise of the Virgin Mary*. We may surmise, too, that she would have had some knowledge of the great German Dominican male mystics: Meister Eckhart (1260–1327) and Johann Tauler (c1300–1361), and that most endearing of the

Dominicans, Henry Suso (1295–1361), a disciple of Eckhart. It was a woman, Elizabeth Stagel, a spiritually gifted Dominican nun of the convent of Tösse in eastern Switzerland who wrote Suso's so-called autobiography, she having requested that he tell her something about his sufferings from his own experience, so that she might be assisted in bearing her own accute afflictions. 'She was drawn by God with great devotion to learn about his life and doctrine. By unobtrusive questioning she learnt the nature of his conversion and then wrote it down, just as it is written.'[16]

But of all the books that influenced Margery, the Bible must take pride of place, the Bible being of very great importance throughout the Middle Ages. Judging by the large number of biblical references in her *BOOK*, her knowledge of the Bible was considerable. She informs us that her acquaintance with the Bible was obtained by hearing it read to her, by the discussions she had with her confessors on biblical topics, and by hearing sermons on biblical themes. The texts and stories which she had heard, were then committed to her sharp and retentive memory, and when opportunity arose, appropriately employed to admonish, rebuke or confound her adversaries, or to encourage and help her friends and supporters. When, for instance, she is reproved because 'she wept and sobbed wondrous sore' she instantly retorts with a verse from the Psalms, 'Those that sow in tears shall reap in joy.' (Ps. 126.5).

Apart from its literal and historical interpretation, the Bible was interpreted spiritually and allegorically, an excellent example of which exists in the Song of Songs, which literally appears to be a beautiful and poetic love song, but which was interpreted by medieval theologians, especially by St Bernard of Clairvaux, as an allegory of the love which Christ has for the Church and the Church for Christ, and also of the love which exists between Christ and the individual soul. A further example of the allegorical interpretation of biblical stories and texts is provided by a sermon preached by Herbert Losinga, Bishop of Norwich and founder of St Margaret's Church in Lynn. He was preaching on the Feast of the Epiphany, which celebrated the manifestation of Christ to the Gentiles, and had described how the wise men had visited, and worshipped the child, Jesus, and resolved not to return to King

Herod, but to go back to their own country by another way. Losinga continues 'This leaves an example to all who should come after, that they who wish to enter upon the way of salvation should in no wise return to Satan. We have left our country of ungodliness … and the uncleanness of our passions and actions. Let us return to our country by the way of faith, by the way of love, by the way of discretion, temperance, patient endurance and justice … In Holy Baptism we renounced the devil; let us not return to the devil. We are bound under an oath to Christ; let us abide in Christ. Let us offer him sincere devotion and a thorough mortification of vices.'[17]

We have listed some of the works of devotional literature which certainly influenced Margery Kempe, and suggested authors of other theological works which she may have heard read to her. In drawing attention to these sources, however, it should not be imagined that Margery herself lacks originality. We all build upon each other's foundations and are influenced by our predecessors and contemporaries. The medieval mystics themselves drew heavily upon earlier sources: the Bible, the writings of the Church Fathers, saints, mystics and theologians, yet each displayed a high degree of originality and each made his or her contribution to our knowledge of God and perception of divine truth. The reader of *THE BOOK OF MARGERY KEMPE* will discover ideas and sayings which occur in the writings of other mystics, yet this does not diminish the originality and value of her own writings. When all the literary and religious influences have been taken into account, there still remains in Margery Kempe a woman who had her own direct and authentic experience of God, which she describes so unaffectedly, and it is this which makes her BOOK so special to us. Nowhere in Christian literature is there a character quite like Margery Kempe, and nowhere is there a book of mystical devotion quite like hers.

AUTHOR'S NOTE

In my translations of the extracts from the *BOOK OF MARGERY KEMPE* I have endeavoured as far as possible to retain the character and spirit of the original Middle English, while at the same time clarifying any obscure expressions. My aim has been to produce a version which is neither so free as to be remote from the original, nor so literal as to perpetuate ambiguous meanings and to retain unnecessary repetitions. Margery's style is essentially plain and straightforward, and therefore much of my translation, I hope, remains true to the original, since no purpose would be served in providing alternative readings when the original is perfectly coherent.

Mount Grace Priory.

Denny Abbey, near Waterbeach, Cambridgeshire.
Engraving in Gent. Mag. Oct. 1828.

CHAPTER ONE

The Spiritual and Devotional Life of Margery Kempe

As a product of the later Middle Ages Margery Kempe was very much part of a religious trend, particularly strong among laypeople, which emphasised personal religion, the pursuit of virtue, the performance of good works and above all a direct encounter with God through prayer. The impetus for this had come partly from a growing sense of disillusionment with the institutional church, its abuses and corruption, its formalism and stress on outward observance, but also from an increasingly educated, independent and literate laity, who aspired to understand and interpret the Bible and the Christian message for themselves. Further impetus came from the reforming zeal of John Wyclif, a stern critic of the church, a champion of the laity and the instigator and supervisor of a translation of the scriptures into the vernacular. The later Middle Ages also saw a proliferation of devotional writings and spiritual handbooks of various kinds, such as studies of the life of Christ, the Virgin Mary, the church's feasts and festivals, the virtues and vices, the Ten Commandments, the creeds, the Mass, and books on prayer and the art of meditation.

Although these works were often addressed to religious professionals, to clergy, monks, nuns and anchorites, they became extremely popular among devout lay people. The mention of them in the numerous wills of the period confirms the ownership of them by a variety of lay folk: by great ladies and patronesses of religion, by wealthy merchants and traders like Margery's father and by ordinary literate lay men and women. Some of these books dealt with the more exalted types of prayer: meditation and contemplation to which Margery Kempe was specially attracted. It was the practice of this kind of prayer which distinguished the mystic and contemplative from the ordinary devout Christian. In the Preface of her *BOOK*, Margery tells us that the adversity she suffered at the hands of her enemies only served to draw her closer to Christ and to these supernatural kinds of prayer, in which her mind was elevated above the ordinary levels of consciousness to perceive divine mysteries.

> **The more slander and reproof she suffered, the more she increased in grace and devotion, in holy meditation and high contemplation, and the more wonderfully did our Lord converse with her in her soul, showing her how she would be despised for love of him, and how she should have patience and put all her trust in him,and give all her love and affection to him only.** [Proem]

Margery's meditations follow the traditional pattern recommended by all the foremost exponents of the spiritual life. The meditator was instructed, at the time of prayer, to adopt a posture of bodily comfort and composure, to pray first for the guidance and illumination of the Holy Spirit, then to reflect in stillness and silence upon some devout subject: a verse from Scripture, a saying of Jesus, an episode from his life, a passage from the Psalms and so forth. With the mind concentrated and wholly given to the selected topic one was then to allow the mind to be receptive to the guidance and instruction of the Holy Spirit.

To bring an episode into sharper focus one was encouraged to imagine oneself present as an observer or participator in the event, as did Margery when she was meditating on Christ's nativity, imagining herself helping to bind the Christ-child in swaddling clothes. Lastly, with the mind enlightened and the heart stirred, one was exhorted to make a firm resolution of will connected with the meditation: to serve God with heightened endeavour, to imitate Christ in this or that virtue, to emulate the humility of our Lady. In this way the emotions elicited by the meditation led the soul to spiritual action and had some kind of practical application.

It was upon the sufferings of Christ that the great teachers of the spiritual life particularly exhorted their disciples to meditate. 'At about midday if possible, if not then at some other time, meditate as fervently as you can on God's cross and on his grievous suffering' said the author of the *Ancrene Riwle*[1] Margery's meditations on the cross follow the events described in the gospel narratives and are interspersed with personal messages from Christ.

'Daughter, these sorrows, and many more, I suffered for love of you, and many pains, more numerous than anyone on earth can tell. Therefore, daughter, you have great cause to love me much, for I have bought you at a high price indeed.' [Ch 79]

Margery meditates on the sorrows of Mary and her grief at parting with her son as he goes to the cross.

'Alas, my dear Son, how shall I endure this sorrow, for I have no joy in all the world except in you only ... I would that I might suffer death for you, my Son, so that you would not have to die, if by that means men's souls might be saved ...' [Ch 79]

Then our Lord took his mother into his arms and kissed her most sweetly. 'Ah blessed mother, be of good cheer' he said, 'for I have often told you that I must suffer death, otherwise no one would be saved or ever come to heaven. It is my Father's will that this should be so. So let it be your will also, for my death will turn to my honour and glory, and you, and all who trust in my Passion, and work in its cause, will profit by it and have great joy ...

So now I pray you, beloved mother, bless me and let me go and do my Father's will, since it is for this cause that I came into the world and took flesh and blood of you.'

Margery proceeds to meditate on the various incidents relating to the Passion. Following Christ's death, his mother returns to her own home, and Margery, in her imagination, tries to comfort her and prepares warm gruel for her. But our Lady's grief is so profound she will take no food. She speaks only of her Son, and in what she says there is a beauty, a lilt and a pathos which make her words sheer poetry.

'Ah, daughter, I tell you truly there was never a woman on earth, who had such great cause to sorrow as I have, for there was never a woman in this world who bore a better child, nor a meeker child to his mother, than my son was to me.' [Ch 81]

Margery laments the indifference of many people to the sufferings of Christ. They weep and sorrow greatly at the loss of their friends and possessions, but they do not mourn the death of their Saviour.

> **Every day we see men and women crying and roaring and wringing their hands, as if they were out of their minds, because they have lost their worldly goods, or a friend or relation, or because they are preoccupied with some earthly love or carnal affection ... Alas, alas, that the death of a creature, who has frequently sinned and trespassed against his Maker, should be so greatly mourned, while the compassionate death of our Saviour, who has restored us to life, goes quite forgotten and unheeded by us unworthy wretches.** [Ch 28]

If Margery in her *BOOK* writes in greater detail of her meditations than her contemplations it is because the latter are of an altogether more lofty and spiritual nature than the former, and therefore more difficult, if not impossible, to describe in human language. Blessed Angela of Foligno, the thirteenth century mystic, gropes for words in an attempt to convey to her readers what her vision of God was like and what she perceived of him in her contemplations. 'I beheld God who spoke with me. But if you seek to know what I beheld, I can tell you nothing, save that I beheld a fulness and a clearness, and felt them abundantly within me. ... I beheld beauty so great that I can say nothing concerning it, except that I saw Supreme Beauty which contains within it all goodness.'[2]

Margery Kempe speaks also of the inexpressible nature of her mystical experiences and her encounter with the Divine Being while engaged in contemplation.

> **They were so holy, so exalted that she hesitated to speak to anyone about them. They were so high above human reason that she could never express in words what she felt in her soul.** [Ch 28]

Experts in the spiritual life tell us that although meditation is of great profit to the soul, contemplation is a more elevated form of prayer. It is a state in which the soul yearns and thirsts for God and aspires to union with him. The devout soul is often compared to the human lover who longs to be in the presence of the beloved and in close union with him or her. The soul, on fire with love for God, desires to be wholly in his presence and to be one with him. The Psalmist cries, 'As the hart panteth after the water brooks/So panteth my soul after thee, O God./My soul thirsteth for God, for the living God.' (Ps. 42.12).

Mystics insist that the initiative is with God. It is he who implants the desire in the soul for himself, draws the soul to himself, takes possession of it, infusing it with his grace and love, and after purging and purifying and illuminating the soul, he enraptures it in mystical union with himself.

Thus the mystical experience of union with God is a pure gift. It cannot be deserved or achieved by human effort. The Holy Spirit pours down upon us a diversity of gifts and the gift of contemplation and union with God is but one of them. In the prayer of contemplation the soul has a foretaste of that bliss which is its ultimate destiny, to be united with God who is the source of its being and for whom it was created.

Those who experience such union of the soul with God declare that all awareness of the body, with its desires and senses, is lost, as is all sense of time and all sense of place, for the soul has been exalted to the realm of eternity. In this sublime state, the soul's rapture may last for seconds or for hours. One is unaware how long it has been. So Margery Kempe informs us that her union with the spirit of Christ so transported her soul that, when she had been at prayer for five or six hours, she thought only one had passed.

> **It was so fervent and sweet that it seemed to her that she was in heaven. She never thought of the time, nor did it trouble her how long she had been at prayer. She was unaware of how the time passed.** [Ch 87]

Jesus converses with her in her soul in a homely and intimate fashion.

> **This woman lay very quietly in the church, hearing and understanding the sweet words of Christ in her soul as clearly as when one friend speaks with another. And when** [Ch 87]

she heard the great promises he made to her, she thanked him and wept and sobbed and had many holy and reverend thoughts and said, 'Lord Jesus, Blessed may you be, for I never deserved such promises as these. I wish I were in heaven where I should never displease you from this time forward.'

By this kind of speech and homely conversation, she was made strong and mighty in the love of our Lord, and greatly stabilised in her faith. And she increased in meekness, in charity, and in other good virtues.

Strongly attached as Margery was to the prayer of meditation and contemplation, she did not omit to engage in the more traditional types of vocal prayer: Praise, thanksgiving, confession, intercession and petition. In a lengthy eulogy of praise to God at the close of her *BOOK*, she offers thanks to Jesus for all manner of mercies and blessings.

'Lord Jesus I thank you for all health and wealth, for riches and poverty, for scorn and hostility and all wrong, and for all tribulations that have befallen me ... and I thank you most highly for letting me suffer pain in this world for the remission of my sins and the increase of my merit in heaven.' [Ch 10] [Bk II]

Penitence and confession figure conspicuously in her religious and devotional life, her confessions being made mostly to a priest but sometimes direct to God.

This woman was very sorry for her sins and felt much grief and shed many tears and sobbed bitterly and loudly because she had been so unkind to her Maker ... When she saw her own wickedness she could only sorrow and weep and pray continually for mercy and forgiveness. [Ch 3]

It would seem that Margery was prey to what the moral theologians called 'scrupulosity', that is over-anxiety about their sins, always doubting whether they had truly been forgiven. Jesus therefore assures her that her sins have been entirely forgiven.

On a Friday before Christmas Day, as this woman was kneeling in the chapel of St John in St Margaret's church in Lynn, crying bitterly and asking mercy and forgiveness for her sins and trespasses, our merciful Lord Jesus Christ [Ch 3]

... enraptured her soul and said to her, 'Daughter, why do you weep so bitterly? It is I, Jesus, who have come to you. I died on the cross for you and suffered grievous pains and torments for you, and I am the very same God who forgives your sins to the uttermost point, and you will never come to hell or to purgatory, but when you pass from this world you will come to the bliss of heaven within the twinkling of an eye.'

Intercession, that is prayer for others, occupied a key role in the religious devotions of all devout Christians. 'During the day sometime, or at night, gather in your heart all the sick and sorrowful who endure misery and poverty, the pains that prisoners endure and feel where they lie, heavily fettered with iron ... Have pity on those who are under severe temptations. Set all their sorrows in your heart and sigh to our Lord that he take pity on them.' So wrote the author of the Rule for anchoresses.[3]

Margery offered intercession for all manner of people: for the pope, the king of England, lords and ladies, clergy of all ranks, sick and needy folk, heretics, thieves, adulterers, prostitutes, prisoners, bed-ridden folk and lepers. She shows particular sympathy for those who, like herself at a time of pregnancy and childbirth, suffered mental derangement; she provides us with a vivid account of one such woman.

As Margery was saying her prayers in St Margaret's church, a man came in and knelt behind her, wringing his hands and showing signs of being distraught with grief. She, perceiving his distress, asked him the cause of his trouble, to which he replied that things were going badly for him, since his wife had recently been delivered of a child, and now had gone out of her mind. [Ch 10]

'And, lady, she does not know me or any of the neighbours. She roars and shrieks and terrifies everyone. She bites and lashes out, so much so that manacles have to be put on her wrists to restrain her.'

Margery proceeds to recount how, in response to the man's entreaties, she visited his demented wife, who, when she saw Margery, welcomed her gladly, though when others visited her she cried and gaped at them as if 'sche wolde an etyn hem'. Each day and sometimes twice a day Margery visited this poor creature and prayed earnestly for her that God would 'restoryn hir to hir wittys a-gayn'. And indeed God did mercifully restore her, for afterwards she went to the church like other women for her purification, and all those who knew about it said that a great miracle had occurred, and the priest who wrote Margery's *BOOK* said he had never seen anyone so alienated from her wits as this woman was, and so difficult to control.

Margery offers her intercessions for the salvation of the world, that Christ would have mercy on the people's sins. To this he replies.

> **'You say, daughter, that I have great patience with the sins of the people, and what you say is true, but if you saw the sins of the people as I see them, you would marvel all the more at my patience, and you would have much more sorrow because of the transgressions of the people than you do have ...** [Ch 20]
>
> **Then she prayed, "Merciful Lord Jesus Christ, in you is all mercy, grace and goodness. Have mercy, have pity, have compassion on the people. Show them your mercy and goodness and help them. Send them true contrition of heart and do not let them die in their sins."**
>
> **Our merciful Lord answered, "I may do no more for them, daughter, than I do do, according to my righteousness. I send them preachers and teachers, pestilence and battles, hunger and famine, the loss of their goods, great sicknesses and many other tribulations, and yet they will not believe my words, nor do they recognise me when I visit them. Therefore I will say to them, 'I made my servants pray for you, but you despised them, their lives and their works.'**

Teachers on the art of prayer traditionally refer to prayer for oneself as petition, to distinguish it from intercession, though petition merely means 'asking' or 'making requests' only in this case it is for oneself. On all sorts of occasions Margery offers up prayers for herself, For example when confronted by a hostile crowd at Canterbury she prays,

> **'Lord, I came here for love of you. Help me and have mercy on me dear Lord.'** [Ch 13]
>
> **At once, as soon as she had uttered this prayer to our**

> **Lord in her heart, two good looking young men came forward and said to her, 'Are you a heretic or a Lollard, young woman?'**
>
> **'No, sirs, I am neither a heretic nor a Lollard,' she replied.**

Violent storms at sea cause her to pray for herself and for her fellow pilgrims.

> **'Now blessed Jesus, remember your manifold mercies** [Ch 3]
> **and fulfil your promises to me. Let me know that you** [Bk II]
> **are truly God and that no evil spirit has brought me here, and to these dangers on the sea ... Help and succour us, Lord, before we perish or fall into despair.'**

Good works, in imitation of Christ who went about doing good and healing all manner of disease among the people, was a vital ingredient of Margery Kempe's spiritual and devotional life. Bernard of Clairvaux, though greatly devoted to solitude and contemplative prayer, was compelled, as abbot of the monastery, to teach and train, and attend to the pastoral needs of the monks and novices. 'The embrace of divine contemplation must often be interrupted in order to give nourishment to the little ones' he wrote.[4] Meister Eckhart too emphasised the need for contemplatives to pay attention to the practical needs of their fellow men. 'If one were in a rapture, like that of St Paul, and a sick man needed help, it were better to come out of the rapture and show love by serving him who was in need.'[5]

Margery Kempe was not lacking in this respect. She visited lepers and other sick folk in Lynn and ministered to the dying. She cared for an aged and destitute woman in Rome, sharing her squalid hovel, being without a bed to lie on or covers to keep herself warm. She fetched water for the poor woman and carried sticks on her back for the fire, and begged food and wine for her.

On one occasion she was urged in her soul to go to Denny Abbey near Waterbeach in Cambridgeshire to comfort the ladies there, who belonged to a house of Franciscan nuns, or Poor Clares, a journey of some thirty miles by boat from Lynn. Strict enclosure was observed by the nuns, no casual visitor being admitted, though the sisters made an exception for the mystic and visionary of Bishop's Lynn, since they derived much comfort and encouragement from her words of spiritual wisdom.

Margery's particular brand of spirituality may be said to be profoundly 'incarnational'. That is, just as God became incarnate in his Son, living on earth among people, immersed in the ordinary everyday affairs of human life, so Margery, everywhere, sees the divine in the human. 'Every ordinary incident in daily life, every commonplace thing, was spontaneously linked with a recollection of the Sacred Humanity. From this, Margery developed the technique of recollecting the presence of Christ, and holding colloquy with him.'[6] The ordinary task of cooking stockfish, for example, brought Christ to her mind, since when the fish is boiled, the skin has the habit of sticking to the hand which reminded Margery of her closeness to Christ and her abiding union with him. And as she reflects on this ordinary event she hears Christ speaking to her.

> **'Daughter, you are compliant to my will, and cleave to me as closely as does the skin of a stockfish to a man's hand when it is boiled. No shame that anyone can cause you, will ever make you forsake me. Therefore I say to you, my most dear daughter, that it is impossible for any soul who is so meek and charitable towards me, to be damned or separated from me.'** [Ch 37]

Incidents in the streets of Lynn or Rome immediately bring Jesus to her mind.

> **Sometimes when she saw a crucifix, or a wounded man, or a man beating a child, or a man beating a horse or some other animal with a whip ... she imagined that she saw our Lord and how he was beaten or wounded.** [Ch 28]
>
> **When she saw women in Rome carrying their children in their arms, and ascertained whether they were male children, she would weep and cry aloud as if she saw Christ himself in his childhood. And if she could have had her wish she would often have taken them from their mothers' arms and kissed them as if she were kissing Christ himself.**
>
> **And if she saw a good looking man, she found it painful to look at him, lest she might see in him the one who was both God and man.**

She is assured that God is always with her, wherever she goes and whatever she does, though she may not always be conscious of his presence.

> **'Wherever God is heaven is. God is in your soul and many angels are around your soul to preserve it by day and by night. When you go to church I go with you; when you sit down to eat, I sit with you; when you go to your bed, I go with you; and when you go out into the town, I go with you.** [Ch 14]
>
> **Daughter, there was never a child so compliant to a father as I will be to you, to help and to keep you. I sometimes do with my grace as I do with the sun. There are times, as you know, when the sun shines everywhere, for all to see, but sometimes it is hidden behind a cloud and none may see it, yet it is still there, shining in its brightness and radiating its warmth. So also I do with you and with my chosen souls.'**

One of the most controversial aspects of Margery's spirituality relates to her propensity to weep copious tears and to sob bitterly and loudly when stirred by any kind of religious emotion, particularly when seeing a crucifix of hearing the gospel story of the Passion read aloud, or hearing a sermon preached on the subject. Martin Thornton, in his otherwise appreciative appraisal of Margery Kempe, writes disparagingly of her 'cries' and suggests that they are an incidental aspect of her spirituality, and could well be eliminated from her *BOOK* without any major impairment to it.[7] Yet it is the sheer number of references to her tears, indeed lengthy passages or whole chapters, which forbids us to regard them as incidental. Rather we may claim they are a fundamental and integral part of her spirituality.

That she was a highly emotional women cannot be doubted, yet we must take into account that holy tears, as opposed to natural tears, belonged to a particular genre of medieval piety and devotion, and were considered a gift of the Spirit, a charism. They were of three specific varieties. There were tears of contrition, or sorrow for sins; tears of devotion which were evoked by any deeply moving religious emotion; and tears of compassion for Christ's sufferings and death on the cross. These three types of Holy tears are referred to by Dame Julian of Norwich, from whom Margery sought spiritual advice. Julian explained to Margery that such gifts are not given to unstable souls.

> **'When God bestows on any person tears of contrition, devotion and compassion, that person may, and indeed should, believe that the Holy Spirit is in his soul ... No evil spirit can bestow such tokens, for St Jerome says that tears torment the devil more than the pains of hell.'** [Ch 18]

Margery's cries would not have caused such hostility had she been able to cry quietly, but at times her cries were so loud and vehement that they drowned a preacher's sermon, which angered the congregation intensely. But it seems that Christ himself was in charge of her tears and modulated them as he chose, now soft, now loud. Furthermore he bestowed them on whomsoever he willed. Both Robert Spryngolde, her parish priest, and Master Aleyn of Lynn, a Carmelite friar, believed without a doubt that Margery's tears were a gift of the Holy Spirit, and that she was only able to cry when God willed it, and had no power to withstand the tears when God sent them.

> **God would sometimes visit her with tears when she was in church, sometimes in the street or in her room at home, or in the fields. She never knew the time nor the hour when God would send them, and they never came without a sense of surpassing sweetness, devotion, and exaltation of soul. As soon as she perceived that she would cry she tried with all her might to restrain herself so that the people would not hear her and be angry, for some of them said that she was vexed with an evil spirit, others that it was caused by some sickness, or that she had drunk too much wine. Some cursed her and wished she was in the harbour, or out at sea in a bottomless boat. Each person had his own thoughts about her, and some spiritual people loved her and favoured her all the more.** [Ch 28]

Often she prayed that God would take her tears away, especially during sermons, or that she might cry when she was alone at home 'only spare me when I am among the people.' But the reply came,

> **'Daughter, do not pray for this, for you shall not have your desire. I shall make you obedient to my will ... for I tell you, daughter, that you are mine and I am yours, and so it shall be for ever.'** [Ch 77]

Many examples of holy tears may be drawn from scripture particularly from the Psalms. The distressed and desolate soul weeps day and night in his longing for God (Ps. 42.3) The prophet Joel exhorts the people of Israel to return to the Lord with fasting and weeping and with mourning, (Joel 2.12). The prostitute repents of her misdeeds and washes the feet of Christ with her tears, (Luke 7.38). Jesus weeps over the city of Jerusalem, (Luke 19.41).

Numerous instances of holy tears occur too in the literature of the Middle Ages, especially, though not exclusively, among women. Blessed Dorothea of Prussia, Elizabeth of Hungary, Bridget of Sweden and Marie of Oignes all wept when hearing about, or meditating upon Christ's Passion. Bridget prayed 'O sweet Jesus, wound my heart, that tears of penitence and love may be my food day and night and bring me entirely to thee.'[8] Marie of Oignes was unable to look at a crucifix or to hear the story of Christ's pains and torments without dissolving into tears of compassion and crying out like a woman in travail, and she would sometimes leave the church for fear she should disturb the priest who was saying Mass. Francis of Assisi became almost blind from excessive weeping at the contemplation of the Passion. 'Lifting up his eyes and hands to heaven he cried with great devotion and fervour "my God, my God" and so saying and weeping bitterly he prayed until morning.'[9]

The friars in particular had the capacity to stir their congregations by their emotional sermons, exercising tremendous power over them. Herculanus of Piegale could speak about the sufferings of Christ in such a way that people could scarcely bear it. Once when preaching at Aquila he had his audience weeping so copiously that one woman begged him to stop as she said she could not stand any more. But Herculanus was adamant. 'No, madam,' he said, 'no, for we cannot weep enough for the Passion of Christ. Christ shed far more blood for us than we can ever shed tears for him.'[10] Johan Huizinga writes of the celebrated Dominican preacher, St Vincent Ferrer, who, when 'he spoke of the Last Judgement or Hell, or the Passion, both he and his hearers wept so copiously that he had to suspend his sermon till the sobbing ceased.'[11]

Christ had warned his disciples that they would face persecution and trial for his sake, (Mark 13.9–13). They would be arrested and brought before the councils, flogged, hated, mocked and scorned for his sake. But they were to endure with a cheerful spirit. 'Exult and be glad, for you will have a rich reward in heaven; for in the same way they persecuted the prophets before you.' (Matt. 5.11–12). Here lies the key to a further aspect of Margery Kempe's spiritual life. She was ready to endure persecution for Christ's sake. Indeed she avowed that she was happier on the days when she was rebuked and persecuted than on the days when she was not. Soon after her conversion and while still a young woman she was forewarned of tribulation that was to come, for as she watched some rats in the fish-markets of Lynn, hungrily tearing fish to pieces she thought she heard Jesus speaking to her.

> **'Daughter, you will be eaten and gnawed by the people of the world, as any rat gnaws a stockfish. But have no fear, for I will give you the victory over all your enemies ... and I swear by my majesty that I will never forsake you in joy or in sorrow.'** [Ch 5]

Blessed Henry Suso was admonished in a similar fashion of troubles that lay in store for him. Opening the window of his cell he saw a dog running about and playing with a tattered mat. The dog 'threw it up and threw it down and tore holes in it ... and a voice spoke within him: "Just so shalt thou be torn and tugged about in the mouths of thy brethren!"[12]

Margery may be said to be one of those chosen souls designated 'a fool for Christ' in conformity with St Paul's statement, 'We are fools for Christ's sake ... People curse us, and we bless; they persecute us, and we submit ... To this day we are treated as the scum of the earth, as the dregs of humanity." (1 Cor. 4.10–13). So Margery relates that,

> **One of her company, a man who had a great affection for her, besought her to go to her fellow pilgrims and to submit herself humbly to them, and ask them if she might continue to travel with them until they came to Constance. And so she did. She continued with them until she reached Constance, putting up with great distress and many troubles, for they treated her shamefully and scolded** [Ch26]

her while on the journey and at various places on the way. The cut her dress so short that it came only a little below her knee, and they made her put on a white canvas garment, like a sacken apron, so she would be considered a fool, a person of no reputation, and be made nothing of by the people.

Compare this with St Francis. 'When the townsfolk of Assisi beheld him unkempt in appearance ... they rushed upon him with mud from the streets and stones, and mocked him with loud shouts as a fool and a madman.'[13] Consider also the case of Jesus. 'Herod and his troops treated him with contempt and ridicule, and sent him back to Pilate dressed in a gorgeous robe.' (Luke 23.11). 'The soldiers ... beat him about the head with a stick and spat at him, and then knelt and paid homage to him. When they had finished their mockery, they stripped off the purple robe and dressed him in his own clothes. Then they led him out to crucify him.' (Mark. 15.16–20).

In many facets of their lives the saints and mystics echo the life of Jesus. Not only was Margery Kempe ready to suffer mockery, derision and contempt for Christ's sake, but she was prepared to suffer death for him. Sometimes she imagined what kind of martrydom she would choose to suffer for love of him. She would, she thought, be tied head and foot to a post and have her head struck off with an axe, for which desire Jesus thanks her and says that he accepts the will for the deed.

'Daughter, whenever you think that you would be willing to suffer death for me, you will have the same reward in heaven as if you truly suffered that death. Yet no one shall slay you, no fire burn you, no water drown you and no wind harm you, for I shall not forget you and how you are written on my hands and on my feet.'[14] [Ch 14]

There is evidence throughout Margery's *BOOK* that she was specially endowed with the gift of prophecy, one of the gifts of the Spirit named by St Paul in his letter to the Corinthians (1 Cor. 12.10). The men of Lincoln, learned men and lawyers, marvelled at her knowledge and wisdom.

'We have attended school for many years,' they said, 'and yet we cannot answer as you do. Where do you [Ch 55]

get this knowledge from?'
'From the Holy Ghost' she replied.

Speaking with the voice of prophecy did not necessarily mean predicting future events, though it might sometimes mean precisely that. It more often meant making utterances which were prompted by God, being God's 'mouthpiece' through whom he made his will and purposes known to individuals, groups or nations. Bridget of Sweden was 'God's fiddle' and Hildegard of Bingen 'God's trumpet'. Margery Kempe made no claim to speak with a prophetic voice on issues of national, political and ecclesiastical importance, as did Bridget of Sweden, who addressed herself to popes and kings and queens, intervening in affairs of state; nor like Catherine of Siena who exerted a powerful influence on Gregory XI and his decision to return to Rome from Avignon. Margery operated on a more lowly and parochial level, addressing herself to individuals she encountered on her travels and at home in Lynn.

A certain vicar came to her and requested that she pray for him to help him discover whether or not he should stay in his parish, since he seemed to be making no headway with his flock. While engaged in prayer Christ spoke to Margery in her mind,

'Tell the vicar to retain his cure and his benefice, and be diligent in preaching and teaching his flock, and procuring the services of others to instruct them in my laws and my commandments, so that he himself may not be at fault. Then if they do no better, he shall not lose his reward because of it.' [Ch 23]

Margery delivered her inspired judgement to the vicar who followed her advice and remained in his parish, his ministry from henceforth flourishing greatly. Many other examples she affords her readers of her supernatural knowledge of how people fared, the state of their souls, their secret sins, whether they would be saved or damned, and whether the sick would recover or die.

One of Margery's great friends, a good man, and one who was kind to the poor, fell sick and suffered for many weeks. People grieved for him and thought he would never recover, so severe was the pain in all his joints and all over [Ch 23]

his body. But our Lord Jesus spoke to her in her soul and said, 'Daughter, do not fear for this man's life, for he will live and do well'. And the man recovered and lived for many years and was in good health and prospered ...

Many more revelations like this were given to this woman, but to write about them all would only hinder and delay the writing of more profitable things. These, however, are written to demonstrate how homely and good our merciful Lord Jesus Christ is, and not to bring praise to this woman.

On one occasion Margery visited an unnamed monastery and was questioned by a monk as to his sins,

'Young woman, I hear it said that God speaks to you. Tell me, I pray you, whether I shall be saved or not, and in which sins I have most displeased God, for unless you tell me my sins I will not believe in you.' [Ch 12]

Margery advised the man to go to Mass, and while Mass was being said she wept in a most wonderful way for this man's sins, and prayed earnestly that Christ would reveal to her the nature of his sins, to which he replied,

'My beloved daughter, speak to him in my name and tell him he has sinned in lechery, in despair and in hoarding worldly goods ... Do not fear, but speak boldly to him in my name, for these are not lies which I tell you.' [Ch 12]

So Margery delivered the message to the monk who was somewhat taken aback by her disclosure of his sins, but sought further proof of her prophetic powers by asking of her whether he had sinned with wives or with single women.

'With wives, sir,' she replied. [Ch 12]
'Shall I be saved then?' he enquired.
'Yes, sir, if you will follow my advice and be sorry for your sins, and I will help you to be sorry. Make your confession and be absolved of your sin, and forsake it with a firm will. Relinquish also the office you hold outside the monastery, and God will give you grace.'

Margery concludes this episode by telling us that the monk took her by the hand, and escorted her to a splendid house and gave her an excellent dinner, and afterwards he gave her money, asking her to pray for him. On a subsequent occasion when she visited this same monastery she was heartened to discover that the monk had relinquished the office he held outside the monastery that he had turned away from his sin and been elevated to the position of sub-prior, and had become a man of good behaviour and amiable disposition.

The enduring of temptation was a further feature of Margery Kempe's spiritual life. The author of the *Ancrene Riwle* had alerted the sisters, for whom he was writing, of the inevitability of temptation. 'Anyone who leads a holy life is sure to be tempted. The higher the tower, the stronger the winds. You yourselves are a tower, my dear sisters.'[15] The *Stimulus Amoris* similarly stated, 'Do not be surprised that you are hindered by temptations, but always be afraid of falling, and always flee to God for help and stay with him and you will not be overcome.'[16] Bridget of Sweden, Margery's spiritual heroine and mentor, declared that 'There are many good and righteous people who are tempted by Satan … This is not to their shame, but to their glory, for the Son of God was tempted in his manhood. It is understandable then that his chosen souls should be tempted for the increase of their merit.'[17]

One of Margery's recurrent temptations was to doubt the authenticity of her visions and revelations. Were they truly from God or from some evil spirit, parading as an angel of light? Reassurance came to her through her confessors who were experts in spiritual matters and avowed that they believed her revelations were from God. In general we may say that visionaries, like Margery, were regarded as genuine if they functioned within the context of the Church, if they endorsed catholic doctrine and supported the Church and its clerical hierarchy. Bridget of Sweden and Catherine of Siena, like Margery Kempe, submitted their visions to their confessors before making them public.[18]

All genuine Christian mysticism in one way or another echoes, or elaborates upon, the traditional doctrines of the Church and its sacred writings, as did Margery Kempe's. The Bible, the worship of the Church, its teachings, sacraments, ceremonies, seasons, festivals and saint's days all figure conspicuously in her *BOOK*, and we may be certain that, when the priest, who was her scribe, came to write down what she dictated to him, he would have corrected any element of heterodoxy that might have crept into her beliefs, omitting any suspect material. Could he, we may wonder, have had some say in her very lucid analysis of true and false revelations, of which we are warned in Scripture? 'My dear friend, do not trust every spirit, but test the spirits, to see whether they are from God; for there are many false prophets about in the world.' (1 John 4.1). Margery writes:

> **Sometimes revelations are hard to understand, and those that people think are revelations are only deceits and illusions. Therefore it is not wise to give immediate credence to every stirring of the mind, but one should wait soberly and prove whether or not they are sent from God.** [Ch 89]

As Margery progressed in the spiritual life she began to experience supernatural manifestations of the Divine Being, and was granted a heightened perception of the senses, so that she heard things, saw things, smelt and felt things beyond the ordinary power of human perception.

> **One night as this woman lay in bed with her husband she heard music, so sweet and delectable, that she thought she was in paradise. At once she sprang from her bed and exclaimed, 'Alas that I ever sinned! There is such joy in heaven'. This music was so exceedingly sweet that it surpassed all other melody that could ever be heard on earth. Nothing could be compared to it. Afterwards when she heard any music and merrymaking she wept abundant tears of great devotion and sobbed and sighed for the bliss of heaven.** [Ch 3]

Richard Rolle, hermit of Hampole, describes a similar experience how, while in the chapel reciting the night psalms, he heard angelic choirs. 'In my prayer I was reaching out to heaven with heartfelt longing when I became aware, in a way I cannot explain, of a symphony of song, and in myself I sensed a corresponding harmony, wholly delectable and heavenly.'[19]

At times Margery perceived 'white things flying' all around her like specks in the sunlight. They appeared wherever she was, in the church, in the town, in the fields and in her room. Sometimes she was afraid, especially when they appeared to her in the darkness. But Christ reassured her.

> **'By this sign, daughter, believe that it is God who speaks in you, for wherever God is heaven is, and wherever God is, there are many angels. God is in you, and you are in him. Therefore do not be afraid, daughter, for these are signs that many angels are round about you, to keep you by day and by night, so that no evil spirit will have power over you and no evil men will harm you.'** [Ch 35]

Margery speaks of beholding the fair beauty of Christ's face.

> **As she lay very still and quietly in the choir, weeping and sorrowing for her sins, suddenly she fell into a kind of sleep. And at once she saw, with her spiritual sight, our Lord's body before her, his head close to her, or so she thought, with his blessed face turned upwards, the most beautiful man that could ever be seen or thought of.** [Ch 85]

Perhaps in this vision she had in mind Psalm 45, a messianic Psalm which prefigures the union between Christ and his Church and which tells of the pre-eminence of Christ among men. 'Thou art fairer than the children of men; Grace is upon thy lips … Thou hast loved righteousness, and hated wickedness:/Therefore God, even thy God, hath anointed thee/With the oil of gladness above thy fellows.'

People of great sanctity tell of their consciousness of heavenly scents and fragrances pervading their nostrils. Angela of Foligno first perceived such indescribable scents following a period of acute suffering of mind, body and soul and after having passed through the fires of temptation. Margery Kempe describes her experience thus,

> **Sometimes she was aware of sweet smells, sweeter, she thought, than any earthly smells. She could never describe how sweet they were, and she felt as if she could have lived by them if they had lasted.** [Ch 35]

Supernatural heat was a further manifestation of the presence of the divine in the human soul. Richard Rolle gives a description of this mystical experience. 'I was sitting in a certain chapel, delighting in the sweetness of prayer and meditation, when suddenly I felt within myself an unusually pleasant heat. At first I wondered where it came from, but it was not long before I realized that it was from none of his creatures but from the Creator himself.'[20]

Similar reports of warmth caused by the fire of divine love can be discovered in the writings of Bridget of Sweden, Marie d'Oignes and Dorothea of Mantau. Margery Kempe describes her experience thus:

> **Our Lord gave her another sign of his presence which lasted for about sixteen years, increasing more and more, and that was a flame of fire, wonderfully hot and very pleasant and comforting.[21] This was the fire of love which never decreased but was always increasing. Even when the weather was very cold she felt this heat burning in her breast and in her heart ... When she first felt this fire of love burning in her breast she was afraid, but our Lord spoke to her in her mind and reassured her, 'Daughter, do not be afraid, for this heat is the heat of the Holy Spirit, which will burn away all your sins, for the fire of divine love quenches all sins. You will know by this sign that the Holy Spirit is in you, and you know very well that where the Holy Spirit is, there too is the Father, and where the Father is, there too is the Son. So you have the whole Trinity in your soul. Therefore you have every cause to love me much, though you will have even greater cause to love me than you ever had before, for you will hear what you have never heard, and see what you have never seen, and feel what you have never felt.[22]** [Ch 35]

As Margery grows in Spiritual maturity she acquires the grace of detachment from earthly creatures and earthly possessions, her love is purified, and her heart is wholly set upon loving God and Jesus Christ. And so she prays that God will withhold everything from her that might draw her love away from him.

> **'I pray you, Lord, withold from me all kinds of earthly goods and honours, and all kinds of earthly loves, which might diminish my love for you and lessen my merit in heaven. Grant me for your mercy's sake, and for your eternal glory, only those loves and possessions, which you know, in the wisdom of your Godhead, would increase my love for you.'** [Ch 56]

In this chapter we have considered some aspects of Margery Kempe's spiritual and devotional life, but what do we know of her ordinary day to day life as the wife of a burgess of Bishop's Lynn, and of the type of conditions that existed in a late medieval town? What do we know too of the religious context within which her spiritual and devotional life evolved? Much of this background material can be discovered from the municipal records of the borough of King's Lynn and from Margery's own writings. In the following two chapters we shall attempt to fill in some of this religious, social environmental background.

CHAPTER TWO

An Outline of the Life of Margery Kempe

Margery Kempe was born in about 1373, in the reign of Edward III. She grew up, married and produced her first few children in the reign of Richard II. But the most dramatic and eventful years of her life belong to the period of English history when the Lancastrian kings were on the throne, and when the stability of the English church was threatened by the Lollard heresy, which emanated from the teachings of John Wyclif. Vigorous efforts were made by the ecclesiastical authorities to stamp out this heresy, suspects being rounded up, tried before the ecclesiastical courts and, if found guilty, handed over to the secular arm and burnt at the stake. Exemption from this ultimate penalty was only granted on condition that the culprits confessed their errors, renounced their heretical beliefs and performed the prescribed penances. In reality the majority of suspects observed these conditions and were never committed to the flames. Because of her habit of citing scripture, appearing to speak with authority about God and criticising the clergy, all of which was forbidden to the laity, Margery Kempe was charged with heresy and brought before the ecclesiastical courts at Leicester, York and Beverley, but emerged from her trials unscathed, her orthodoxy vindicated.

Margery was the daughter of John Brunham of Bishop's Lynn, in Norfolk, a wealthy and successful member of the merchant class, the nouveaux riches of the later Middle Ages, which in the fourteenth and fifteenth centuries was growing in influence and prosperity. What sort of merchandise and business he was associated with we are not told, but perhaps with some branch of the lucrative woollen industry. It is certain, however, that John Brunham was a citizen and burgess of considerable importance in Lynn, as the many references to him in the municipal registers

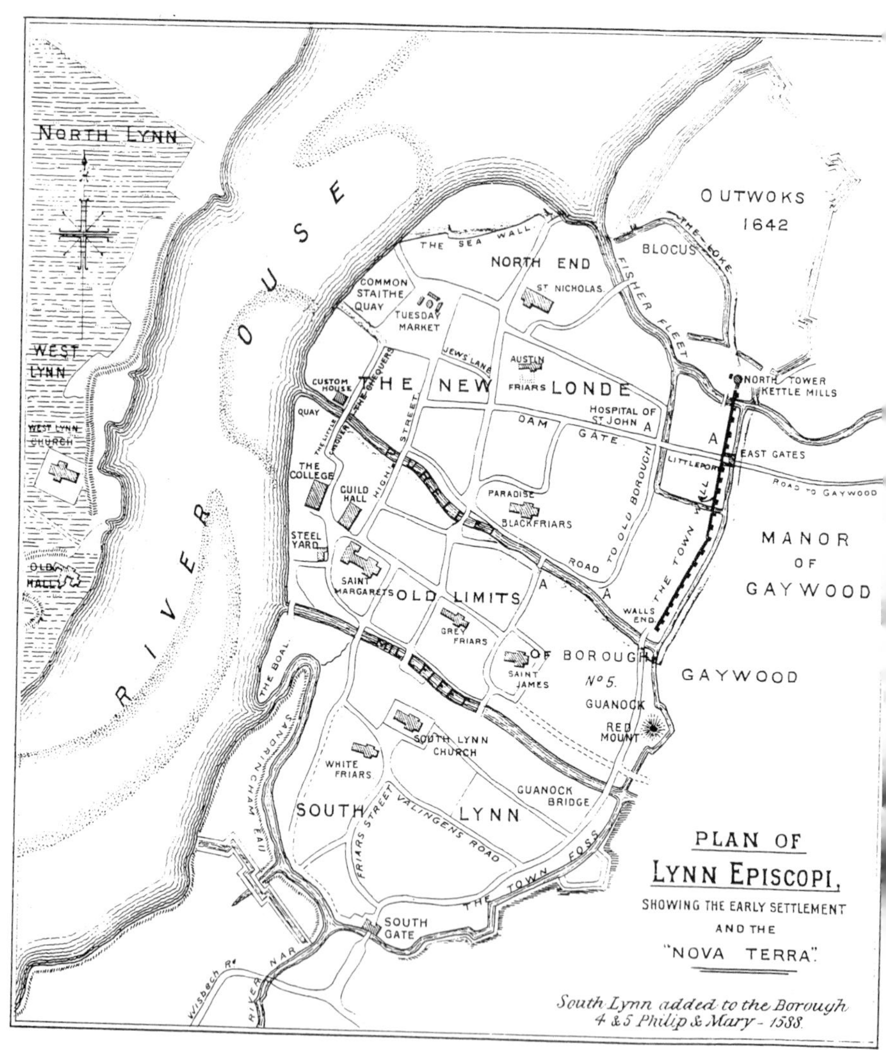

Map 3 from 'Our Borough, Our Churches: King's Lynn'. E. M. Beloe. Cambridge 1899.

testify. His name appears six times in the Red Register as one of the two members of parliament for the borough between the dates 1364 and 1384, and five times as mayor of Lynn. At various times he also held the offices of chamberlain, coroner and justice of the peace, and participated in the discussions relating to the electing of mayors, jurats and burgesses. He played a conspicuous role too in the contentious issue of the parochial status of St Nicholas' Chapel, a chapel of ease of the mother church of St Margaret's in Lynn.[1] In addition to occupying these positions of civic importance in the town, John Brunham was alderman of the prestigious Guild of the Holy Trinity, a guild of immense wealth and influence in Lynn and in the great trading centres of northern Europe, drawing its members principally from the rich burgess and merchant class.

In *c*1393, when Margery was about twenty years old, she married John Kempe, also a burgess of Lynn, though of less distinction than his father-in-law, figuring in the municipal registers only as jurat and one of the borough's four chamberlains or treasurers. His name appears in the registers in connection with a tenement in Fincham Street (now New Conduit Street), which may possibly have been the home of Margery and John Kempe for part of their married life, until, in 1413, about twenty years after their marriage, they took a mutual vow of chastity and subsequently, for a while, occupied separate tenements. The registers also contain a reference to John Kempe's brother, Simon, who figures in connection with tenements in Bridgegate (High Street), Purfleet Street, and Damgate (Norfolk Street). Since Simon Kempe predeceased his brother, John, one or other of these dwellings may have passed to John and been occupied either by John himself or by Margery, following their vow of chastity. However, we cannot be sure of the precise location of John and Margery's residences, though they would almost certainly have lived in, or fairly near the centre of the town, where burgesses usually dwelt.

Neither can we be sure what kind of craft or trade John Kempe pursued. The Lynn archives designate a John Kempe, probably his father, and a Simon Kempe, his brother, 'skinners', all three Kempes belonging to the Guild of Corpus Christi. There is a reference too to a John Kempe, 'brewer' in the first decade of the fifteenth century.[2] Margery informs us that she herself went in for brewing during the early part of her married life, though the manner in which she describes this business venture suggests that it was an occupation quite independent of that of her husband. It is of course possible that John Kempe was also a brewer at some stage of his career.

But whatever his craft or trade, it appears that John Kempe lacked business acumen, since he incurred debts from which Margery had to rescue him, probably by means of a proportion of the legacy bequeathed to her by her father. Professor Meech has estimated that John Brunham died between the dates 19 December 1412 and 16 October 1413, and that Margery departed from Lynn for her pilgrimage to the Holy Land in the autumn of 1413, having promised to pay her husband's debts. By the time she left Lynn she must have received the bequest from her father and been in a position to provide her husband with financial assistance.[3]

Margery relates in her *BOOK* how, shortly after her marriage, she found herself pregnant and that both before and after the birth of the child she suffered acute sickness of mind and body. Pregnancy in medieval times was one of the numerous health hazards which women faced, many women dying in childbirth or from its after-effects, their survival depending on natural strength, uncomplicated births and sufficient time for recuperation.[4] Margery was evidently one of those women who were fortunate enough to possess the fundamental good health and stamina to see her through her numerous pregnancies and the birth of fourteen children. Yet this first pregnancy was accompanied by such fearful sickness that she despaired of her life, and thinking that she would soon die, she sent for her confessor,

> **For she had something on her conscience which she had never disclosed to anyone in all her life.** [Ch 1]

Confessions were normally made to a priest in the church, but in cases of severe illness or impending death the priest might visit the penitent to hear the confession and to dispense absolution, as is stated in the following piece of ecclesiastical legislation. 'Let the priest choose for himself a common place for hearing confessions, where he may be seen by all the church. Do not let him hear anyone, especially any woman, in a private place, except in great necessity and because of the infirmity of the penitent.'[5]

On this occasion therefore the priest visited Margery in her home and all proceeded smoothly until she came to naming the undisclosed sin, and then courage failed her and she wavered, at which wavering her confessor, almost certainly Master Robert Spryngolde, parish priest of St Margaret's church, grew impatient with her, spoke sharply to her and rebuked her. Unfortunately this only increased her distress and confusion and she would say no more, with the consequence that the sin went unconfessed. Then what with one thing and another: her confessor's sharp rebuke, her precarious state of health and her dread of damnation, she went clean out of her mind.

Gruesome visions of hell assailed her, of the sort that medieval folk were accustomed to hear about in sermons or in the ever-popular mystery and miracle plays, or to see vividly portrayed in the wall-paintings and stained glass windows of their churches.

> **She thought she was devils opening their mouths, all ablaze with flames of fire, as if they would have swallowed her up. By day and by night they ramped and raged at her, threatening her, calling her and pulling her about ... commanding her to give up her Christian faith, to deny her God, our Lady and all the saints in heaven, and to turn against all virtues and all good works, against her father and mother and all her friends. And so she did.** [Ch 1]

Seized with bouts of fury and violence she tore the skin from her body, close to her heart, with her nails, and bit her hands with such ferocity that scars remained on them for the rest of her life. Fetters had to be placed on her for fear she would destroy herself. Then in the midst of all this turmoil and anguish our Lord lovingly appeared to her. She describes the vision thus:

> **As she lay alone one day, her guardians having left her for a while, our merciful Lord Jesus Christ, who is always to be trusted, his name always honoured, and who never forsakes his servants in time of need, graciously appeared to this woman in his blessed manhood. He was more beautiful, more comely, more amiable than anyone one** [Ch 1]

might ever set eyes upon. He was clothed in a garment of purple silk, and sat at her bedside, looking at her with so blessed a face that she was at once strengthened in spirit. Then he spoke to her and said, 'Daughter, why have you forsaken me, for I have never forsaken you?' As soon as he had spoken these words she saw how the air opened up and became as bright as lightning and he ascended into the air, not hastily or suddenly, but gently and most becomingly, so that she could watch him until the air closed upon him again.

At once Margery recovered her reason and was as calm and sensible as she had ever been before. She asked her husband for the keys to the buttery so that she could get herself something to eat and drink. But her maidservants and attendants advised him not to give her the keys, for they said she was out of her mind and would only give away such provisions as they had.

However, her husband, who was always tender and compassionate towards her, commanded them to give her the keys. So she took food and drink, as much as her strength would allow, and she recognised her friends and the members of her household and all the other folk who came to see her and to witness the grace that our Lord Jesus Christ had worked in her. [Ch 2]

Margery now resumed all her normal household duties and she performed them wisely and sensibly, but she still did not know our Lord's wonderful power to draw the soul to himself, and as time passed and the vision of Jesus had faded from her mind, she relapsed into worldly ways and gave in to vanity and pride, cherishing ambitions to grandeur and luxurious living. She loved nothing better than to be admired and worshipped by the world, and to this end she went in for costly clothes and bright colours to catch the eyes of men. Her dresses, hoods and tippets were decorated with serrated or 'dagged' edges, which were all the rage among great ladies of the day. 'The fourteenth century was an era of dagged edges. This strange method of decorating a garment by cutting its edges into various jagged shapes began in the time of Henry II and was mostly used on men's clothes, but in the last decade of the fourteenth century dagges became fashionable for women also.' [6] Hair-styles and head-dresses of medieval women were also extremely elaborate and of infinite-variety and novelty. Margery tells us that she wore 'gold pypys on hir hevyd' which probably refer to the cylindrical cauls that fashionable ladies wore on either side of their face; these were made of gold mesh, and had a solid band at top and bottom, into which coiled plaits could be inserted.[7]

Personal adornment and ostentation in dress was a popular subject of pulpit invective in the Middle Ages. 'Those great lords and ladies who come to church and before our Lord God Almighty, richly arrayed in gold and silver, pearls and precious stones and other worldly splendour, ought to follow the example of the noble Queen, Esther, who did away with all her rich apparel and humbled herself meekly before God.' [8] Richard Rolle of Hampole in Yorkshire, whose religious treatise, *Incendium Amoris*, Margery Kempe was to hear read to her by one of her learned clergy friends, was also critical of those who indulged in novel and elaborate fashions. 'These women of today need to be rebuked, for they have invented new fashions of great and fantastic conceit ... They put widespreading horns on their heads, extremely horrible, made up of hair not their own ... and men and women alike in their excessive vanity wear clothes cut in the latest style regardless of natural decency.' [9]

As the daughter of a prosperous merchant and burgess of Bishop's Lynn, Margery would have been accustomed to a fairly affluent way of life. Hence her love of finery and her ambition to keep up with the latest fashions. In medieval society a considerable amount of social climbing took place, particularly among the rich merchant class. Parents were accustomed to send their daughters into the families of the gentry to wait on the lady of the house, where they would receive training in good manners and genteel behaviour, so that they might better themselves and possibly marry into the families of the gentry. Personal appearance, tasteful dress and adornment went a long way towards their being accepted in a stratum of society above that into which they were born. But Christine de Pisan, an Italian woman of letters, the wife of a French nobleman, and a champion of women, advised her sex to keep to their station and not to try to ape the upper classes by dressing like them. 'It is a great folly to dress up in clothes more suitable for someone else, when everyone knows very well to whom they rightly belong; in other words to take up the grander style that belongs to another.' [10]

When Margery's husband reproached her for her proud and pompous ways she haughtily retorted that he should never have married her, for she came of a highly respected family, her father having been mayor of Lynn and alderman of the noble Guild of the Holy Trinity. Moreover she firmly meant to live up to her family's honourable reputation. But John Kempe was a man of modest means and his financial resources would not stretch to Margery's extravagant demands. Margery, therefore, in order to indulge her love of rich attire, resolved to supplement her husband's meagre income with an income of her own. This was not at all uncommon in medieval society; married women often assisted their husbands in a trade or craft, but also frequently pursued a quite separate one of their own, such as combing and carding wool, spinning or brewing. Indeed brewing was largely in the hands of women.[11] It was to brewing that Margery first turned her hand, and for three or four years she was one of the foremost brewers in the town, until her endeavours suffered a change of fortune and her business enterprise collapsed with the consequences that she lost a great deal of money.

> **However skilled her workmen were, and however familiar with brewing, suddenly nothing would go right for them. When the ale had as good a head of froth on as anyone could wish to see, the froth would unexpectedly go flat and fail to settle, and all the ale would be lost. This happened with one brewing after another, so her servants were ashamed of their failure and would not stay and work for her any longer ... Then she gave up brewing and never brewed again.** [Ch 2]

Margery blamed herself for her failure and said it was due to her pride and obstinacy and her refusal to take her husband's good advice, but that now she intended to mend her ways. But, alas, her good intentions were short-lived and she was very soon mulling over in her mind what fresh occupation she could embark upon to make herself rich. She settled for milling and purchased a horse-mill and two sturdy horses and engaged a servant to work for her and to grind people's corn. But this venture was no more successful than the other, for although the horses pulled well at the mill in the first instance, they suddenly and unaccountabily turned obstinate and would not pull at all. The workman tried by every means to make the animals perform their appointed task, but to no avail. He led them, coaxed them, beat them, rode on them and dug his spurs into them, but they refused to move an inch, but 'would rather go backwards than forwards'. At last the man quit Margery's service, and rumours spread around the town that neither man nor beast would work for this woman and that God was taking vengeance on her, because of her pride. Some said one thing and some another, but wise and discerning folk said that God was showing great mercy on her and was calling her away from the vanity of this wicked world.

Then seeing all these adversities coming upon her on every side, she thought they were like the scourges of our Lord, punishing her for her sin. So she asked for God's mercy and forsook her pride and her covetousness and her desire to be worshipped by the world, and she practised great bodily penance and began to walk in the way that leads to everlasting life. [Ch 2]

If we take into account the information which Margery provides us with: that she was married when she was twenty years old 'or somewhat more', that she was ill for about eight months during and following her first pregnancy, that she was a successful brewer for three or four years, and a miller for only a short while, we may estimate that she was in her middle to late twenties when she made her decision to forsake the world. Although some of the dates that occur in her *BOOK* are established certainties and can be deduced from historical events, others are open to conjecture, for she herself admits that the events she describes are not written in chronological order, but just as they came into her mind when the *BOOK* was written.

For it was so long before the book was written that she had forgotten the time and order of events as they occurred. But she would allow nothing to be written except that which she knew to be the truth. [Proem]

It was a combination of the events which we have outlined above: her severe illness, her vision of Jesus, her miraculous recovery, her failure in business, which gave impetus to a complete transformation in Margery's life, prompting her to take her religion more seriously, to pray with greater fervour and to practise more rigorous austerities. We have already observed that she lived at a period of history when there was a remarkable burgeoning of personal religion and that she was following in a tradition of English spirituality, encouraged by Richard Rolle, Walter Hilton, the anonymous author of the Cloud of Unknowing and Dame Julian of Norwich. Of powerful influence too were some of the great continental men and women mystics whose particular type of mysticism included the practice of rigorous bodily austerities, which Margery took as a pattern for her own religious life.

> **She gave herself up to great fastings and vigils. She rose at two or three o'clock and prayed in the church until noon and sometimes all afternoon too. People slandered her and rebuked her because she lived so strict a life. She obtained a hair-cloth from a kiln, the sort that people use to dry malt on, and she put it in her under-gown as secretly and discreetly as she could, so that her husband would not see it. Nor did he ever see it, though she lay beside him every night in his bed, and she wore the hair-shirt every day too, and she was bearing children at that time.** [Ch 3]

The wearing of a hair-shirt was a common form of ascetic discipline among the saints and mystics. Perhaps Margery Kempe had heard of the wandering preacher, poet and disciple of St Francis of Assisi, Jacopone de Todi, a wealthy, ambitious lawyer, who, it is said, was converted by the sudden death of his beautiful young wife when he discovered that beneath her splendid clothes she wore the hair-shirt of a penitent. This prompted Jacopone to renounce his wealth and worldly ambition and to follow the way of poverty and humility. Having recognised the incomparable beauty of Christ he wrote in one of his 'Lauds',

> Now on no creature can I turn my sight;
> But on my Maker all my mind is set ...
> For Christ's dear love all else I clean forget;
> All else seems vile, and day as dark as night.
> Cherubin, seraphim, in whom are met

Wisdom and love, must yet
Give place, give place,
To that one Face,
To my dear Lord of love.[12]

Following Margery's conversion, her manner of life was the very opposite of that of other married women of the medieval period who occupied themselves almost entirely in managing their households, purchasing foodstuffs, preparing meals, baking bread, brewing ale, sewing and mending garments, spinning and weaving, attending to the needs of husbands and children. Margery would, inevitably have had to involve herself also to some extent in these and other domestic activities, but without such single-minded dedication as other women did. Her failure to conform to the traditional role of housewife and mother aroused the animosity of the town and country folk of Beverley and Hessle in Yorkshire, to which places she had travelled and which were a great distance from her home in Lynn.

> **The two friars and the two yeomen escorted her again to Hessle, and the men of that district called her 'Lollard', and the women came running out of their houses with their distaffs crying out to the people, 'Burn this false heretic!' Then she went on towards Beverley with the friars and yeomen and they met people who said to her, 'Woman, give up this kind of life you lead and go and spin and card wool like other women do, and do not put up with all this shame and sorrow that you do. We wouldn't suffer what you do for any amount of money on earth.'** [Ch 53]

But the people's entreaty fell upon deaf ears, for Margery had a star to follow, a vocation to respond to, and respond to it she did with courage and tenacity, the most amazing aspect of that vocation being the constraint she felt upon herself to travel round the country visiting bishops, clergy, monks, nuns, friars, anchorites and devout laypeople. Entertaining and socialising was high on the agenda of the social graces in medieval times and Margery, though an unlettered laywoman, appears to have been a welcome guest in bishop's palaces, monasteries and nunneries, where, at their tables she would enliven the conversation with her religious tales, her shrewd observations and her quick rejoinders. With remarkable energy and zest she travelled the length and breadth of England, from Canterbury in the south to Bridlington in the north, from Yarmouth in the east to Bristol in the west, and always in response to what she believed were divine commands and no whims or fancies of her own.

> **She felt moved in her soul to visit certain places ... but she could not go without her husband's consent, so she asked his permission, which he readily gave, believing that it was God's will. Then they travelled together to such places as she felt inclined to visit ... And they came to a house of monks, where she was warmly welcomed, except that there was one monk, who held high office in the monastery, who despised her and made nothing of her. However, when she was seated at table with the abott she often uttered inspired words during the meal, good and devout words, just as God put them into her mind. The monk, who had so despised her was present and many others too, who wished to hear what she would say, and because of her conversation this monk felt strongly drawn towards her and began to savour every word she spoke.** [Ch 10 & 12]

We have already seen in the previous chapter how this very same monk was to come under Margery Kempe's benevolent influence and how, through divine inspiration, she was to discern his sins and describe to him how they could be remedied.

These numerous journeys which Margery made are all the more remarkable when we consider that they were undertaken almost entirely on foot. Only wealthy aristocrats and nobles, or gentlefolk like the Pastons in Norfolk, or well-to-do urban folk owned horses and could travel on horseback. Women travelled by this means much less frequently than men, and then only when the journeys were urgent. Only twice do we hear of Margery Kempe travelling on horseback and on both occasions she was accompanied, assisted and led by men. At Leicester her friend and guide, Patrick, put her upon his horse and brought her to his home in Melton Mowbray, a distance of about twelve to fifteen miles. At Dover she was taken on horseback to Canterbury by a poor countryman.

She was up early in the morning and came to a poor man's house and knocked at the door. The good fellow hurried into his clothes, unbuttoned and unfastened, and came to the door to see what she wanted. She enquired whether he had a horse and could help her to get to Canterbury, saying that she would reward him for his labour. The poor man, wishing to help her for our Lord's sake, complied with her wishes and led her to Canterbury. [Ch 8] [Bk II]

Although Margery was an energetic traveller and visited many far-flung places, it would be a mistake to imagine that she was away from home a great deal or for long periods at a time, especially during the early years of her married life. In the Table of Events, which relate to the chronology of her life, there is a marked dearth of entries for the period between the years 1393 and 1413, which indicates that for the first twenty years of her married life she was, as we would expect, heavily occupied at home with child-bearing, child-care and domestic responsibilities, with the occasional excursion to Norwich or some other place not too far from home. This scarcity of entries for the period we have specified contrasts sharply with the year 1413, for which there are numerous entries, suggesting that the year 1413, when she was about forty years old, was one of critical importance to Margery. In that year her father died; she and her husband took an oath of chastity; they travelled to Lincoln to obtain ratification of their vow from Bishop Philip Repingdon; they visited Archbishop Thomas Arundel at Lambeth Palace; and Margery departed from Lynn on her pilgrimage to Jerusalem, Rome and Assisi.[13]

If there is one single regretable omission in Margery Kempe's *BOOK* it is an almost total lack of any reference to her children. She tells us that she prays for them and that Jesus assures her that they, and her husband, will all be saved, and she furnishes us with a detailed account of her grown-up son's fall from, and return to, the path of virtue. Her silence, however, on the subject of her children may be defended on the grounds that, although her *BOOK* has been described as an autobiography, it is more accurately a spiritual autobiography, the story of a soul's journey to God. It contains little of the usual material that goes to make a conventional autobiography, such as details of the author's childhood, youth, adult life, marriage, husband's occupation, children, friendships, interests and so forth. It is true that we are provided with smatterings of information on some of these aspects of Margery's life, but principally for the reason that they contribute to the overall purpose of her *BOOK*, which is essentially a religious one. Thus we are told of her business ventures, not because of any intrinsic interest which they have in themselves – though of course they are of considerable interest to the modern reader – but because they illustrate the humbling of her pride and her conversion from a materialistic outlook on life to a spiritual one. Similarly the saga of her wayward son is not related because of any special significance it has, but because it enshrines a moral lesson for the edification of the reader and demonstrates the power and efficacy of Margery's prayers, which eventually effect his conversion.

Yet the very silence of Margery on the subject of her children induces the reader to wonder how they fared when she was absent from home on her travels in England or on pilgrimage abroad. We can but speculate upon this matter, since Margery provides us with no information as to how her family managed without her. Our speculation can, however, be substantiated to some extent by the knowledge we possess in relation to the conditions that prevailed in the realm of home and family life in the Middle Ages, and this will go some way to explain the apparent indifference and callousness of Margery towards her children.

First it should be pointed out that infant mortality was tremendously high in medieval times, especially in the towns where overcrowded living conditions, lack of proper sanitation and domestic hygiene, unspeakably dirty streets and a want of medical knowledge encouraged the spread of disease. It is therefore most unlikely that all of Margery's children survived even into early childhood, which would have reduced the number of children to be cared for. Plague, dysentery, smallpox, tuberculosis and many other contagious diseases carried off an enormous number of children who were especially susceptible to infection.[14] Contemporary sources witness to the fact that sometimes contagious diseases claimed almost entire families, for example the great Italian mystic, Angela of Foligno, describes how her mother, her husband and all her children died within a short space of time, probably from the

1. The Joys and Sorrows of Mary, c 1485. Nativity window, East Harling, Norfolk.

2. River Jordan – Place of Jesus's Baptism.

3. Sea of Galilee, Road along shore.

plague, outbreaks of which sporadically swept through Europe in the Middle Ages.[15]

We have also seen that there were maidservants in the Kempe household, who would have assisted with the care of the younger children as well as performing household duties during Margery's absence from home. It is probable too that the Kempe family followed the popular English custom of boarding their children out to other families, and taking the children of other families into their own homes for domestic labour as well as for training in the social graces. Although this custom prevailed chiefly in the families of the gentry and upper classes, the wealthy merchant class liked to imitate the fashion. It was a custom deplored by the citizens of other countries, the author of the *Italian Relation* drawing attention to the want of affection in the English for their children. 'For after keeping them at home till they arrive at the age of seven or nine years, they put them out, both males and females, to hard service in the houses of other people ... and few are exempted from this fate.'[16]

In urban societies it was also the custom to send children, both boys and girls, to the households of others to be apprenticed to a craft or trade. Apprentices went to live in the house of the master and his wife as one of the family, where they were fed and clothed, learnt a trade and received some training in manners and morals. Fathers who were domiciled in towns would leave money in their wills for their daughters, to put them to a trade, or for dowry when they were married. Sometimes children were sent out at a very early age, the boys being under the tuition of the master, and the girls under the wife. Children as young as three or four were sometimes taken in to learn the elementary aspects of a trade or craft, although the guilds opposed child labour at too early an age. As Eileen Power observes 'the exploitation of child labour was by no means an invention of the Industrial Revolution'.[17]

In connection with her children we should also note that Margery's father, John Brunham, was still alive until 1413, continuing as a wealthy and prominent citizen of Lynn and exercising an influence on the activities of his daughter and her family and probably giving financial and other support and advice. By the year 1413, when Margery went on her overseas pilgrimages, some of her older children could have been married, or mature enough to assist with the care of the younger ones, which was a common policy in most large families of the bourgeois class like Margery's.

But however vigorously we attempt to defend Margery Kempe's attitude towards her children, it must be said that the medieval period was not notable for the high value it placed upon its children, nor for the compassionate way in which it treated them. 'The idea that they had any natural rights was impossible to the medieval mind. Children were just chattels, and therefore entirely at the direction and disposal of their fathers ... As to the mother's attitude to her children, nothing can overcome the love of women for their children, especially when they are still young. But as the complete dependence and intimacy of babyhood drew to a close, and the children became noisy human beings, then slowly the repressive influence of the age did its work.' [18]

This short summary of Margery Kempe's life would be incomplete without some mention of the important role played by John Kempe in her story. Despite the scathing remark which Margery made to her husband, that he should never have married her, he was in reality an admirable husband for Margery, being kind, easy-going and commendably tolerant towards his wife's faults, fobiles and eccentricities, faithfully accompanying her on many of her journeys, and only on rare occasions leaving her to her own devices.

But he always came back to her and had compassion on her and spoke up for her ... When everyone else failed he was always ready at hand to help her. To whatever place our Lord wished to send her, he travelled with her, trusting that everything was for the best and would come right in the end. [Ch 15]

Both Margery and John Kempe lived into their sixties, Margery outliving her husband, who died in the summer or early autumn of 1431, he having been incapacitated for some years following a fall down the stairs. Margery gives us a dramatic account of this accident and the subsequent troubles she experienced in looking after him.

It happened at one time that this creature's husband, now a man of great age, over sixty years old, was coming [Ch 76]

> **from his bedroom, bare-footed and bare-legged, and slithered or somehow lost his footing, and fell down the stairs to the ground below, his head caught beneath him. His head was so seriously injured and bruised that he had to have five linent plugs put in the wounds to drain them, and these were kept there for many days while his head was healing.**

The din, which he created as he fell, alerted neighbours to his plight and on entering the house they found John Kempe only half alive, his head covered in blood. At once Margery was sent for, and his wounds stitched and dressed, but he was a long time recovering, sympathy for poor John Kempe rousing the neighbours to anger against Margery. If he died, they declared, she should be hanged for his death, for if she had been living with him the accident might not have occurred. Margery explains to the reader that they were living apart at the time to facilitate the keeping of the vow which they had made by mutual agreement to abstain from marital intercourse.

> **For at first they lived together after they had taken their vow, but then people slandered them and said they indulged the lust of their bodies as they did before they had taken the vow. When she and her husband went on pilgrimage or to see and speak with other religious folk, many wicked people, without any fear or love of our Lord Jesus Christ, whose tongues were their own destruction, said they were went rather into the woods, groves and valleys to indulge the lust of their bodies, where no one should see them or find out about it.** [Ch 76]
>
> **Knowing how prone people were to think evil of them, and wishing to avoid all such occasion ... they parted from each other as regards bed and board, and went to live in different places. This was why she was not with him at the time of his fall.**

Dismayed by the accusations of the people, Margery prayed that, if it pleased the Lord, her husband might live; and the Lord replied that he would live and that she must take him home and care for him. But if she obeyed this command, she said, she would not be able to devote herself to her prayers and meditations as she was accustomed to do. She wished to be a good and dutiful wife and to win the approval of her friends and neighbours in Lynn, but on the other hand her devotion to Christ required that she spend her days in prayer. As she agonized over this conflict, caught between her family and spiritual commitments, she heard our Lord commanding her to nurse her husband.[19]

> **'Do as I say, daughter, for you will have as much reward for looking after him and helping him in his need at home as if you were praying in the church. You have often said that you would be happy to look after me, so I pray you now, look after him for love of me, for he has been obedient to both your will and my will, and has made your body freely available to me, so that you should serve me and live chaste and clean. Therefore I wish you to be free now to help him in his need.'** [Ch 76]

Margery therefore took her husband home and looked after him for a number of years until his death, enduring many hardships in caring for him. Age, decrepitude and the serious injury to his head had left him childish and unable to control his natural functions, with the consequence that he either would not, or could not, relieve himself on the 'stool of easement',

> **But like a child emptied his bowels in his linen clothes as he sat by the fire, or at the table, or wherever he was. He spared no place. All this added to her labour, what with the washing and wringing of clothes. The cost of fuel too added to her expenses.** [Ch 76]

While Margery was tending and caring for her husband, tragedy struck a second time in the Kempe household when her son, who had married a German woman and had one child and lived abroad for some years, returned with his wife to Bishop's Lynn to visit his mother. Margery observed how her son, after his marriage, had markedly changed for the better both in appearance and behaviour, for some years before, while on business abroad, he had fallen into the sin of lechery, keeping company with loose women, for which he received a stern rebuke from his mother.

> **'Since you refuse to forsake your worldly ways, as I have counselled you to do, I strongly urge you at least to keep your body clean from associating with women until such time as you take a wife according to the church's law.** [Ch 1] [Bk II]

And if you do not, I pray that God will chastise you and punish you for your misbehaviour.'

Her son, however, paid no heed to his mother's warning, but rather shunned her company and continued in his immoral ways, with disastrous consequences. Sickness fell upon him, and from Margery's description of his ailment, he appears to have contracted some kind of venereal disease, possibly syphilis. His face suffered a horrifying change of colour and became covered in pimples and pustules (whelys and bloberys) which gave him the appearance of a leper, and prompted his master to dismiss him from his employment.

But now, some years later, the young man was a reformed character, had repented of his sins, taken a wife, and greatly pleased his mother by his modest, sober and clean appearance. But perhaps remnants of his disease lingered, for his mother relates how in 1431,

When they arrived home on a Saturday they were both in good health, but on the next day, Sunday, at about midday, while they were having a meal together with some of their good friends, her son became seriously ill and had to rise from the table and lie down on his bed. He was sick for about a month, then passed away to our merciful Lord in a virtuous state of life and in right belief. Shortly after his death, his father went the same way, the way that everyone must go. [Ch 2] [Bk II]

The two women now widowed, the younger remained in Lynn for eighteen months with the older, until friends in Germany wrote to Margery's daughter-in-law pressing her to return to her own country and to the little daughter she had left behind, and this the young woman decided to do. Margery was at once faced with a dilemma; should she accompany her daughter-in-law to Germany, and brave the ocean waves which she feared most terribly, or should she stay at home and allow her daughter-in-law to travel unaccompanied except by a strange man who had come to fetch her. After praying and pondering the matter and seeking the advice of her confessor and others, it became clear to Margery that, she should not only travel to Ipswich with her daughter-in-law, but also undertake the voyage to Danzig with her. And so

Margery embarked upon what was to be her last voyage overseas, followed by two arduous pilgrimages, to Wilsnak and Aachen.

Home again in Lynn in 1433 or 1434, Margery was now free to attend to an undertaking that had long occupied her mind, namely the writing of her spiritual memoirs. An attempt had been made some years earlier to get this done, but the scribe who did the writing for Margery, probably her own son, produced such an illegible script 'neither in good English nor in good German' that she was obliged to procure the services of a local priest to revise the first draft and to make a fresh copy. The priest, we are told, commenced his work on 23 July 1436, completing Book One of her memoirs. He then began Book Two on 28 April 1438.

Margery has bequeathed us a vivid account of how her *BOOK* came to be written and the obstacles that accompanied its production. She relates that in order that the task should proceed speedily she was more at her home with the priest than in the church praying. We may envisage the scene as Margery describes it, the priest poring over this original and badly written script, deciphering a word here and there, gradually piecing it together, Margery beside him, correcting or confirming what he reads out, he, in his accomplished hand producing a fresh and legible copy.

Day after day, week after week, by daylight and by candlelight they pursue their task. The priest complains at times that he cannot see properly to form his letters or to mend his pen, so he puts a pair of spectacles on his nose, but that makes matters worse, and Margery tells him that the devil is envious of his good work and is trying to hinder him, but that he must not give up. Then to his astonishment when he returns to the task he discovers that he can see perfectly clearly.

As the work proceeds Margery feels a flame of fire at her breast, hot and wonderful, the fire of the Holy Spirit, and she hears the voice of a sweet bird singing in her ear, and other heavenly melodies beyond her power to describe. And as she recalls the sweet words that Jesus had spoken to her and the marvellous way in which he had led her and taught her and manifested himself to her, she sheds tears of love and devotion, and the priest, catching something of her deep emotion, cannot restrain himself from weeping too.

Sometimes during the period of writing Margery becomes ill, but as soon as she stirs herself to resume the work she miraculously recovers and feels fit and well again. Always there is a sense of urgency about the task, and if ever she grows weary of it, she is commanded in her soul to return to it with haste, and God speaks words of encouragement to her,

> **'Have no fear, daughter ... for the effort you exert to get these things written down, and to describe the grace that I have shown you, pleases me very much, and so does the man who is doing the writing for you ... for by means of this book, daughter, many people will turn to me and believe.'** [Ch 88]

The last official record we have of Margery Kempe in the Lynn archives is dated 1438, when she was admitted to the Guild of the Holy Trinity, an event which witnesses to the high esteem in which she was held in the borough of Bishop's Lynn.[20] But did she end her days as an anchoress, we may wonder, as the printer, Henry Pepwell, in 1521, states?

Pepwell was reissuing a booklet, printed by his eminent predecessor in the printing trade, Wynkyn de Worde, who, in *c*1501, had published a seven page booklet about Margery, entitled *A Shorte Treatyse of Contemplatyon Taught by our Lorde Ihesu Cryste, or Taken out of the Boke of Margerie Kempe of Lynn.* Wynkyn de Worde had a special interest in works of English devotional and mystical literature, which found a ready readership among devout laypeople and members of religious orders like the Carthusians and Bridgettines who favoured such writings.[21] In Pepwell's reissue of the booklet he designates Margery Kempe 'a devout anchoress'. Although Margery paid many visits to anchoresses, and must have especially valued the spiritual counsel of Dame Julian of Norwich, and may well have admired and wished to emulate their kind of life, there is no indication in her *BOOK* that she ever became an anchoress. Professor Meech, however, suggests that Pepwell, or a collaborator, might have possessed authentic knowledge that she was indeed an anchoress in the latter part of her life.[21]

Yet the notion of Margery Kempe as a recluse living in seclusion and silence is not quite consistent with everything else we know about her as a much-travelled, loquacious and gregarious housewife, though by the time she had reached her middle sixties, she could have mellowed considerably, and become a more stable and serene character. With her husband no longer alive, her children off her hands, she would have been free to adopt a solitary existence and to devote herself more earnestly to her most cherished occupation, that of prayer, meditation and contemplation.

CHAPTER THREE

Medieval Lynn

Bishop's Lynn, in the Middle Ages, scene of many of Margery Kempe's religious experiences, was one of England's busiest and most flourishing seaports, plying a lively trade with Germany, the Low Countries, the Baltic and Scandinavia, and ferrying goods inland by means of the river Ouse and its numerous tributaries. Grain, wool and salt were exported to various parts of Europe, and, in the fourteenth and fifteenth centuries, when the cloth industry was expanding, large quantities of cloth. Imports entering the country through Lynn included timber, furs, oil, bitumen and wax from the Baltic, fish from Norway, Denmark and Iceland, and mill-stones from the Rhineland. Fine silks and wine arrived from southern Europe, the latter particularly from the English possessions in Gascony. Five million gallons a year were being shipped to England towards the close of the thirteenth century, mainly through London and the east coast ports.[1]

The charter which relates to the founding of the parish church of St Margaret, St Mary Magdalene, and All the Virgin Saints in 1101, indicates that its founder, Herbert de Losigna, Bishop of Norwich, was responding to a request of a band of traders for a church to serve the local community, the traders having already recognised the potential of the area as a centre of trade and commerce and gained a footing in the locality. Alongside the church, Losinga built a Benedictine Priory and transferred to it a small group of monks from the mother house of the Cathedral Church of the Holy Trinity in Norwich. Thus the Lynn priory was a cell of Norwich and subordinate to it, the prior of Norwich having jurisdiction over the Lynn priory, with the right to receive the revenues and profits from its endowments.[2]

To ensure the prosperity of the region Losinga endowed the monks with a market, a fair, land and property. The market, to serve the interests of local and foreign traders, was to be held weekly on a Saturday and to be situated on a plot of land to the north of the church, which today retains the street name of Saturday market. The annual fair, or mart, was to be held on St Margaret's Day, 20 July, and would also serve local and foreign merchants. A new mill in the Gaywood Marsh was made over to the monks of Lynn priory, and in addition, a number of saltworks, salt being a highly valuable commodity in the Middle Ages, used for a variety of culinary purposes, particularly for the curing of fish and meat. Domesday Book records a hundred and eighty saltworks in the region round King's Lynn, and active salt-making was taking place in the eleventh century on all the coasts of the Wash.[3]

Bishop's Lynn was one of about eighty European towns belonging to the powerful Hanseatic League, formed to protect trade, safeguard trade routes, and to ensure the safety of merchandise when stored in foreign markets. The most important of Britain's depots was the Steelyard in London, though others existed at Hull, Bristol, Boston, Yarmouth and Lynn. The north German town which had especially close trading links with Lynn was Danzig, which figures in Margery Kempe's *BOOK*, since her son, employed by a wealthy Lynn merchant, often had occasion to visit the town on his business ventures overseas, selling and purchasing merchandise.

Apart from its trading connections with the Continent, important commercial links existed between Lynn and other seaports round the English coast. Ships from Scotland, Newcastle and Scarborough brought coal and fish to Lynn, and Lynn merchants imported large quantities of raw hides also from Newcastle. Yarmouth was a notable centre of the herring industry, immense quantities of fish being harvested from the North Sea and then salted, packed in barrels and transported inland by packhorses or sent by ship to other coastal regions. Margaret Paston writes to her husband about her Lentern supplies of food and comments that she has been unable to obtain any supplies of eels, but 'as for herring I have bought a horse-load for 4s. 6d.'[4] Margery Kempe several times mentions stockfish, which applied to cod, codling, haddock and other similar fish, cured by being split and dried in the sun, and which were apparently in great demand. Certain streets in Lynn, Codling Lane and Stockfish Row, were particularly associated with the curing and sale of this type of fish. One has only to read of the immense quantity and variety of fish consumed by the guests at a feast given by Thomas Arundel, then Bishop to Ely, to realise how important a part of the English diet fish was, especially during the season of Lent and the great feast days. For the Feast of the Translation of St Etheldreda of Ely (17 October) the menu included codling, plaice, turbot, eels, lamprey, pike, merlin, sturgeon, and herring. And for the Feast of the Assumption (15 August), when Arundel's sister, Joan, was staying at his Downham residence, the fish was equally plentiful, with the addition of porpoise, crab, lobster, perch and roach.[5]

The prosperity of Lynn depended largely upon its strategic position on the estuary of the river Ouse, not only because of the convenience of importing and exporting goods to and from Europe, but because of the convenience of transporting commodities inland by means of the Ouse and its network of tributaries, to the counties of Norfolk, Suffolk, Cambridgeshire, Bedfordshire, Northamptonshire, Leicestershire and Warwickshire. These counties in turn sent local products to Lynn and other parts of Norfolk, for example sedge, reeds and turf from the Fens and stone from the quarries of Northamptonshire and Leicestershire. The abbeys of Crowland and Ramsey, the cathedrals at Ely, Bury St Edmunds and Peterborough and many fenland churches were constructed of the freestone from quarries at Barnack. Stone was also required for the construction of walls, with which the majority of medieval towns were surrounded. Scattered remains survive in Lynn at Kettlewell Lane, the Walks and Wyatt Street.

As well as rivers being utilised extensively by merchant vessels in the Middle Ages, they were often used for passenger travel. The sacrist of Ely, during the fourteenth century, regularly travelled by boat along the Ouse and the Cam to the synods at Barnwell in Cambridge and by the same means to Lynn. Thomas Arundel travelled around his diocese of Ely as much by barge as on horseback. Manorial accounts show too that his personal baggage and household possessions were conveyed by water. Heavier commodities were likewise transported along the Ouse, as was, for example, a mill-stone purchased at Lynn in 1383 for the mill at

Great Shelford in Cambridge.[6] Sailing was especially well suited to the conditions which existed in the flat marshlands around Ely, where there were few trees to break or divert the wind.[7]

A characteristic feature of Bishop's Lynn were its many 'fleets' or tidal channels which intersected the town in every direction, and flowed into the river Ouse through openings in the embankment, filling up at high tide and being left shallow at low water. Fresh water supplies for the use of the inhabitants of Lynn were obtained from the river Gay, which rises about eight miles to the east of the town from the chalklands near the village of Grimston. In order that the fresh water supplies from the uplands should not become polluted by the salt water from the fleets, strong stone sluices with stout gates were constructed to keep the tidal waters back. A supply of fresh water for domestic purposes was retained in what was called the 'Common Ditch'. The municipal records tell of an irresponsible citizen, who maliciously permitted salt water to enter the Common Ditch, thus polluting the town's supply of fresh water, for which crime he was placed in the pillory on the Tuesday Marketplace for one day and then ordered to abjure the realm. Despite the numerous sluices that were constructed to prevent the rising tides from flooding the town, the citizens were in daily fear of being inundated with the sea water. Repairs to the sluices, walls and banks caused the townsfolk constant anxiety and expense. In the reign of Henry IV there is a record of the rents and profits of the Guild of St George being spent on 'repairing the banks, walls, fleets and watercourses of Lynn, without which the said village could not be preserved from the violence of the sea'.[8]

The two main fleets were the Purfleet to the north and the Millfleet to the south, and it was between these two fleets that the original, or first medieval town, developed, the nucleus of the town being in the region of St Margaret's Church. In this area the population was most densely concentrated, which soon resulted in the building of tenements, workshops, merchant houses, warehouses, guildhalls, quays and staithes. The growth of the town was rapid and by the time Bishop Turbe was in office as Bishop of Norwich (1146–1174) it had begun to extend northwards beyond the Purfleet to what became known as The New Land, the second

St George's Guildhall (north view), King's Lynn from a drawing by Revd E. Edwards, 1861.

Guildhall of the Holy Trinity, King's Lynn. Deeds and Records of the Borough of King's Lynn, Henry Harrod, London, 1874.

medieval town, or North Lynn. This new urban area had its own church, a chapel of ease to St Margaret's, called St Nicholas' Chapel. It had, too, a weekly market and an annual fair both of which were held on the Tuesday Market, one of the most magnificent and expansive areas of Lynn, which at that time opened onto the waterfront, thus facilitating the loading and unloading of cargoes. These two settlements, the first medieval town and the second medieval town, remained virtually separate towns until the year 1204, when they were united to form one borough and were granted a charter by King John under the name Bishop's Lynn, a name which was retained until the time of Henry VIII, when in 1537 it was renamed King's Lynn.

A third town developed to the south of the Millfleet, known as South Lynn, which was largely agricultural, outside the Bishop's jurisdiction, and had no market or fair of its own, with the consequence that it flourished less than the other two regions. Margery Kempe makes no specific mention of South Lynn, though she must certainly have known it well and travelled through it on her various journeys southwards. It was in South Lynn that one of her staunchest supporters, Aleyn of Lynn, lived as a member of the Carmelite order. Margery makes no reference either to the charming little church in South Lynn, All Saints, of greater antiquity than St Margaret's, where an anchorite occupied a cell on the south side, a cell which for centuries has been in a ruinous condition, but which has recently been beautifully restored.

The wealth and prosperity of Lynn is evidenced by its splendid buildings: its guildhalls, its elegant churches, merchant houses, town walls and fine stone gateways. Many of these have perished with the passing of time, but sufficient remain to impress and delight the visitor. Two guildhalls survive: the Guildhall of the Holy Trinity, with its imposing chequered facade of flint flushwork, in the Saturday Market, and the Guildhall of St George in King Street (then Checker Street). The Guildhall of the Trinity was built in Margery's time in 1422, when she would have been about fifty years old. She would also have known the earlier guidhall, which stood near to the north porch of the church, and which was destroyed by fire on January 3 1420/1421, together with the messuage of Geoffrey Cantley.[9] The municipal records of course preserve a reference to this disastrous event, but it is of interest to possess an account of a first hand witness, that of Margery Kempe. She writes,

> **It happened at one time that there was a great fire in Bishop's Lynn, which burnt down the guildhall of the Trinity, and if it had not been for the grace of God and a miracle, the whole town might have been set alight and the parish church destroyed. This church, dedicated to St Margaret, is a noble and stately building, revered by all.** [Ch 67]

Margery proceeds to relate how she witnessed the dreadful raging of the fire and the sparks entering the lantern of the church, and of how she besought the Lord that he would have mercy on the people and send them some favourable weather to put out the flames. Then, to the astonishment of all, three men came into the church, their clothes covered in snow.

> **'Look, Margery!' they exclaimed, 'see how gracious our Lord God has been to us. He has sent us a heavy fall of snow to quench this fire. So cheer up and thank God for his goodness.'** [Ch 67]

The second guildhall, St George's, in King Street, dates from the early fifteenth century, and like the Guildhall of the Trinity, has a large upper floor room, used in medieval times for guild meetings, commercial activities and for various feasts and festivities. King Street was the location of a further guildhall, the Guildhall of Corpus Christi, of which nothing now survives. An entry in the Lynn Registers states that Margery's father, John Brunham, granted the Guild of Corpus Christi a messuage, a shop and the financial profits from a ferry boat, which probably refers to the ferry, which then as now, ran from Ferry Lane (Cowgate) across the river to West Lynn.

The merchant Guild of the Trinity, the most powerful of all the guilds in Lynn, acquired much of its wealth from donations and legacies of wealthy members of the borough and from the high fee charged for membership. It also imposed heavy fines for failure to attend the general meetings, and for misbehaviour at the meetings, such as appearing barefooted or unsuitably clad, or for sleeping during meetings and ceremonies. But, while the Trinity Guild was an opulent society, it was also a magnanimous one, since it contributed to a variety of good causes, charitable institutions and needy individuals, to the lame, the leprous, the blind, the poor. It initiated and funded local projects, and undertook the building and repair of churches and gave assistance to hermits and anchorites in and around Lynn. The Guild had its own special chapel in St Margaret's Church, where daily celebrations of Mass took place, and where annual celebrations were held on the Eve of Trinity Day and on Trinity Day itself. Prayers were continually offered for departed members and lavish funerals held for those who had died, all services being marked by the use of many lights and torches.[10]

Like every other medieval town, Lynn was the scene of a multitude of crafts, trades and industries each with its own craft guild. There were masons, tilers, sadlers, glaziers, tanners, chandlers, parchment-makers, combers and carders of wool, spinners, weavers, fullers, dyers, drapers and numerous others, the workers in each craft or trade tending to congregate in occupational zones, often giving their name to the streets and localities in which they operated.[11] For example in Lynn, skinners and parchment-makers practised their trade in Skinners Row; meat was on sale in Butchers Lane and the wool market was in Woolpack Street.

Beautiful as medieval Lynn must have been, nevertheless it had its grim and sordid aspects: its narrow, dark and dirty streets, its muckhills and common privies, its rowdy taverns and ale-houses, its drunkards, thieves and brawlers, its rats and rotting fish; its diseases and pestilences. The squalid conditions that prevailed in all urban environments has been vividly described by a modern historian. 'Standards of housing and nutrition depended largely on family income, but other features of urban life – filth running in open ditches in the streets, fly-blown meat and stinking fish, contaminated and adulterated ale, polluted well-water, unspeakable privies, epidemic diseases, casual interpersonal violence, disastrous fires – were all experienced indiscriminately by all social classes.'[12] A bye-law was passed in Lynn in 1424 forbidding butchers to slaughter their animals in the streets; and in Norwich in 1390 a William Gerard was fined 20s. for leaving a dead horse for a long time in the King's Highway 'to the abominable offence and poisoning of the air'.[13] Margery Kempe speaks of the 'ooze and muck' that filled the gutters, or channels, which ran down the middle of the streets in Lynn. She complains too of a wretched fellow who deliberately threw a bowlful of water on her head as she was coming along the street, not an uncommon occurrence, since irresponsible folk would often dispose of their rubbish and dirty water by pitching it from an upper story window into the street below.

Overcrowded and insanitary living conditions, the consumption of contaminated food and water, unsatisfactory means of the disposal of garbage and sewage, and ignorance of the most elementary aspects of hygiene, caused disease in the medieval town to thrive. The diagnosis and treatment of sickness was a haphazard affair, depending on a certain amount of accurate medical knowledge and experience of previous cases, on a familiarity with the curative properties of herbs, a belief in astrology and magic, and the use of charms and potions. Qualified doctors were few, and only the rich could afford to take advantage of their services. Most of the educated doctors of the time were clergy, but the Church forbade the practice of surgery, because of taboos about the shedding of blood and contact with blood. Surgical operations, therefore, were in the hands of barber-surgeons and other similar humble practitioners. One ailment was often confused with another, almost every skin disease being identified as leprosy, even syphilis being included in this general term. Real leprosy was common in England before the Crusades, but the disease was rare in England after 1400.

In Margery's day the number of lepers therefore was comparatively small. That they existed in Lynn is evidenced by the fact that she visited a leper house, fired with zeal to be like Jesus who had compassion on lepers and like St Francis who embraced and kissed them.

She began to love what she had once hated most, for in the days of her worldly prosperity and pride, there was nothing more loathsome and horrible to her than the sight of a leper, but now, through the mercy of our Lord, she desired to embrace and kiss them, for the love of Jesus. [Ch 74]

She therefore asked permission of her confessor to go to a leper house so that she might kiss lepers, and to this he agreed, ordering her, presumably for propriety's sake, only to kiss women who had the disease.

> **She was overjoyed that he had given her leave to kiss sick women. So she went to a place where there were women full of the disease ... and while she was there she kissed two sick women and had many holy thoughts and shed many devout tears, and encouraged them with many kind words, urging them to be meek and patient and not to complain about their sickness.** [Ch 74]

To which lazar-house in Lynn Margery went we do not know, though it was very probably the Hospital of St Mary Magdalene on the Gaywood Causeway, since it was there that Margery's learned friend, Aleyn of Lynn, was reader in divinity. The hospital was governed by a prior, housed twelve brethren and took in men and women lepers. The regulations stipulated that the lepers were to refrain from wandering about in public and were to keep to the places assigned to them. They were to attend the seven Canonical Hours and Mass, and on Maundy Thursday they were each to be given a herring and a farthing.

There were other hospitals in and around Lynn which admitted lepers. These were in Cowgate (between the present High Street and King Street, running into Ferry Lane), at Gaywood, Setchey, Harwick (a hamlet in the parish of North Runcton) and one across the river at West Lynn. There was a further hospital of some importance in Damgate, though there is no mention of lepers being admitted to it. The hospital, dedicated to John the Baptist, was run by a master and a few brethren, and was composed of an infirmary, a church, houses and a hall, the decrees ruling that the Prior of Lynn was to visit the hospital every year and to bury the dead in the graveyard of St Margaret's church.[14]

To the medieval mind with its clearly defined sense of good and evil, right and wrong, sickness was commonly regarded as a punishment for sin. Thus Margery prefaces her account of her own illnesses with the comment, 'The God punished her with many great sicknesses'. She reports that, following her return from her overseas pilgrimages, she suffered from intermittent attacks of dysentery, which reduced her to extreme weakness. At another time she experienced 'a great sickness in her head, and later in her back' and this was followed by an ailment in her right side, which lasted on and off for over eight years, and during one of these attacks,

> **She would vomit all that was in her stomach and it was as bitter as gall, and while the sickness lasted she could neither eat nor drink, but could only groan until it had passed ... and then she would pray 'Ah, dear Lord, because of your great pain, have mercy on my little pain'.** [Ch 56]

After returning to England from the warmer climates of Italy and the Middle East, she found Lynn uncomfortably cold, and as winter approached she complained of poverty and being unable to purchase fuel to keep herself warm. Contemporary records make frequent reference to fuel required for heating, cooking and lighting. In 1372 John of Gaunt sent the poor lazars of Leicester three cartloads of wood for fuel for the winter, and the same for the prisoners of Newgate. England was still comparatively well supplied with woods and forests, and therefore logs and faggots were readily available, though turf was a valuable substitute and very plentiful in the Fens.

The principal means of lighting houses was by candles of wax or tallow, wax being an expensive item of the household budget. The wealthy possessed numerous candlesticks and candelabras, but the very poor depended mainly on cresset lamps, which consisted of bowls in which wicks floated in liquid wax or tallow. Most families, however, depended heavily on natural daylight, ordering their lives and activities to fit into a routine of rising at sunrise and retiring to bed at sunset.

As an ecclesiastical centre Bishop's Lynn was one of the most notable in Norfolk, with its fine parish church and priory, its two chapels of ease and its four orders of friars: the Franciscans, the Dominicans, the Carmelites and the Augustinians. Throughout her *BOOK*, Margery speaks of the parish church of St Margaret's and of her profound indebtedness to its parish priest, Master Robert Spryngolde. Officially the parson of the parish was the prior of the Benedictine priory, but parochial duties, such as the conducting of services, the celebration of the sacraments, and the pastoral care of the parishioners, was delegated to chaplains or secular (non-monastic) priests, who nevertheless remained subordinate to the prior. Thus while Thomas Hevingham was prior of Lynn, we hear Margery Kempe speaking of Master Robert as her 'parish priest'.

Apart from the prior of Lynn, Thomas Hevingham, Margery refers to another prior, though not by name, who temporarily supplanted and ultimately succeeded Thomas Hevingham. He was John Derham, who, according to Margery's account, was despatched to Lynn while Hevingham, for some undisclosed reason, was recalled to the Norwich priory. Derham remained in Lynn for only a short while, for Hevingham soon returned to resume his duties as prior. Hevingham, however, was now an old man and continued as prior for only about four years until his death, after which John Derham was promptly despatched to Lynn again, where he remained as full-time prior. He was a learned and eminent cleric and evidently in the king's favour, being appointed, together with other notable clergy, to go overseas with Henry V, who was engaged in his third military campaign against the French. John Derham, therefore, made preparations for his departure from Lynn and sorrowfully took leave of his friends, thinking that he might never return to Lynn again, since he was a man of weak constitution and frail health. But as events turned out he was never to go to France,for the king died of dysentery, a disease which claimed many of his soldiers. The year was 1422.

First and foremost St Margaret's was a conventual church, a private place of worship for the prior and convent, though it also served as a parish church for parishioners, who had access to the nave in the daytime and at night. Benedictine and Augustinian houses frequently allowed the nave of their churches to be used for parochial worship, the altar for the laity being placed by the rood screen. We have already observed how Margery Kempe rose at two or three o'clock in the morning before the first light of day, and proceeded to the church to pray. It is of interest to note that two o'clock was the precise time when the monks said their first

The Braunche Brass (Robert Braunche and his wives Letita and Margaret), St Margaret's Church, King's Lynn, 1364. (Brass 8ft 10in x 5ft 2in).

office of the day, Vigils (or Nocturns). Carrying their lanterns with them, they left the dorter by the night stairs which led direct to the choir. If we are right in supposing that Margery lived in Fincham Street or possibly Stonegate, where her father owned a tenement, then she would not have had a great distance to walk in the early hours of the morning for her devotions, since both streets are in the town centre, near to St Margaret's church.

Compared to the medieval churches of today, which are comparatively plain and unadorned, medieval churches as they existed in their own period of history, were lavishly decorated and resplendent with colour. Scarcely any part of the church was without some form of artistic embellishment. Walls, roofs, choirstalls, screens, fonts, font-covers, pulpits, misericords were all enriched with either paint and gilding or carvings and sculptures. Scenes from the Bible, stories and legends of saints, apostles, prophets, martyrs, all were colourfully portrayed to beautify the church and to instruct the unlettered layfolk. And to crown all these decorative devices, there were the marvellous great windows, like the west window of St Nicholas' Chapel, filled with multi-coloured glass, which, when the sun shone through them, created a glorious blaze of colour in the interior of the churches. Brass enthusiasts will be familiar with the two fine flemish brasses in the south chancel aisle, which portray Adam de Walsokne (Walsoken) and his wife (1349), and Robert Braunche and his two wives (1364). The latter brass depicts, at the base, minstrels heralding the commencement of the famous Peacock Feast which Braunche, as mayor of Lynn, gave to Edward III during his visit to the town.

Drawing of frieze at base of Braunche Bras

Art, literature and drama, all combined to form one cohesive and didactic force, each medium of communication coming under the aegis and direction of the Church, no medium operating independently of the others, each contributing to the propagation of the Church's message of man's salvation in Christ, each amplifying and reinforcing the Church's formal and traditional teaching. So interdependent and intertwined are the images and illustrations which appear in art, literature and drama, that it is often impossible to discover the origin of any one particular piece of imagery or symbolism, whether the artist drew his inspiration from literature, or literature from the artist, whether the manuscript illuminator was dependent on the glass painter or vice versa.

From Margery Kempe's account of the great fire which destroyed the Guildhall of the Holy Trinity we gather that there was a lantern tower on the summit of St Margaret's church, which was similar to that of Ely Cathedral. But she was never to witness the magnificent pinnacle which was erected on the top of the lantern in 1484, some years after her death. Nor did Margery live to see the graceful spire built on the north west tower as shown in some ancient prints. But neither the lantern nor the spire were to survive, for in 1741 a fearful storm brought the spire crashing to the ground, damaging the lantern as it fell, and neither was rebuilt.[15]

On the south side of the church were the buildings of the priory, none of which survive except for the broad archway of the southern range, now incorporated into one of the houses in Priory Lane. The Priory consisted of living quarters, hall, parlour, kitchen, dormitory, guest house, library and chapel. The compre-

in St Margaret's, King's Lynn, Norfolk

hensive inventory witnesses to the comparatively comfortable conditions in which the monks lived, neither too affluent nor too spartan. Such moderation is consistent with the Benedictine Rule, which did not demand excessive austerity of the brethren. Included in the inventory are such items as tables, chairs, benches and chests, cushions, quilts, bed-covers, tapestries, wall-hangings, fine red curtains, candelabras and gold and silver plate.[16]

The second medieval town, North Lynn, was conspicuous for its very fine chapel of ease, that of St Nicholas, with its richly carved porch, large west window and spacious interior. Founded in 1146, and rebuilt in Margery's day, in the late fourteenth and early fifteenth centuries, it was at the centre of a controversy concerning its status as a chapel of ease, subordinate to St Margaret's. Margery was about five years old when, in 1378, an attempt was made to obtain certain ecclesiastical privileges for the chapel, of which the parishioners were justly proud. A number of wealthy and influential persons wished to have St Nicholas' elevated to the status of a parish church, with a font of its own, so that baptisms might be celebrated there without the necessity of having to resort to St Margaret's. They wished also to obtain the permission to have marriages celebrated in the chapel, and the churching of women. But as F. A. Gasquet informs us 'by the ordinary law of the Middle Ages a font could only be set up in a parish church; and in the case of a chapel of ease, children had generally to be brought to the mother church for baptisms'.[17]

The Red Register of Lynn furnishes us with details as to how this dispute was resolved, which may be summarised as follows: A certain John Peye, chaplain of St Nicholas' had 'fraudulently and surrepticiously' obtained a bull from Pope Urban VI, authorising the celebration of baptisms, marriages and the churching of women in the chapel, on condition that this would not be to the detriment and derogation of the mother church. At a large assembly of eighty two burgesses, including Margery's father, then mayor for the second time, the matter was discussed, and both John Peye and the papal bull utterly denounced, since it was claimed that the granting of such privileges to the Chapel would be prejudicial to the mother church of St Margaret's. Furthermore it was claimed that the distance between the two churches was but 'three stadia' (one stadia being equivalent to about 184 metres) and that the way was safe for the parishioners to make the short journey to the mother church. The matter was then referred to the learned and distinguished prior of the neighbouring Augustinian Priory of Pentney, who perused the relevant documents, and deciding that each and every parishioner residing near St Nicholas' Chapel should go to the parish church of St Margaret's for the sacraments and the services concerned.[18]

But the dispute over the font rumbled on for a number of years, and in 1431–2, when John Derham was prior of Lynn, a further request was made for a font to be installed in St Nicholas's Chapel. Margery Kempe, desiring the pre-eminence of the parish church to be maintained, vigorously opposed the request, and being a woman of prophetic gifts, assured the priest, who later became her scribe and amanuensis, that even if the people paid large sums of money to have their way, they would not succeed in having it. The matter was finally resolved when the Bishop of Norwich, William Alnwick (1426–1436) consented to permit the parishioners to place a font in St Nicholas' Chapel on certain conditions, but as the parishioners rejected the conditions, no font was put into the Chapel until two centuries later.

A further chapel of ease, that of St James, also figures in Margery's *BOOK*. Built in the first half of the twelfth century in what is now London Road, opposite to the Police Station, the chapel in Margery's time was the scene of vigorous religious activity when a celebrated Franciscan friar, probably William Melton, arrived in the town and was invited to preach at St James's. The priest in charge of St James's had warned this eminent preacher of Margery's inclination to cry during sermons.

> **'Do not be displeased about what I am going to tell you sir, but there is a woman here who will come and hear your sermon, who weeps and sobs when she hears about the Passion of our Lord, or any other subject of high devotion. Her crying does not last long, so endure it patiently good sir, and if she makes any noise during your sermon do not be dismayed.'** [Ch 61]

Friars in their long black, white or grey robes were a familiar sight in the streets of Lynn. The Franciscans, or Grey friars, followers of that mild and gentle saint, Francis of Assisi, had arrived in England in 1224, and in Bishop's Lynn in about 1230, the first of the mendicant orders to come to the town. They built their friary and church in the district between what is now Tower Street and St James Street, its location easily identified by the Grey Friars Tower, which dominates the town centre and is a familiar landmark. If this elegant, octagonal lantern tower of the late fourteenth century is any indication of what the remainder of the church and monastic buildings were like, then they were truly magnificent.

The Dominicans, Black Friars or Preaching Friars, established their house on the east side of Lynn, north of the Purfleet, in the district now occupied by South Clough Lane and Blackfriars Street. Their order was apparently much favoured by the people, especially by the wealthy urban folk who made handsome bequests to them in their wills. All three of the King Edwards made generous gifts to the Black friars of Lynn when they visited the town.

The Carmelites, or White Friars settled in South Lynn, near to All Saints' Church overlooking the river Nar, a tributary of the Ouse. All that survives of this once large and imposing religious house is the fourteenth century gateway, near the junction of Bridge Street and Birdcage Walk.

The fourth order of friars were the Austin friars, not to be confused with the Augustinian Canons, of which we shall hear more later. These friars chose a site in North Lynn for the foundation of their friary, near to the Tuesday Market, on the east side of Chapel Street (then Listergate Street) and bounded to the north by Austin Street (Hopmans Way). Thomas Arundel, then Bishop of Ely, accompanied by his sister, Joan, Countess of Hereford, and a large retinue, were entertained to supper by the Austin friars of Lynn on 11 August 1383, breakfasting with them the next day, the Bishop reimbursing them for the expenses they had incurred. He and his sister were staying at Wisbech Castle at the time, and their visit to Lynn was apparently a costly business, for their sixty horses had to be transported across the river Ouse.[19]

Hermits and anchorites were a common feature of the religious scene in medieval England, the principal difference between them being that hermits were free to roam the country, while anchorites remained in their anchorholds and normally took a vow of enclosure. The anchorhold was not always, as is often supposed, a tiny cell, where the anchorite was walled in, though it could sometimes have been precisely that. It might, however, have consisted of a two or three-roomed house, with a parlour, a kitchen, a guest room and perhaps a walled garden. Often an anchorage was constructed against the wall of a church, and had a window looking into the church, so that the recluse could take part in the religious services and receive communion. One of their most important functions, apart from prayer and contemplation, was to dispense advice to all who sought it, as did Margery Kempe from Dame Julian of Norwich.

Men and woman who chose to live this secluded or semi-secluded life, took vows of claustration before the bishop of the diocese in which they intended to dwell, a license being given to them by the bishop, who alone could release them from their vow and revoke their license. Thus we find Bishop Goldwell of Norwich, in the late fifteenth century giving an aged and ill anchoress of Lynn permission to quit her cell in Lynn for a bed in the infirmary at Denny Abbey in Cambridgeshire.[20] From the thirteenth to the fifteenth century the wealthy merchant class was renowned for the generous donations they made to this group of religious enthusiasts who depended on charity for their livelihood, often placing almsboxes outside their cells to receive gifts of money or food. The Lynn archives contain a number of entries in connection with anchorites, for instance in 1386 a payment of 20s was made to the anchorite dwelling in the cell attached to All Saints Church. In medieval wills anchorites figure prominently too. Bishops John Wakering of Norwich (1416–1425) left a sum of about a hundred marks to be shared by the anchorites, recluses and other poor folk in his diocese, especially in the rural areas.[21]

Hermits were usually, though not exclusively male, and, like anchorites, were required to receive a license from the bishop in whose diocese they occupied their hermitage. Too much wandering was disapproved of by the ecclesiastical authorities and could result in the loss of the license, as could any other kind of misbehaviour, since not all hermits were holy and virtuous men.

St Nicholas Church, King's Lynn from a drawing by J. B. Ladbrooke, 1826.

Part of Old Town Wall with White Tower, Lynn, as they appeared in 1800.

Some were imposters, thriving on the charity of others, frequenting ale-houses, eating and drinking abundantly, and idly passing their time in gossip and merry-making. But the conscientious hermits, like Richard Rolle of Hampole, devoted themselves to study, prayer and good works. 'These men fasted, had ecstasies, were tempted by the devil ... and pilgrims flocked to their cells in order to be sanctified by their advice and presence.'[22]

As well as engaging in spiritual activities, the hermit also served the community in a multitude of practical ways. He repaired roads and bridges, his hermitage often being positioned on or close to a bridge; he guarded the town gates; he maintained beacons at the estuaries of rivers or other coastal areas for the guidance of seafarers; he conducted travellers across rivers and over treacherous parts of the country and the highways. For these, and other valuable services to the community he received a modest renumeration, a pension and gifts and bequests from appreciative citizens. Numerous records survive of the benevolence displayed towards hermits, since the whole community depended on them. At Lynn a hermit received an annuity of 13s to keep the town bridge in order. A William Warde, hermit of Beccles, kept the great bridge and chapel there in a state of repair.[23] The accounts of the Guild of the Holy Trinity in Lynn state that a donation was made in the reign of Edward III of 5s to the hermit of St Nicholas' Chapel, and in the reign of Richard II 6s 8d was paid to Thomas, the hermit at the South Gates, and 5s to the female hermit, Ann Whyote at the East Gate.[24]

The main highway into Lynn was by Damgate (Norfolk Street) and entered the town by the East Gate, which stood in the vicinity of what is in the present day the Hob-in-the-Well public house in Littleport Street. This gate was commonly known as St Catherine's Gate, since a chapel was built on the site and was dedicated to St Catherine of Alexandria. This chapel was sold in 1549 as a private dwelling 'because John Consolif wished to live there in a solitary life, depending on the alms of good people'.[25]

King's Lynn looking across from West Lynn.
M. Booth. Norwich 1780.

CHAPTER FOUR

Margery Kempe and the Secular Clergy

As we would expect of a religious enthusiast like Margery Kempe, she associates much with the clergy. The charming pen portraits she provides of individual clergy with whom she came into contact, constitute one of the most delightful aspects of her *BOOK*. As with clergy of all epochs of history, they were a motley collection, some eminent and at the pinnacle of the ecclesiastical hierarchy, some learned, some virtuous, some idle, neglectful and worldly and some like Chaucer's poor parson: 'A holy minded man ... benign and diligent and patient when adversity was sent ... Christ and his disciples and their lore he taught, but followed it himself before.'[1]

Of the eminent, virtuous and learned Margery writes a great deal, for it is with these that she chiefly associated, to these she resorted for instruction, advice and edification, to these she made her confessions, and to these she disclosed her visions and her homely discourses with Jesus. But first and foremost it was her parish priest in Lynn, her spiritual father and confessor, who was of special importance to her. When asked by Jesus whom she would choose to be her companion and friend in heaven, she replies that she would choose her parish priest, Master Robert Spryngolde. But why, asks Jesus, would she not choose her natural father to be her companion in heaven, to which she replies,

> **'Because I can never repay Master Robert for his goodness to me and his gracious work in hearing my confessions.'** [Ch 8]

By giving priority to her spiritual father over her earthly father, Margery is affirming her belief in the primacy of spirit over flesh, soul over body, which accords with the teaching of the gospel.[2] She considers that those who help her spiritually deserve her highest gratitude and praise, for by instructing her, ministering to her and setting an example to her, they show her the path to heaven and help her to walk along it. After declaring her choice of Master Robert to be her companion in heaven, Jesus informs Margery that she will be granted her wish, and assures her that her earthly father, her husband and all her children will be saved. As to Master Robert, Jesus promises her that she and he will rejoice together in heaven.

> **'Believe it for a certainty, daughter, that you and he will have much joy in heaven at the last, and will bless the time that you ever knew one another. And, daughter, you will be everlastingly thankful to me for giving you such a true spiritual father, for although he has sometimes been sharp with you, this has been very much to your profit, for if it had not been so, you would have had too much personal affection for him ... You have great faith in his words, and so you should have, for he is not a man to flatter you.'** [Ch 88]

The clergy in the Middle Ages were divided into two main categories. They were the secular clergy, of whom Robert Spryngolde was one, who formed the majority of men in holy orders and who lived, and conducted their ministry in the world (in seculo). Then there were the regulars, who belonged to a religious community and followed a Rule (regula). The secular clergy occupied positions as archbishops, bishops, archdeacons, deans of cathedrals, parish priests, vicars, curates and chaplains. Some bishops, however, belonged also to religious communities, as did Bishop Peverel of Worcester, a Carmelite, or White friar. In 1265, the pope offered the see of York to the eminent Franciscan theologian, St Bonaventure. John Peckham, an outstanding archbishop of Canterbury (1279–92), was also a Franciscan friar, who had studied at Paris and Oxford and then joined the Franciscans, becoming Provincial of his Order, rising to power as theologian and lecturer at the papal curia and being appointed Archbishop of Canterbury by the pope. A great number of bishops were the nominees of popes. Royal patronage also played an important role in a man's elevation to a bishopric, which was often the reward for some kind of service to the king. 'The road to a bishopric was not

4. The Miraculous Draught of Fishes – detail from 13th c. Bible Window III, North Quire Aisle, Canterbury Cathedral.

5. Judgement, 15th c. Window, Fairford, Oxon.

6. Corporal Acts of Mercy (15th c.) window, All Saints, York.

7. Jesus is nailed to the cross. Nave Roof Boss, Norwich Cathedral.

success as a parish priest, but by distinction in the more aristocratic world of monasteries, the universities, and the bureaucracies of bishops, popes and kings.'[3]

Numerous other men were classed as 'clergy', though they did not hold high office, nor did they hold benefices, but might have been employed as chantry priests, domestic chaplains, stand-ins for absentee rectors, tutors, lawyers, secretaries, confidential advisers, custodians of legal documents or keepers of small schools. These unbeneficed clergy were very numerous and often outnumbered the beneficed clergy. Some parishes has resident rectors, though it was also possible for a rector, with permission, to live elsewhere as a university scholar or as an ecclesiastical official, supported by the income from his parish. John Wyclif, for example, held three parishes in succession between the dates 1361 and 1384, but habitually resided at Oxford until the last two years of his life.[4]

The clerical profession was immensely popular in the Middle Ages, since it assured those who entered it a fixed, though often meagre, means of livelihood. It also gave such men a status above their fellows, and an opportunity, if they were able and diligent, to rise in the ranks of the hierarchy, and because of their education they were often involved in secular affairs, in the judiciary, for example, in business, education, agriculture, diplomatic service and so forth. The higher clergy were particularly involved in affairs of state, archbishops and bishops often being as adept, shrewd and competent in political matters as they were in religious.

We may gain some idea of the numerical strength of the clergy by looking at two typical English dioceses in the fourteenth century. In the diocese of Exeter, from March to December in the year 1373, Bishop Brantyngham ordained 500 men. Of these he ordained 85 to the priesthood, 88 to the diaconate and numerous others to minor orders. William of Wykeham, during his thirty seven years as bishop of Winchester (1367–1404) ordained 1,273 men to the priesthood, 1,382 to the office of sub-deacon and 1,334 as acolytes. The country swarmed with clerics, though only a small proportion of them ever became ministers of religion or held benefices.[5]

There was a great variation in educational attainments of the clergy in the Middle Ages, and no uniform system of theological training as there is today. Some had a university training, though the expense was an obstacle to many. The register of Bishop Stapledon in the fourteenth century states that there were only 25 Masters among the whole cathedral and parish clergy of his diocese of Exeter who had stayed for the whole university course. The training at the universities tended to be directed towards the qualifying of professional theologians, canon lawyers and administrators and not to the training of parish priests. Full courses at the universities of Oxford and Cambridge were very protracted: six years for a mastership in the Arts, and a further eight years for theology. Oxford trainied the intelligentia, its scholars being mostly clerics, but many of these did not end up serving in parochial work but took up academic or administrative posts.[6]

Those clergy who did not have the benefit of a university education would have received their training at cathedral schools, at the schools of the friars, or at grammar schools, of which there were many in the fifteenth century, or they may have gained their knowledge and experience from a senior priest. Numerous manuals were in current use for the instruction of parish priests, notable among them John Mirk's *Instruction for Parish Priests* in the vernacular, which dealt with such matters as how the priest should dress and behave, how to hear confessions and instruct the laity in the Ten Commandments, the Seven Deadly Sins, the Seven Virtues, the Creed, the Hail Mary and the Lord's Prayer. John Mirk also wrote a manual for the more educated clergy which contained more elaborate instructions. This was *Manuale Sacerdotis*.[7]

Among the secular clergy who played an influential role in Margery's spiritual growth was Richard of Caister, vicar of St Stephen's church in Norwich from 1402 to 1420, a man very much like Chaucer's poor parson though more in character and disposition, than in poverty, for Caister was not poor, and had money to leave in his will. Margery provides us with an engaging account of her first meeting with this saintly man.

Dressed in black at this time, she made her way to Norwich, and arrived at the church a little before noon ... She greeted the vicar and asked if she might speak to him about the love of God, for an hour or perhaps two, in the [Ch 17]

> **afternoon when he had eaten. Then he lifted up his hands in amazement and said, "Bless us! however could a woman spend an hour or two speaking of the love of God? Indeed I will not eat anything until I have heard what you can say about God within the space of one hour.**
>
> **Then he sat himself down in the church, she a little aside from him, and she told him all that God had revealed to her in her soul. She described the kind of life she had lived since her childhood, as near as things came into her mind, how unkind she had been to our Lord Jesus Christ, how proud and vain in her behaviour, how rebellious against the laws of God and how envious towards her fellow-Christians. She told him too how, when it pleased our Lord, he chastised her with many trials and temptations, after which she was sustained and comforted by her meditations, especially when she thought about our Lord's Passion.**

She related to him how sometimes the Father in heaven spoke to her in her soul and sometimes the Son or the Holy Spirit, or our Lady, and how her 'dalliance' with our Lord was so sweet, so holy and devout, that she could scarcely endure it and she would cry and sob so passionately that she thought she would die. Richard of Caister listened with rapt attention to what she had to say and was convinced of her sincerity, and from now on, he took on the role as her confessor and gave her Communion whenever she came to Norwich and became one of her most loyal advocates, defending her against her enemies.

For about five years before becoming vicar of St Stephen's in Norwich, Richard of Caister had been Vicar of Sedgeford, a small village a mile or two east of Heacham in Norfolk. It is of interest to learn that in 1397, the prior and convent of Norwich presented the benefice of Sedgeford to Richard, which suggests that he was possibly one of the regular benedictine clergy of Norwich at the time of his appointment to Sedgeford, though the living could have been merely in the gift of Norwich Priory. But as Richard of Caister was parish priest of both Sedgeford and St Stephen's Norwich, which covered the major part of his career, he may be classed as one of the secular clergy of the Norwich Diocese.

Caister was alleged to have been a secret admirer of John

Sedgeford Church, Norfolk, from a drawing by H. D. Holbeach.

Wyclif, as no doubt many of the clergy were, and to have been much opposed to the decline in moral standards of his day. The emphasis which he placed on personal religion and good conduct, as well as his inclination towards mysticism and a personal approach to God through prayer, must certainly have been an important element in the attraction which he and Margery felt for one another. When commanded to appear before the bishop's officers to answer charges that had been brought against her, it was Caister who accompanied her and spoke up for her as her friend and advocate. In his will, we are told, he bequeathed the bulk of his possessions and wealth to the poor, which is consistent with Lollard doctrine which condemned the wealth of the religious orders and urged the end of property owning.[8]

A number of didactic works are attributed to Richard of Caister, including treatises on the Eight Beatitudes and the Ten Commandments. To him also is attributed the beautiful and widely known medieval lyric, *A Hymn to Jesus*.

Jesu, Lorde, that madeste me,
And with thy blessed blode hast bought,
Foryeve that I have greved thee
In worde, werke, will and thought.

Jesus, for thy woundes smerte
Of body, fete and hondes too,
Make me meke and lowe in herte,
And thee to love as I shulde do ...[9]

A further secular priest, of undisclosed name, was to bring great benefit to Margery and she to him. She relates how he was a newcomer to Lynn and had hired a room in the town where he lodged with his mother. He first encountered Margery in the streets of Lynn and felt powerfully moved to speak to her, but first he enquired of others what kind of woman she was. When they replied that they thought she was 'a right good woman' he sent for her, saying that he and his mother would like to speak with her. Both mother and son welcomed her warmly and as they talked together the priest took a book and read aloud the account of how Jesus wept over the city of Jerusalem. 'O Jerusalem, Jerusalem, which killeth the prophets, and stoneth them that are sent unto her! how often would I have gathered thy children together, even as a hen gathereth her chickens under her wings, and ye would not!' It was no doubt the pathos of the Bible passage and the tears of Jesus at his rejection that touched Margery's heart and moved her to break out into bitter sobs, neither the priest nor his mother knowing the cause of her weeping. When Margery had departed the priest remarked to his mother,

> **'I am absolutely amazed at the way this woman cries so much, and why she does so, but I think she is a good woman and I should like very much to speak with her again.' His mother was pleased about this and encouraged him to do so. Afterwards this same priest grew to love and trust her very much and to be thankful for the day that he met her, and to find much spiritual comfort in her. She caused him to look up many passages of scripture, and references to the doctors of the church, which he would not otherwise have done if she had not been there.** [Ch 58]

Margery reports that apart from the Bible and Bible commentaries this priest read other books to her, including books on contemplation, Hilton's book, Bridget's Revelations, The Goad of Love, Richard Rolle's Fire of Love and many more. These reading sessions covered a period of seven or eight years, so Margery would have been introduced to a great number of theological and devotional works during this time. The readings benefitted both Margery and the priest, the priest's knowledge being greatly extended because of his having to read and look up many religious works and Bible references, and as a result he was promoted to a benefice 'a great cure of souls'.

It was not only those clergy on the lower rungs of the ecclesiastical ladder, parish priests and humble friars, with whom Margery associated. She mixed freely with those at the top, with bishops and archbishops, doctors of divinity and doctors of the law, for as Professor Knowles says, 'Margery Kempe, like Teresa of Avila, made contact with some of the most eminent prelates, distinguished theologians, preachers and holy persons of her day.'[10] It was her ardent zeal for religion which attracted her to the clergy, and the clergy's education, learning and scholarship which she, as an illiterate laywoman, especially valued. The clergy, for their part, must have reacted variously towards this devout, eccentric and voluble lay-woman, some, like the priest we have described above, or Richard of Caister, greatly favouring her, siding with her, supporting her and showing a sympathetic attitude to her 'gifts of tears'. Others were less sympathetic and found her irritating, provoking and troublesome, as did the famous Grey friar, whose sermons she disturbed in St James's church in Lynn.

Margery's most illustrous acquaintance was Thomas Arundel, Archbishop of Canterbury, who talked with her in the garden of Lambeth Palace in the afternoon until the stars came out in the evening. Her encounter with the archbishop proved to be an altogether pleasant and amicable one, and for Arundel, who must have had weighty matters of Church and State on his mind, her visit no doubt provided some light relief and would have been a relaxed affair, since Margery was an easy conversationalist and never lost for words. She confided the secrets of her soul to him and told him of her manner of life and how our Lord spoke to her in her mind, revealing many truths and mysteries to her.

> **And her found no fault in her, and was full of praise for her way of life, and expressed his joy that our merciful Lord Jesus Christ was showing such grace in our own day.** [Ch 16]

The Archbishop responded magnanimously to her request that he give her permission to choose her confessor, and to receive communion every Sunday if God willed it. She requested also that he give her a letter of authority, which she could carry with her wherever she went within his province of Canterbury, allowing her to receive such weekly communion, for frequent communion was very rare in the Middle Ages, and required special authority. This he gladly gave and would take no payment, nor allow his secretaries to take any money for writing and sealing the letter.

Thomas Arundel (1353–1414) was of noble and royal parentage, his father, the wealthy and influential Richard Fitz Alan, earl of Arundel, his mother, Eleanor, the daughter of Henry Plantagenet, earl of Lancaster. In 1373, at the age of twenty he was ordained deacon and priest and consecrated bishop, all on the same day, and eight months later was consecrated to the see of Ely, which he occupied for fifteen years. Except for Easter visits,

Thomas Arundel seems rarely to have resided at his official palace at Ely, but chose instead to instal himself at his episcopal manor at Fen Ditton, from where he could readily attend meetings of the Bishops' Consistory Court at various churches in Cambridge, and which afforded him easy access to Ely by river. But like other bishops he possessed a number of manors, his favourite being at Little Downham. Others were at Wisbech Castle, Doddington, Somersham, Willingham and Balsham in Cambridgeshire, Little Hadham and Toteridge in Hertfordshire, and the finest and grandest of all, his residence at Holborn in London.

As Bishop of Ely, Thomas Arundel was occupied with a multitude of episcopal duties, more than at any other period of his tenure of high office. These duties included travelling round his diocese, which he executed with great diligence, ordaining, confirming, conferring tonsures, attending to unruly convents, dedicating churches, transacting diocesan business and attending to legal matters at the Consistory Courts, many of them concerning matrimonial offences and the misconduct of the clergy. For example, disciplinary action had to be taken over John Podington, rector of Newton in Cambridgeshire, who was accused of failing to conduct services and to bring communion to the sick, of allowing the chancel of the church to fall into ruins so that rain fell on the altar, and of being a public fornicator with many of his parishioners.[11] At this early stage of his career as Bishop of Ely he was also showing great concern about the spread of Lollardy, and writing to clergy warning them of deceitful men, parading as clergy, and taking upon themselves, without any ecclesiastical authority, the priestly duty of hearing confessions, preaching to the simple people, pretending to be bishops and conferring orders.

These great ecclesiastical figures of the past, like Thomas Arundel, appear to have an unreal quality about them, surrounded as they were by pomp, ceremonial and grandeur, but when we read about the ordinary everyday events of their lives, their domestic circumstances, their dwellings, their diet, their families, their parents, brothers and sisters, servants and so forth, they come to life, enabling us to see them as real human beings. The splendour and magnitude of Arundel's retinue and his lavish manner of living were not without their critics. Bishop Brinton (d. 1389) of

Rochester, for instance, who occupied one of the poorest sees in England, compared his retinue of twenty nine with Arundel's seventy eight, which included a number of clerks, squires, yeomen, grooms, pages, choristers and personal servants. And when on parliamentary duty in London and residing at his luxurious manor at Holborn, he kept a stable of about seventy to eighty horses with over twenty grooms, each receiving a daily wage.[12]

Thomas Arundel appears to have been on extremely good terms with his sister Joan, Countess of Hereford, who was frequently to be seen in his company, perhaps partly because of her premature state of widowhood. She possessed her own manor at Kimbolton and was widowed in 1373, her two daughters being about seven and four years of age when their father died. Joan was then in her late twenties, never remarried, and was to survive until 1419, aged about seventy two, outliving her brother Thomas by approximately three years. The visit of Margery Kempe to Lambeth Palace took place in the summer or early autumn of 1413, shortly before her departure from England for her tour of the Holy Places in Palestine and Italy, and only a few months before Arundel's death. Although the visit did not merit any mention in Arundel's official records, it must have been a very memorable occasion because of Margery's highly unusual character and extreme religious fervour, providing, as H. S. Bennett says 'the strongest possible evidence of the strength of personality and the essential orthodoxy of her views'.[13] This great prelate would hardly have frittered away his time speaking at such length to a woman of heretical opinions, for he was a passionate foe of heretics.

On arrival at the Archbishop's palace, Margery and her husband entered the hall and were confronted by some members of his retinue, clerks, yeomen and squires, who horrified Margery by the blasphemous oaths they swore and the other forms of reprehensible conduct they displayed. Not only did Margery rebuke them for their bad behaviour, but she put in a word of warning to the Archbishop as well.

> **'My lord, Archbishop, Almighty God has not given you your benefice and your wordly wealth to employ those who are traitors to our Lord, and by their great oaths, crucify him afresh every day. You will have to answer for** [Ch 16]

> **them, unless you either correct them or dismiss them from your service.'**

The Archbishop very kindly and meekly allowed her to speak her mind and responded favourably so that she had reason to believe that things would improve in this respect.

Margery also relates that she visited Thomas Arundel's successor, Henry Chichele, though she provides us with no details of this visit, which probably took place in the autumn of 1417. The purpose of the visit was to obtain from the Archbishop a letter of authority, the precise nature of which we are not told, though it was most likely an endorsement of that given to her by Thomas Arundel, granting her permission to choose her confessor and to receive weekly communion.

Henry Chichele had none of his predecessor's aristocratic lineage, his father being a small landowner and prominent merchant and burgess of Higham Ferrers in Northamptonshire. Educated at William of Wykeham's school at Winchester, and later at New College Oxford, Chichele's legal training and thorough knowledge of canon law, established him firmly on the road to ecclesiastical advancement. Following his ordination as deacon in 1392 he was to hold numerous appointments in the Church including Rector of St Stephen's Walbrook, Prebend of Rafyn, Archdeacon of Dorset, Archdeacon and Chancellor of Salisbury where he resided in the Close, and was appointed Vicar-General to the Bishop. In 1411 he was made Bishop of St David's while simultaneously being immersed in royal service at home and on diplomatic missions overseas. Finally he was appointed Archbishop of Canterbury by Henry V in 1414, an office which he held until 1443, the king having known him as a member of the Royal Court and valued him as a competent lawyer and diplomat and a person of good character, patient and humane. Chichele was generally well liked, was at home with the laity, had the goodwill of London and was a man of sharp intelligence.[14]

Chichele was an enthusiastic promoter of education. He built a cathedral library at Canterbury, and in 1438 founded, jointly with Henry VI, All Souls College Oxford, a place of graduate study in the arts, in theology, canon and civil law and ecclesiastical administration. He was, by all accounts, a devout and compassionate man, less severe in his attitude towards the Lollards than Thomas Arundel, endeavouring by education and reason to wean them away from their beliefs, always aiming to raise the standards of learning among the clergy.

Near to the church in Higham Ferrers stands a splendid Bede House, founded, or rather refounded – since there was a Bede House there before Chichele's time – by Chichele, the statutes of which reflect his concern for the ageing batchelor and widower. The hall consisted of six cubicles on either side where the poor men slept. A garden was provided where they could grow vegetables, and 1d a day was paid to them, with which they could purchase meat. This was cooked for them by a female housekeeper, who looked after them and tended them when they were sick. The regulations stated that the woman was to be of good reputation, honest, quiet and not a brawler or a chider, friendly, patient, able to cook and of the age of fifty. She was to make the men a fire every morning and prepare a pan of water for them to wash their hands, and she was to attend to the washing of their clothes.

It was Henry Chichele who, as Archbishop of Canterbury, received King Henry V and his returning troops at the cathedral on 17 November 1415, after their glorious victory at the battle of Agincourt. Chichele lived to the age of eighty one, a great age in medieval times, but he was then to say of himself that he was 'broken and wearied by the burden and cares, which, in my time I have borne upon my shoulders'.[15]

A further prelate of great eminence, who was to make the acquaintance of Margery Kempe, was Henry Bowet, Archbishop of York. Henry had been one of Thomas Arundel's protégés, ordaining him acolyte in 1376, when Arundel was Bishop of Ely. By 1380 Bowet was clerk and chaplain to the warlike Bishop of Norwich, Henry Despenser, acting in his service and becoming involved in international and ecclesiastical politics. In 1386 he was appointed archdeacon and prebendary of Lincoln, high in the favour of both Richard II and Henry IV, the latter rewarding him for his loyalty in 1401 with the see of Bath and Wells, which he occupied until 1407, when he was promoted to the Archbishopric of York. It was during his office as Archbishop that he was to encounter this strange, fanatical and fervent laywoman from Norfolk, Margery Kempe, and of this encounter we shall hear more presently.

In 1406 Henry Bowet, while still Bishop of Bath and Wells, was one of the prominent persons who accompanied the royal court to Bishop's Lynn, and from thence on a mission to Sweden, to escort the Princess Philippa, daughter of Henry IV, who was to marry King Erik XIII of Sweden. It was largely due to this union between the English and Swedish royal families that the cult of St Bridget of Sweden received impetus in England and led to the founding of the Brigettine Convent on the banks of the Thames, a convent which Margery Kempe visited towards the end of her life. Soon after Bowet's return from his Scandinavian mission he was elevated to York, where involvement in important ecclesiastical affairs necessitated his partial withdrawal from matters of State. Like Thomas Arundel, Henry Bowet was a zealous opponent of Lollardy, the two men officiating at the trial of the Evesham tailor, John Badby. In 1417 Margery Kempe was commanded to appear before this daunting, overbearing and sharply-spoken archbishop on a charge of heresy, when 'her flesh [Ch 52]
trembled and quaked in a most astonishing fashion, so that she was compelled to put her hands under her clothes, in order that no one should see how they shook'. But by now Henry Bowet's health was beginning to fail and he had to be carried in a litter; no wonder he found Margery an extremely tiresome woman, though he commended her for her sound knowledge of the faith.

Philip Repingdon, Bishop of Lincoln, was another of Margery's eminent clerical acquaintances. As a young man at Oxford in 1382, he had been a supporter of John Wyclif, preaching a sermon to the university in defence of his views, calling Wyclif 'an eminently Catholic doctor'. This, and another sermon preached in Brackley church on the Eucharist, elicited from the ecclesiastical authorities a charge of heresy. However, when he was condemned by Archbishop Courtenay, Arundel's predecessor, he abjured his heresies and returned to the path of orthodoxy, whether for reasons of a genuine change of heart and mind, or from fear of persecution and death we cannot know. Perhaps it was predominantly for reasons of self-interest, for his intellectual, practical and administrative abilities promised him a bright future in the Church and at court, all of which would have failed to reach fruition if he had persisted in his heretical beliefs. His recanting, however, secured him a place on the road to promotion.

In 1394 he was elected abbot of Leicester, a house of Augustinian Canons, which, with the exception of Cirencester, was the wealthiest Augustinian house in England at the time, possessing numerous large manors in various parts of the country, with their attendant revenues in the form of tithes and rents, a considerable amount of its wealth being spent by Repingdon on repairs to the church and the abbey buildings. But his term of office as abbot was short, for in 1404, at the request of Henry IV, he was presented with the bishopric of Lincoln, where he was a paragon of orthodoxy, rigorously hunting down heretics. It was in June 1413, or some months later, that Margery, now something of a curiosity, and already heard about by Repingdon, descended on this ex-Lollard of Lincoln. As he was absent from his palace at the time of her arrival, she and her husband had to wait for three weeks before gaining an audience.

When the bishop came home and heard that this woman had waited for him for so long and wished to speak with him, he sent for her at once to find out the cause of her visit. Then she came into his presence and greeted him, and he welcomed her warmly and said that he had for a long time wished to speak with her, so now he was glad she had come. She asked if she might talk to him privately and tell him the secrets of her soul, so he arranged a convenient time. [Ch 15]

When the time came she told him about her meditations and high contemplations and all the secret things God had disclosed to her about the living and the dead, and he was truly glad to hear them, and with great kindness allowed her to say whatever she wished. He commended her for her religious feelings and meditations, saying that these were very lofty matters, very devout matters, and inspired by the Holy Spirit. He urged her very seriously to have them written down, but she said that it was not God's will that they should be written so soon. Nor were they written for twenty years or more.

In the summer of 1417 Margery was in Bristol, awaiting a ship to take her to St James Compostela, when she was summoned to appear before the Bishop of Worcester, Thomas Peverel, at his manor in Henbury, three miles from Bristol. Peverel was educated at Oxford where he became a Carmelite friar. It is of interest to note that he was acquainted with Margery's father, who, as a prominent citizen and mayor of Lynn, would have had many contacts with people both in his native Norfolk and with those in the adjoining county of Suffolk, from which county Thomas Peveral came. His acquaintance with John Brunham may account for the special kindness and hospitality which he extended towards Margery when she was in the area. Being a White friar, or Carmelite, he may also have known of Margery and her family through her friend and supporter, Aleyn of Lynn, also a White friar. Peverel may possibly have stayed at the splendid Carmelite house in Lynn, since members of religious communities were accustomed to travel from one religious house to another, and were hospitably received in all branches of their order. East Anglia was particularly well supplied with Carmelite houses, others, apart from the Lynn house, being at Norwich, Yarmouth and Ipswich.[16]

While Margery awaited an audience with the Bishop – for it was early when she arrived at his residence and he had not yet risen from his bed – she was led into the hall, where there were many of the Bishop's men, clerks, squires and others, all decked out in fashionable clothes with dagged edges. Lifting up her hands in horror at the appearance of these men, she said, 'God bless my soul!' At which the men displayed some anger,

> **'What the devil's the matter with you?' they said.** [Ch 45]
> **'Whose men are you? she enquired.**
> **'The Bishop's men' they replied.**
> **'No, indeed! you are more like the devil's men.'**
> **Then they were very angry and scolded her and spoke sharply to her, but she took it all very meekly. And afterwards she spoke seriously against sin and the way they behaved, which silenced them, showing that they were well pleased with what she said.**

When Margery had had her say and put the Bishop's men in their place, she retired to the church and waited for the Bishop to appear, and when he arrived she respectfully knelt down before him and asked him why he had sent for her, since she was a pilgrim on her way to St James Compostela, and this visit to Henbury delayed her.

> **'Margery, I know well that you are John Brunham's daughter of Lynn' he replied. 'I beg you do not be angry with me, but be fair with me and I shall be fair with you, for you must come and eat with me today.'** [Ch 45]

So Margery dined with the Bishop and he and his household made her very welcome, and she remained at his residence until the weather was favourable for sailing. The Bishop heard her confession and gave her absolution, and asked her to pray for him that he might die in charity, for a certain holy man had warned him that he would die within two years, and indeed it occurred as the holy man had predicted. Bishop Peverel died on 1 March 1419.

Two other bishops were to cross Margery's path. They were John Wakering, Bishop of Norwich (1415–1425), who preached at St Margaret's Lynn, and did not object to her crying, but 'endured it full meekly and patiently' and Bishop William Alnwick, also of Norwich (1426–1436), who, as we have already stated, figured in the controversy over the status of St Nicholas' Chapel.

At a time when laypeople were still expected to adopt a submissive and deferential attitude towards the clergy, as they had done in the early Middle Ages, Margery showed remarkable boldness and outspokenness. Though generally respectful and appreciative of their ministrations as confessors, advisers and teachers, she was never intimidated by them, never cringing and servile towards them, especially if she saw any evil in them which she thought required correction. But there was nothing unusual in this critical attitude towards the clergy, for in the later Middle Ages the laity were showing increasing independence and initiative in religious matters and greater concern for the quality of the priesthood. As Christopher Harper-Bill informs us, 'Lord Grey, touring his Welsh estates in the 1440s embarked on a personal campaign to enforce celibacy. The civil authorities in London expelled scandalous priests from the city, and many wills stipulated that the

St Margaret's Church, King's Lynn, from a drawing by E. M. Beloe, in 'Our Borough, Our Churches,' Cambridge, 1899.

priest employed to celebrate soul masses should be chaste and worthy'.[17]

One should note also that it was not the laity alone who showed dissatisfaction with the clergy. The laity were but echoing some of the denunciations which the clergy voiced against their fellow-clergy; the clergy were the worst critics of their own profession, for as Harper-Bill comments, 'It is salutary to remember that many identifyable authors of such polemic, and all the preachers who thundered from their pulpits, were themselves clerics, and that their anger was directed against those of their order who tarnished the priestly image'.[18]

Like Joan of Arc, who, when she was asked by her interrogators if she was obedient to the laws of the Church, answered 'Yes, our Lord first being served' Margery on two occasions demonstrates that she believed Christ should take priority over the Church, since the Church took its origin from Christ and not Christ from the Church. On the first occasion she hears Christ telling her that he is pleased that she obeys the Church and her confessors, who have the authority to absolve her from her sins and to exempt her from the necessity of going on further pilgrimages to Rome and St James Compostela.

> **'Despite all this, daughter, I command you in my name to visit these holy places and do as I bid you, for I am above Holy Church, and I shall go with you and keep you from all harm.'** [Ch 29]

The second occasion concerns her projected voyage to Germany with her daughter-in-law, which she is not at all keen to undertake, since she is now old, dreads the thought of sea-voyages and has not obtained permission from her confessor, to whom she is bound by a promise of obedience, to embark on the journey. To this Jesus replies,

> **'I command you to go in my name – in the name of Jesus – for I am above your spiritual father, and I shall excuse you, and guide you there and bring you back safely again.'** [Ch 2] [Bk II]

The discipline of the clergy in regard to various offences was the responsibility of the bishops in their ecclesiastical courts, assisted by the archdeacons. For example in the diocese of Durham a

Robert Segefeld was ordered by the court by pay 6s 8d to St Cuthbert's shrine, and to do penance for immorality by walking barefoot in linen vestments, and carrying a candle in the front of the procession on Sunday. Among the letters of the distinguished Bishop of Lincoln, Robert Grosseteste (1235–1255) is one addressed to a cleric, castigating him for his luxurious and licentious way of life, telling him plainly that he is 'a blot on the clergy, a shame to theologians and a delight to the enemies of religion'.[19]

Officially the clergy were celibate, though many were in fact married and had children who were passed off as their nieces and nephews. From a civil and secular point of view these marriages were not illegal, though they were regarded by Canon Law as 'concubinages' and the offspring of such unions were classed as 'bastards', who could not inherit property, and their sons were barred from ordination. But a bishop could, if he wished, give a dispensation, subject to papal approval, which allowed an illegitimate son of a cleric to be ordained, and there are many examples of this actually occurring. We find, for instance, that in 1398, Bishop Grandisson of Exeter, received a grant of dispensation from Pope Clement VI, for fifty priests and scholars to receive ordination and to hold benefices, thirty of whom were classed as illegitimate, ten being the sons of Priests or other persons in holy orders.[20]

But no doubt the vast majority of the clergy were conscientious hard-working and virtuous men. The bad ones hit the headlines, and just how bad the bad ones could be is illustrated by a somewhat indelicate tale told by Margery Kempe before Archbishop Henry Bowet and a distinguished company of monks, friars, clerics and doctors of the law in York Minster, Margery impressing upon the Archbishop that she was not speaking of priests in general, but only of one particular priest by way of example,thus exonerating herself from anti-clericalism, a distinctive feature of Lollardy.

A certain priest, began Margery, had lost his way in a wood and took shelter for the night in a beautiful orchard in the midst of which was a pear tree 'all flourished with flowers and embellished with blooms, delightful to behold'. Then along came a great and terrible bear to that place and shook the tree, making all the blossoms fall. Greedily the beast devoured those beautiful flowers and 'turning his tail-end in the priest's presence, he voided them from his hinder parts'. Disgusted by this loathsome sight and troubled at what it might mean, the priest, the next day, wandered off in a sad and disconsolate mood. By good fortune he met a wise, good-looking old man, a pilgrim or wayfaring monk, who enquired of the priest why he looked so downcast. The priest then rehearsed the story to the pilgrim, who, by his wise interpretation, proved that he was a messenger from God.

> **'Priest' he said, 'you yourself are that pear tree, sometimes flourishing and blossoming because of the services you say and the sacraments you administer, even though you perform them without much devotion. You care little how you say Matins and the other services so long as you are able to gabble them through to the end. Then you go to Mass, but without any devotion and little repentance for your sins, and you receive the sacrament of the altar, the fruit of everlasting life, with a lukewarm spirit. All the day afterwards you misspend your time, giving yourself over to buying and selling, bartering and haggling, like a man of the world. You sit at your beer and abandon yourself to gluttony and excess, to lust of your body, lewdness and uncleanness. You break God's commandments by swearing, lying, slandering, back-biting and other such sins.** [Ch 52]
>
> **By your ill-behaviour you are like this loathsome bear, devouring and destroying the flowers and blossoms of virtuous living, and doing so to your own eternal damnation and to the harm of many others, unless you have the grace to repent and to amend your life.'**

The Archbishop expressed his approval of the story. He liked it very much and said it was a good tale. But one of the clerks who had examined Margery said, 'Sir, this tale cuts me to the heart'.

South Porch of St Nicholas Chapel, King's Lynn.
Engraving by S. Noble from a drawing by F. Mackenzie.
Published 1 Oct. 1811.

CHAPTER FIVE

Margery Kempe and the Regular Clergy

One cannot read *THE BOOK OF MARGERY KEMPE* without immediately becoming aware of the ubiquity of religious orders in medieval England. There were houses of Benedictine monks, Cistercians, Cluniacs, Augustinian Canons Carthusians, Bridgettines and other smaller orders. The friars too were classed as 'regulars' and belonged to the orders of St Francis, St Dominic, St Augustine and St Mary of Mount Carmel. 'Turn where we will in the later Middle Ages, we find towns and countryside sprinkled with communities of *religiosi* of many different kinds, but all united in one respect; they had taken life-long vows which set them apart from ordinary members of the Church.'[1] Regulars were, in theory, enclosed in monasteries, though some, like the Augustinian Canons, were, with the pope's and the bishop's permission, allowed to leave the cloister and serve in parishes.

Principal and earliest among the religious orders were the Benedictines or Black Monks, so named because of their black habits. Their founder was St Benedict (480–547), who at his famous monastery at Monte Cassino, had drawn up a Rule for his small group of monks, which was to provide 'an authoritative standard of religious life, more ancient, more dignified, and more stable than any other'.[2] There in the convent the monk or the nun had the opportunity, par excellence, of living the Christian life, of putting into practice the gospel precepts of loving God and neighbour, of praying fasting, renouncing self-will, renouncing wealth, practising virtue, living chastely, labouring with hands and brain. St Augustine, in his Commentary on the Psalms, furnishes us with an idyllic and harmonious picture of monastic life at its best where 'great and holy men spend their time in hymns and prayers and praises to God. Their occupation is reading; they labour with their

Benedictine Monk.

hands, and by this means they support themselves. They seek nothing covetously. Whatever is brought in for them by pious brethren, they use with contentment and charity; no one claims as his own what another has not; all love and support one another mutually'.[3]

In the early centuries of monasticism we may assume that, apart from the occasional rule-breaker and offender, Benedictine houses were places where virtue and obedience flourished and where monks lived ordered and disciplined lives, but the accounts which Margery Kempe gives of some monasteries, indicate that by the early fifteenth century decay had firmly set in. Indeed it was particularly during the fifteenth century that a marked deterioration took place in the religious houses, the high standards of learning and virtuous living that had characterised the early centuries, having sunk to a low ebb. Bishop Goldwell of Norwich, in the latter part of the century, during his visitation of the Benedictine house at Norwich, revealed that the observance of the Rule had grow slack, especially the rule of silence, and that learning was little evident in the monastery. There were reports of money being stolen, valuables disappearing, and indiscreet gossipping taking place in the church between monks and women of dubious character. Matters were even worse twenty or so years later when there were reports of buildings being dilapidated, of monks wearing new-fangled garb, dancing in the guest-hall at night, women going in and out at leisure, services being conducted in a slovenly manner, the monastery being in debt and the sub-prior being a profligate and evil-example.[4]

Even as early as 1330 we hear of monks and nuns who had grown negligent about the performance of the monastic hours, cutting services, and behaving with the greatest flippancy. At Exeter 'the canons giggled, joked and quarrelled during the services and dropped candle wax from the upper stalls on the shaven heads of the singers in the stalls below'.[5] Visitors and boarders were considered to be a major cause of the evils that crept into the monastic system, for they brought with them worldly ideas and standards of behaviour which were contrary to those expected of professed monks and nuns. 'Great ladies of the day loved to amuse themselves with pet animals, and nuns were quick to follow their example ... William of Wykeham in 1387 issued an injunction forbidding the nuns of Romsey Abbey to bring birds, rabbits, hounds or other frivolous things into the church'.[6] The reason for this prohibition was that the creatures diverted the nuns' attention from their offices, promoted indiscipline, befouled the church and caused a very great noise and disturbance to the divine service.

However, A. R. Myers utters a word of warning against painting too gloomy a picture of the state of religious houses in the fourteenth and fifteenth centuries or of stressing too much the prevalence of unseemly behaviour among their inmates. 'Holiness was still to be found among the monks, and the friars were by no means inactive in the performance of good works ... It was the business of the episcopal visitors to reveal and correct what was wrong, not to record success or sanctity; hence episcopal registers have much to say about corruption, and very little about satisfactory houses'.[7]

In addition to the Benedictine monastery at Bishop's Lynn, there were two other cells of the Norwich Priory in Norfolk. These were at Yarmouth and at Aldeby, the latter a mile or so north of Beccles. A further cell was at Hoxne in Suffolk, about six miles south east of Diss. A Benedictine house of nuns existed at Carrow just outside Norwich, where Julian of Norwich had her anchorhold and was visited by Margery Kempe. The Benedictine abbeys at Binham and Wymondham in Norfolk were daughter houses not of Norwich but of St Albans.

Other smaller Benedictine convents existed in Norfolk which may have been known to Margery Kempe. There was Blackborough Priory, which she may well have visited since it was but a few miles south of Lynn, near to the village of Middleton. This house was founded in *c*1150 for monks but was soon handed over to nuns. It was here at Blackborough convent that Margery Paston and Richard Calle stayed, awaiting the time of their marriage, a real love-match, though not regarded favourably or as socially acceptable by her parents and family, since Mr Calle was a mere head bailiff to Margery's father. Another Benedictine house was situated at Horsham St Faith, several miles north of Norwich, of which considerable remains survive, principally the fine

Norman entry to the Chapter House and the two perpendicular windows.

England's most celebrated Benedictine abbey was that of Christ Church, Canterbury, where the shrine of the murdered archbishop, St Thomas Becket attracted a tremendous number of pilgrims. It was here that Margery faced hostility from the monks because she cried incessantly and appeared to speak with authority about God, and here too she encountered an aged monk, John Kynton, who, before joining Christ Church monastery, had been a powerful man of the world and treasurer to the wife of Henry IV, Queen Joanna.

'What can you say about God?' he enquired of Margery, taking her by the hand. [Ch 13]

'Sir, I will both speak about God, and listen to what others say of him,' she replied. Then she rehearsed a story from scripture, at which the monk exclaimed, 'I wish you were shut up in a house of stone, so that no one could speak with you!'

'Ah, sir' she replied, 'you should support God's servants, yet you are the first to oppose them. May our Lord stir you to mend your ways.'

When Margery departed from the monastery the monks and people followed her and shouted words of abuse at her, screaming out that she should be burnt, for she was a 'false Lollard', and that they had a barrel ready to put her in, and a cartful of thorns to set light to her. Trembling and alone, for her husband had gone off and she did not know his whereabouts, she stood outside the gates of Canterbury. The curfew bell was rung at 8pm in the winter and at 9pm in the summer, after which hours the gate was closed, so Margery could no longer find refuge in the city. Shaking with terror, she offered up her heartful prayers to God for mercy and help, and much to her relief two young men came to her assistance and took her back to her hostel, where she found her husband.

One of the most splendid monastic houses in Norfolk, four miles north of Swaffham, was Castle Acre Priory, of the order of Cluniac, named after their mother house of Cluny in Burgundy. The Cluniacs were reformed Benedictines, who followed a simplified and more austere Rule and abandoned the requirement of manual labour, which the Benedictines insisted upon. Instead the Cluniacs devoted themselves more assiduously to the exercise of the mind and spirit. The priory, with its magnificent west front still remaining, is about fifteen miles east of Lynn and housed thirty monks, a small number compared to the size and splendour of the monastery. Other Cluniac houses in Norfolk were at Thetford and Bacton (Bromholm), the latter being renowned as a pilgrim site because of its relic of the Holy Cross. The prior and monks of this house regarded the Paston family as their friends and benefactors.

The Cistercians, like the Cluniacs, were a reformed Benedictine order whose virtual founder was the saintly Bernard of Clairvaux, a man of singular charm and beauty of character, and whose face was described by one who knew him as 'radiant with light not of earth, but of heaven; his eyes shone with angelic purity and dove-like simplicity'.[8] The first abbey was founded at Citeaux in Burgundy in 1098, soon to be followed by foundations in many parts of Europe, the greatest monastery in England being at Rieuvaulx in Yorkshire, famous for its abbot, Ailred, whose devotional classic, *The Mirror of Charity*, Margery Kempe would almost certainly have heard read to her by one of her clergy friends. The Cistercians, or White Monks, excelled at farming and horticulture and acquired their great wealth mainly from the huge flocks of sheep which roamed the moors and hills of Yorkshire, the wool produced in that area being much sought after, not only by the English, but by overseas wool merchants. Despite the large number of Cistercian houses in England as a whole, Norfolk was particularly lacking in Cistercian abbeys, its only house being a small nunnery at Marham. Unfortunately Margery Kempe does not always name the monasteries she visits, but the one Cistercian house she does name is Hailes Abbey in Gloucestershire where she was welcomed by the monks who were amazed by her 'boistrous weepings' and by the boldness with which she rebuked them for swearing 'great and horrible oaths'.

A further religious order, founded a few years before the Cistercians was that of the Augustinian Canons, or Black Canons so named because of their black cassocks, cloaks and cowls. They first settled in England in about 1100, establishing their monastery

Cistercian Monk.

probably at Colchester in 1103 and constructing their buildings largely of the bricks from the old Roman town, remains of which can still be seen today.

The Rule adopted by the Augustinian Canons was based not on that of St Benedict, but on a letter of instruction written by St Augustine to some religious women in North Africa in the fifth century, who were forming themselves into a religious community. He instructed them to have all things in common, to pray together at appointed times, to dress without distinction and to obey their superior. The Rule was moderate in its demands, flexible and adaptable to suit the different communities who followed it, and as one of the canons of the house at Barnwell in Cambridge wrote, 'The rule of the canons regular is the Rule of St Augustine, who drew his brethren together and tempered the rigour of his rule to their infirmity. Like a kind master, he did not drive his disciples with a rod of iron, but invited those who love the beauty of holiness to the door of salvation under a moderate rule.'[9]

In general it may be said that the Augustinian Canons were the least ascetic and the most liberal of the religious orders, spending less time on the daily offices, allowing the eating of meat, giving themselves to conversation rather than to silence and being free to move outside the monastery walls. In the thirteenth century a member of their order wrote, 'Among the Augustinian Canons one is well-shod, well-clothed and well-fed. They go out when they like, mix with the world and talk at table.'[10] Their aim was to serve the people among whom they lived, teaching, preaching, emphasising practical works such as running small schools, hospitals, places of retirement for the sick, the aged, lepers and the blind. It was these practical works which made them so popular among the laity.[11]

Of all the Augustinian Priories in Norfolk, Walsingham was the richest and most illustrious, attracting, in its hey day, vast numbers of pilgrims, including many royal parsonages who donated generously to its maintenance. By the end of the fifteenth century the bishop on his visitation reported terrible goings-on at this priory. 'The prior was living a scandalous and dissolute life, engaging in an illicit relationship with the wife of one of his servants, robbing the treasury of many jewels and behaving brutally towards the canons, with the result that the canons themselves became dissipated and quarrelsome, frequenting taverns, hunting and hawking ... and some sat up all night drinking and rolled into chapel in the early morning and fell asleep and snored.'[12]

West Acre, a few miles west of Castle Acre, in the valley of the river Nar, was another extremely wealthy Norfolk house of Augustinian Canons, founded in *c*1100 and built on the same sumptous scale as the Cluniac monastery at Castle Acre. West Acre was greatly favoured by the rich merchants of Lynn and Norwich who sent their sons to join the community of brothers there. Bishop Goldwell's visitation of the house revealed that the convent was in debt and inefficiently run, but otherwise there were no outstanding evils taking place.

Among the Augustinian houses in Norfolk visited by the bishops of the later Middle Ages was that of Penteney, which alone was outstanding for its consistently high reputation. The visitations disclose that there were no complaints, no dissentions, nothing in need of reform and that the canons of that house maintained their high standards of behaviour to the end. We have already observed that the documents relating to the installation of a font in St Nicholas' Chapel in Lynn were sent to the prior of Penteney for his scrutiny, which indicates that he was a man of learning and legal knowledge. Indeed the priors of Penteney, from the time of King John, had invariably been men of influence and importance in the diocese of Norwich.[13]

It is perhaps rather surprising that two very devout and influential clerics should emerge from the Augustinian order which Sir Richard Southern describes as 'neither very rich, nor very learned, nor very religious, nor very influential ... Like the ragwort which adheres so tenaciously to the stone walls of Oxford, or the sparrows of the English towns, they were not a handsome species'.[14] The two men were St John of Bridlington and Walter Hilton, of Thurgarten in Nottinghamshire, author of the devotional classic, *The Scale of Perfection*, already mentioned.

John of Bridlington, a Yorkshire man from Twinge, nine miles west of Bridlington, studied at Oxford, after which he returned north and, in 1340, became a novice at the Augustinian Priory of St Mary at Bridlington where he progressed to the positions of precentor, almoner, sub-prior and finally in 1361/2 prior. In his position as prior it was said of him that he assiduously observed the Rule of St Augustine, despised rich food and clothing, was never idle, set a good example to others by his blameless life and maintained poor scholars out of the wealth of the monastery. He was also reputed to have been the recipient of the charism of 'holy tears', a gift which would have endeared him to Margery Kempe.

After spending the whole of his adult life at Bridlington apart from the two years at Oxford, John died of the plague in 1379, and because of his great sanctity and the miracles which he reputedly performed during his life and those which occurred at his shrine after his death, he was canonized in 1401. Bridlington Priory then became a popular place of pilgrimage and attracted people of every rank including Henry IV, Henry V and other members of the royal family, who made handsome grants to the Priory, resulting in its becoming extremely wealthy. It was said that Henry V attributed his victory at Agincourt and the birth of his son partly to the intercessions of St John of Bridlington. The dissolution of the monasteries saw the almost total destruction of the Priory except for the gatehouse and the impressive nave of the conventual church, now in use as a parish church.[15]

Margery Kempe was about six years old when John of Bridlington died in 1379 and twenty eight years old when he was canonized in 1401. The agreement between Margery and her husband 'to live chaste' took place in June 1413 when they were travelling together from York to Bridlington. We may surmise that their purpose in making this detour from York to Bridlington, involving a journey of forty or so miles north east, instead of striking due south for home, was to make their offerings and prayers at this famous shrine. It is very likely too that on this occasion Margery made her confession to William Sleightholm, for she refers to him on a later occasion as 'my confessor'. It is noteworthy that William Sleightholm was also the confessor and chaplain to John of Bridlington himself, so Margery was in saintly and elevated company in sharing her confessor with the saint.

In the autumn of 1417, following her trial before Henry Bowet of York, Margery had gained the Archbishop's permission not to vacate his diocese until she had been to Bridlington to speak with her confessor, William Sleightholm. Wishing to be rid of this troublesome woman, the Archbishop issued the command,

> **'Lay your hand on this book before me and swear that you will leave my diocese as soon as you are able to ...'** [Ch 52/3]
>
> **'But, sir, I cannot leave this diocese so quickly,' replied Margery, 'for there are certain good folk I must speak with before I depart, and with your permission I must go to Bridlington to talk to my confessor, a virtuous man, who was the confessor of John of Bridlington, the prior who has recently been canonized.'**

Then the Archbishop gave five shillings to a man to escort Margery out of the town and to Bridlington, where she made her confession and spoke with William Sleightholm, who gave her some money with the request that she should pray for him. Four years later in 1421 Sleightholm died.

We have spoken in the Introduction of *THE BOOK OF MARGERY KEMPE* once belonging to the Carthusian Priory of Mount Grace in the North Riding of Yorkshire. The Carthusians in England were a small select community, occupying only nine houses and probably numbering little more than a hundred brethren, but despite their numerical weakness theirs was an influential order, well-organised, disciplined and maintaining a strict adherence to the monastic rule. Their order had been founded in 1084 by St Bruno at the Grande Chartreuse, a wild and desolate spot in the mountains near Grenoble in France. From the start they had adopted an austere way of life, wearing a hair-shirt next to the skin, living on bread and water for three days of the week, feeding on fish, cheese, eggs, fruit and vegetables for the remainder of the week, observing a strict rule of silence and rising at 5.45am for the first office of the day. Much of the day was spent in praying, reading, writing, copying books and cultivating their individual gardens. Unlike the other religious orders, the Carthusian order was semi-communal, each monk occupying a separate little house with a walled garden. On the lower floor of the house was a living room with a fire-place, a study and a bedroom which also served as an oratory; on the upper floor was a workshop. Of this seemingly luxurious living accommodation it has been observed that 'the amount of space allowed to each monk was remarkably generous, and one can but think that the hardship imposed by the Carthusian vow of silence must have been adequately compensated for by the privacy enjoyed by each monk; privacy was a rare luxury in the Middle Ages'.[16] The monks, however, did not live in total seclusion, for they met together in the chapel for Matins, Laudes and Vespers, and shared a common meal on Sundays and feast days.

The first Carthusian house, situated at Witham in Somerset, was founded by Henry II as part of his penance for his involvement in the murder of Archbishop Thomas Becket of Canterbury. Other prominent houses were in north west London, which became Charterhouse school; at Sheen on the south bank of the Thames; and the one we have mentioned near Northallerton, founded in 1398 when Margery was about twenty five years old. The emphasis of the Carthusians was on the fostering of the spiritual life, achieved chiefly by contemplation of, and devotion to the crucified Christ. By their dedication to a harsh, self-denying way of life they could more readily identify themselves with their self-denying, suffering and dying Lord. It is not surprising then that they were particularly attracted to works of devotional and contemplative literature and possessed copies of the writings of the fourteenth century English mystics, Richard Rolle, Walter Hilton and the anonymous author of *The Cloud of Unknowing*.

Early in the fifteenth century a prior of the Carthusian house of Mount Grace, Nicholas Love, translated part of the Pseudo-Bonaventura's *Meditations*, which he called *The Mirror of the Blessed Life of Jesus Christ*. He presented this translation to Thomas Arundel, Archbishop of Canterbury, in support of Arundel's campaign against the Lollards.[17] The book was immensely popular in fifteenth century England and was written for laypeople, clergy and 'for those who are of simple understanding'. Among the many devotional works that were read to Margery we may be sure that this was one of them, for it contains much that would have arrested her interest and sympathy, especially for its stress on the contemplations of Christ's manhood, suffering and death.[18]

It is worth noting that one of the most attractive and saintly characters of medieval England was a Carthusian monk of the Grande Chartreuse, Hugh of Lincoln, whom Henry II, in 1180,

8. St Anne. Window c. 1450, All Saints, York.

9. Our Lady of Pity, "Pieta", 15th c. window, Long Melford, Suffolk.

persuaded to come to England to govern the Charterhouse at Witham. After governing the monastery for six years as prior, he was elevated to the see of Lincoln, the largest diocese in England, stretching from the Humber to the Thames, where he remained as bishop until his death in 1200. He is remembered in the pages of history as an energetic educator, preacher and builder, a fearless opponent of injustice, patient, humble, tender, caring towards the sick and a lover of children and animals – his pet swan became his emblem in ecclesiastical art.[19]

That most devout and religious king, Henry V, in 1415, founded a Carthusian monastery on the south bank of the river Thames at Sheen (Richmond), the largest of the English Charterhouses, and on the opposite bank, on the Middlesex side of the Thames at Twickenham he founded a second religious house, the Convent of the Holy Saviour, St Mary and St Bridget, known as Mount Syon. This convent was to become the richest and most important religious house founded in England in the later part of the Middle Ages, and was a daughter house of that founded by Bridget of Sweden (*c*1303–1373) at Vadstena in the diocese of Lincopen. The community of Mount Syon was composed chiefly by nuns but included a small number of monks, some of whom acted as confessors and chaplains to the nuns, thus qualifying the convent to be designated a double monastery under the government of an abbess, similar to the double monasteries of Anglo-Saxon England. St Bridget had based her Rule on that of St Augustine but extended it to include her own Bridgettine additions to suit the particular circumstances of her convent at Vadstena.

The popularity of Bridget of Sweden in England in the early fifteenth century flowed largely from the connection between the royal houses of both countries, for in 1406, the Princess Philippa, daughter of Henry IV and sister of Henry V, married King Eric XIII of Sweden and Denmark, the princess travelling to Sweden under the care of a granddaughter of Bridget. Also accompanying the royal party to Sweden was Sir Henry Fitzhugh, Baron of Ravensworth and Constable of England, who attended the coronation of Henry V. Both Philippa and Fitzhugh visited the famous religious house at Vadstena, with the result that Fitzhugh was fired

Carthusian Monk.

with enthusiasm for Bridget's religious foundation, and desiring to see a similar foundation in England, devoted his land and property at Cherryhinton, near Cambridge, to the establishment of a Bridgettine convent. So popular and widespread was the cult of St Bridget that convents of the Bridgettine order were at that time springing up in many parts of Europe. But Fitzhugh's plan failed to come to fruition, though it was probably he who advised and encouraged Henry V on the founding of the convent at Twickenham in February 1415.

Several sisters and brothers arrived in England from the convent at Vadstena to form the nucleus of the new order and soon they were joined by some English sisters. The first formal profession of the nuns took place on 1 April 1420, the true foundation day, when Archbishop Chichele admitted twenty seven sisters, five priests, two deacons and four lay brothers to the new convent. The location of the convent at Twickenham, however, proved to be too damp and the buildings too small for a permanent residence for the sisters, and in 1431 the community moved to a site a short distance down the river to Isleworth, the community here being enriched by Henry VI with manors, land, tenements in many parts of England, as well as generous financial endowments, gifts, and bequests from well-wishers. The convent continued to flourish until the dissolution 120 years later 'wealthy and fervent to the end' as David Knowles comments, adding that the Carthusian house on opposite bank 'kept alive an almost unceasing round of prayer with nightly signal bells across the river flats'.[20]

It was to this monastery of Syon that Margery Kempe proceeded at Lammas-tide, probably in the year 1434, before the buildings were finally completed, where she amazed the people in the church by her loud and fervent weeping. Among them was a young man, who himself aspired to take the habit of a monk, and who was especially curious as to why this woman wept so passionately. When therefore he had to chance to speak to her privately he asked her the cause of her crying.

She, very meekly and kindly, and with gladness of spirit, commended his intention, and so far as she thought it right, told him, partly the cause of her weeping and sobbing. It was, she said, because of her great unkindness [Ch 10] [Bk II]

> **to her Maker, whom she had often offended, though he had been so good to her. The thought of her sins appalled her and caused her to sob and to weep. She was also moved to tears when she contemplated the profound love of her redeemer, who by his Passion and the shedding of his precious blood, had saved her, and made her an heir of everlasting joy and bliss.**

Syon is known to have been an important centre of mystical devotion in the fifteenth century with a pronounced interest in feminine piety which arose from the female founder of the order, Bridget herself being a mystic and visionary. Miss Hope Emily Allen has remarked of Syon Abbey, 'The affection for this foundation of such a learned ecclesiastic as Dr Thomas Gascoigne must be taken as an indication of the importance of the Bridgettine movement even in university circles'.[21] Dr Gascoigne, was chancellor of Oxford university in 1434 and again in 1439 and a widely respected preacher and theologian and author of a two-volume dictionary of theology, which in addition to its theological information, contains some fascinating material on the state of the church of his day. He also translated into English a life of St Bridget for the edification of the sisters of Syon Abbey and bequeathed numerous books for the library of this newly founded monastery. A devotional treatise, *The Myroure of Oure Ladye*, written for the use of Syon, may also, according to Dr J. H. Blunt, have been written by Dr Gascoigne. This beautiful little book comprises an English translation from the Latin, with explanation and commentary on the Hours and Masses of the Blessed Virgin, to assist the sisters in understanding their services.

The content and literary style of the *Myoure* is characterised by a simplicity, compassion and tenderness which the sisters must have found spiritually comforting and most delightful to read. For example in the commentary on the Lord's Prayer, they are exhorted to 'think of the way a child, when he is in any kind of trouble, will go trustingly to his father. So, when you are in trouble or distress, temptation or sin, go humbly and confidently to God your Father. Lift up your hearts to him and tell him what troubles you and say Our Father.' Commenting on the petition 'Lead us not into temptation, but deliver us from evil' the sisters are told that they must 'pray this prayer wholeheartedly and with great devotion, for no one can grow in virtue unless they are tempted, although none of us, even the most perfect, can withstand any temptation without the special help and grace of God ... Therefore with meekness and holy fear, and being aware of our own weakness, we ask God to keep us from the evil of sin.'[22]

CHAPTER SIX

Margery Kempe and the Friars

The immense influence which the friars exerted upon the religious life of Europe from the thirteenth to the fifteenth centuries can hardly be over-emphasised, for the friars were among the most learned and educated men in the medieval church, many having been trained at one or other of the great centres of learning: Paris, Bologna, Oxford and Cambridge, from whence emerged such luminaries in the sphere of philosophy and theology as Alexander of Hales, Roger Bacon, Duns Scotus, William of Ockham and Bonaventure – all Franciscans – and Thomas Aquinas and Meister Eckhart among the Dominicans.

Before being appointed Bishop of Lincoln in 1235, Robert Grosseteste had been Oxford's most distinguished scholar and teacher, attracting great numbers of students to hear his lectures, the school of theology, which he founded in the house of the Friars Minor, becoming one of the most important academic centres in the world. Reporting to Pope Gregory IX on the progress of the Franciscan movement in England, Grosseteste declared that the friars were illuminating the whole country with the bright light of their preaching and teaching, for the friars excelled at preaching.[1] They possessed great skills at combining the promulgation of sound doctrinal and moral teaching with a lively style of delivery, peppering their sermons with wit, humour, and the rehearsal of sensational tales and miracles. 'To go to hear a friar preach was a recognised holiday attraction; their racy stories, direct moral and emotional style gave them great power to move their hearers.'[2]

It was to the towns that the friars principally came, for in the towns they found the greatest concentrations of people to whom they could preach their message, and from among whom they could recruit new members to their order. Wealthy burgesses, like Margery's father, were enthusiastic supporters of the friars, providing them with funds for the building of their churches and friaries, and for their day to day needs. Although the friars built splendid churches, which were large, spacious and free from aisles and pillars, so as to accommodate as many people as possible, their friaries were nothing like as fine and capacious as the monasteries, for the monasteries owned great wealth and treasure, land and property, and went in for business enterprises like sheep rearing and other manual occupations, which were often specifically enjoined upon them by their monastic Rule. The friars on the other hand were mendicants, beggars, and depended largely upon the charity of others, upon donations and legacies, and fees for burials and for saying masses for the dead. 'The gifts on which the friars lived are known to us mainly through the numberless wills which have survived from the later medieval centuries ... The gifts were small in comparison with the endowments of monastic foundations, but they were very numerous and they came from a wider area of society than any previous religious benefactions of which a record survives.'[3]

One marked difference between the friars and the monks was that the friars were gregarious, frequently left their friaries and mingled with the people, conversing with them, preaching to them, being earnstly intent upon converting the world, while the monks stayed mostly in their monasteries, secluded from the outside world. Of the friars E. M. Beloe writes, 'Their abnegation of wealth, for they had no lands beyond the sites of their convents, their ascetic life and their great power of preaching, soon got a marvellous hold on the mind of the middle classes'.[4] When it was known that a friar was to preach at a certain church, the people would swarm to that church like bees to a honeypot. This is made abundantly clear by Margery Kempe's account of the delight which the inhabitants of Lynn displayed when the eminent Grey friar arrived to take up residence in the Lynn friary.

> **He was renowned for his holiness and was greatly favoured by the people, so much so, that some would go with him into the country if they knew he was preaching there, or they would follow him from town to town to hear him, since it was a great pleasure to them to listen to his sermons.** [Ch 62

The two principal orders of friars were the Franciscans and the Dominicans. St Francis (1181–1226) belonged to a wealthy family, his father being a prosperous cloth merchant, yet the essence of Francis' life and teaching was centred on the concept of poverty and renunciation, on selling everything and giving to the poor, on making oneself bare for Christ, which was based on such gospel commands and precepts as 'Go, sell all your possessions and give to the poor' (Matt 19.21) and 'None of you can be a disciple of mine without parting with all his possessions' (Luke 14.33). These, and other hard sayings of Jesus, Francis took literally, applying them to himself and enjoining them on his followers. But renunciations were not to be undertaken for their own sakes, but that having emptied oneself, one might be filled with Christ, having become naked for him, one might be clothed with him, having divested oneself of the clutter and impediment of money and possessions, one might be free to follow him.

The call to poverty and renunciation, therefore, was combined with a devotion to Christ and identification with him, particularly to, and with, his Passion, his suffering and death, which in Francis' case led to his receiving the stigmata, the marks on his hands and feet and side corresponding to those of Christ. This uncompromising message and way of life met with a response from, at first, a small number of men, who followed Francis and became the nucleus of the new order of friars. By contact with this holy man, by listening to his message and witnessing his example, the Lady Clare was inspired to pioneer a movement for women, according to the pattern set by Francis, and so began the Second Order of Poor Clares. This was followed by a Third Order (the Tertiaries) composed of men and women living in the world, pursuing their ordinary secular occupations, some married, some widowed, some single, yet who, wished to obey a Christian Rule of Life that embraced all those elements of religion propounded and practised by St Francis: the cultivation of the virtues of humility, simplicity, renunciation and generosity, and above all love for Christ and obedience to the gospel. To this Third Order belonged countless men and women committed to the pursuit of this worthy and heroic ideal, some of outstanding virtue and holiness whom the Church beatified or canonised, such as Bl Angela of Foligno, St

Franciscan or Grey Friar.

Bridget of Sweden, St Elizabeth of Hungary, all Franciscan Tertiaries. And perhaps we might add to their number Margery Kempe, who in her modest way, attempted to emulate St Francis, and who, while in Rome distributed all her money to the poor. We have, however, no concrete evidence that Margery ever officially joined the Order of Franciscan Tertiaries.

The Dominicans, the second of the two greatest orders of friars, drew their members chiefly from the cultured classes, the intelligentia, and emphasised learning and scholarship, which equipped the friars for their principal task of educating people, of preaching and teaching and combating heresy. Their founder was Dominic (1170–1221) a Spaniard, a member of the Augustinian Canons, a champion of orthodoxy and a vehement opponent of an heretical sect, the Albigenses, who, like the Manichees, propounded a doctrine of 'dualism', the notion that two contending powers, those of good and evil, God and Satan, ruled the universe. Thus they denied the absolute and omnipotent power of God, the creator of all things. Dominic believed that heresy could only be refuted by education, by reason and persuasion and by lives modelled on Christ and his apostles, on lives of humility and simplicity, like those of Francis and his followers. The two men were to meet each other, and both were eager to promote and extend their own order, and to this end they borrowed from one another, emulated each other and assimilated the strongest points in each other's orders. The Franciscans adopted the organisational skills of the Dominicans and followed them into the universities, and the Dominicans adopted the Franciscan feeling for a spirituality characterised by poverty and simplicity. 'In a large sense the Dominicans provided the intellect and the Franciscans the instincts which led to universal success ... Standing together against the rest of the world, while bitterly contesting every inch of the ground occupied by the other, they grew with astonishing speed.'[5]

At the Franciscan friary in Norwich was a distinguished friar, sympathetic towards Margery and evidently one of her trusted confidants, being familiar with her eccentric ways, her sincere piety and her emotional response whenever she heard Christ's Passion spoken of. This friar, she explains, was a very learned man, a doctor of divinity, whose advice she sought as to whether she should travel overseas with her daughter-in-law, the prospect of which filled her with dismay, for she was ever fearful of sea voyages. She must obey the will of God and the promptings of the Holy Spirit, replied the friar, and with this advice Margery was satisfied and reassured.

Could this friar, we may wonder, have been the celebrated Franciscan of Norwich, John Brackley, a distinguished academic, famous preacher and a close associate of the Paston family? Knowing Margery's customary manner of fraternising with the learned, the great and the famous, we may surmise that he could in all probability have been this very friar. John Brackley, a colourful character, who signs himself in letters 'Frater J. Brackley, Minorum minimus', was much in demand as a preacher in East Anglia, and not unaware, indeed sometimes boastful, of his gifts as a preacher. Margery Kempe's visit to this friendly friar of Norwich, whom she does not name, took place in the Spring of 1433, which would coincide with the dates of John Brackley.[6]

In her accounts of her pilgrimages Margery speaks of the Grey friars in Jerusalem and other parts of the Holy Land, where they had custody of a number of the holy places, and were responsible for guiding pilgrims from one place to another, explaining the significance of each. Their principal convent in Jerusalem was that of Mount Zion, but they also owned a smaller house adjoining the Church of the Holy Sepulchre. They had a convent also in Bethlehem and were in charge of the Grotto of the Nativity, the reputed birth place of Jesus, in the Church of the Holy Nativity.

The profound devotion which Margery exhibited at the holy places won the favour and admiration of the Grey friars, and prompted them to take her under their wing and place her at their table, so that she would not have to eat alone, for her compatriots had excluded her from their company, being irritated by her displays of emotion and her copious tears. 'Is this the English woman, whom we have heard, speaks with God?' enquired one of the Grey friars. When Margery heard of the friar's enquiry she understood the meaning of what our Lord had told her before she left England.

'Daughter, I will make all the world to wonder at you, and many men and women, will speak of me, for love of you, and they will worship me because of you.' [Ch 29]

Because of their training in pastoral counselling and the guidance of souls, the friars were much in demand as confessors, though some acquired a reputation for dispensing absolution too readily, especially if the penitent promised them a reward. Margery's Dominican confessor proved to be a wise and sympathetic counsellor and a formative influence on her spiritual progress, since he too cherished an interest in mystical theology, which gave him a special affinity with Margery and a sympathetic understanding of her particular type of spirituality. When first she told him of her mystical experiences of the divine presence, and how she conversed with Christ in so intimate and homely a manner, he was deeply moved and wept and thanked God and said,

'Daughter, you already have a foretaste of heaven and suck on Christ's breast.' [Ch 5]

As a man of learning and a doctor of divinity this Dominican anchorite would have been familiar with the doctrine of the maternal nature of God and Christ, first propounded by the Church Fathers; Clement of Alexandria, Augustine, Origen, Irenaeus and others, and later enlarged upon by medieval theologians and mystics. The doctrine asserted that Christ, because of his life-giving death, and his nourishment of his children with his body and blood in the eucharist, was like a mother who feeds her young with her milk. The idea is dealt with in some detail by Julian of Norwich in six chapters of her *Revelations of Divine Love* in which she writes, 'The human mother will suckle her child with milk, but our beloved Mother, Jesus, feeds us with himself... and does it by means of the Blessed Sacrament.'[7] Margery however makes no further mention of the motherhood of Jesus for it is his Blessed Manhood to which she is most attracted.

When she complains to the Dominican that her other confessor, Master Robert Spryngolde, is very sharp with her and will not believe her visions, but rather makes light of them, the Dominican judges the matter wisely and explains that God has appointed Master Robert to chastise her,

Dominican or Black Friar.

'For he deals with you as a smith does with a file when he wants to make a rusty and discoloured piece of iron bright and clean. The more sharpe he is with you, the brighter your soul will shine before God. But as for myself, God has chosen me to be like a nurse to you, to comfort and console you. You must be meek and lowly and thank God for both of us.' [Ch 18]

This piece of advice surely reveals the Dominican friar's knowledge of the early thirteenth century devotional treatise *The Ancrene Riwle* (the Anchoresses' Rule) in which the author exhorts the ladies, for whom the Rule was written, to endure opposition in the right spirit. 'If anyone speaks evil of you or does you some wrong, consider and understand that, for you, he is a file such as metal-workers use, and that he is filing away all your rust and the roughness of sin ... making you bright and smooth'.[8]

We have already spoken of Margery's eminent friend and unwavering supporter, Aleyn of Lynn, a Carmelite, or White friar, a reader in divinity at the flourishing little community of St Mary Magdalene on the Gaywood Causeway in Lynn. A doctor of divinity, trained at Cambridge, this worthy clerk was the author of a number of scholarly works, which included a compilation of indexes of sermon writers, and the theological works of over fifty authors. He also assiduously studied and made indexes of the extensive corpus of writings of Bridget of Sweden, which contain accounts of her visions, revelations and prophecies. That a cleric of such distinction as Aleyn of Lynn should befriend, encourage and support a woman like Margery Kempe and believe implicitly in her visions and revelations, lends considerable credibility to the authenticity and veracity of her religious experiences, for a scholar of such renown would not have easily been gulled by a highly emotional and fanatical woman if he had not believed there was more to her than that.

It was Aleyn of Lynn who defended Margery against the antagonism and adverse criticism of the Franciscan friar, the famous preacher, who so objected to her crying during his sermons. It was Aleyn too who investigated the fall onto Margery's back of a heavy piece of masonry and part of a wooden beam from the roof of St Margaret's Church. This unfortunate accident could well have killed or seriously injured her, but left her unharmed when she cried out 'Jesus, have mercy!' On hearing of this event Master Alan wished everyone to know about it, since he regarded it a great miracle and wanted God to be glorified. He therefore recovered the piece of stone and the section of beam, weighed them and found that the stone weighed three pounds and the beam six.

> **This highly respected doctor said that a marvellous miracle had occurred, and that our Lord was to be greatly glorified for preserving this woman against the malice of her enemy, the devil. He told many people about it, and many glorified God because of this woman.** [Ch 9]

The White friars belonged to the Order of the Blessed Virgin Mary of Mount Carmel, their English province being the largest in the Order, with a preponderance of houses in East Anglia. Austerity was the hallmark of their regime, strict silence being observed except when pastoral duties as confessors or spiritual advisers demanded otherwise. Their intellectual training was stringent and protracted, a doctorate only being awarded at the age of thirty two or more, after eighteen years of study. The Carmelites' most distinguished Provincial was Thomas Netter of Walden (1372–c1430), theologian, diplomat, preacher at the funeral of Henry IV and confessor to Henry V. Netter approved of genuine female anchoresses and recluses who operated within the church's authority, but was suspicious of freelance religious mystics and averse to women capturing too much public attention as did Margery Kempe.

There were certain people who envied Margery's friendship with Master Aleyn and complained to Thomas Netter, that she was associating with him too much. This called for disciplinary action on the part of Thomas Netter, who was a vigorous opponent of Lollards, and of laypeople taking too much interest in the study of Scripture. Netter, therefore, imposed a ban on Master Alan, forbidding him to speak with Margery or to answer any queries she might have relating to Scripture.

> **This was a great sorrow to him, as he told certain people, he would rather have lost a hundred pounds – if he had it – than lose his conversations with Margery, because they were of such spiritual benefit to him.** [Ch 69]

When Margery's confessor was informed that this respected doctor, Master Aleyn, was commanded not to have any communication with her, then to avoid all such occasion of this occurring, her confessor also warned Margery not to go to the friar's house anymore, nor to speak with Master Aleyn, nor to ask him questions as she had done before.

Margery faithfully obeyed her confessor's orders, and Aleyn his Provincial's, neither of them speaking to the other if they happened to meet in the street. However, after Master Aleyn had suffered a spell of serious illness and had recovered, he was released from the ban, presumably when Netter had examined the case carefully and decided that no fear of heresy was involved and no harm would be done by their resuming their friendship. So it happened one day that when Master Aleyn was dining in the house of a lady who had taken a vow of chastity and been clothed and adorned with the mantle and the ring, he sent for Margery to come and join them and speak with him again. Greatly elated and speechless with joy, Margery set out for the noble lady's house.

Then the honourable doctor said to her, 'Margery, you are most welcome. I have been prevented from seeing you for a long while, but now our Lord has sent you here so that I can speak with you again ...' [Ch 70]

The dinner that followed was a joyous and happy occasion, more for its spiritual than its bodily sustenance, for it was sauced and savoured with tales from Holy Scripture.

Two other Carmelite houses existed in Norfolk, both on the north Norfolk coast, one at Burnham Norton, the other at Blakeney. The former was founded in 1241, its most illustrious friar being the historian Robert Bale, who spent part of every year at the Carmelite houses at Oxford and Cambridge, bequeathing his valuable library to his own friary at Burnham Norton. The Gatehouse and vestiges of the friary survive, but nothing to speak of remains of the Blakeney house, whose most famous son was John de Baconsthorpe, educated by the Carmelites at Blakeney, proceeding to Oxford and to Paris and becoming Provincial of the English Carmelites in 1329.

Margery writes beautifully of the advice given to her by a further Carmelite of her acquaintance who was a member of the friary at Norwich. He was William Southfield, a man of great goodness and virtue and of a bright and pleasing countenance. Margery rehearsed to him how graciously God worked in her soul, but like many of the mystics she was fearful of being deluded by the devil. Were her visions and other religious experiences from God or from the devil? William Southfield listened to all that she told him and then reassured her of the truth of her visions.

> **'Have no fear, sister, in respect of your manner of life, for it is the Holy Spirit who works so bountifully with his grace in your soul. Thank him exceedingly for his goodness; indeed we are all bound to thank him for you, and for working such grace in our own day. We are greatly helped and comforted by you, and supported by your prayers and by the prayers of others like you ... Blessed be Almighty God for his goodness. Therefore, sister, I advise you to put yourself in the right disposition to receive God's gifts with lowliness and humility, and not to put any obstacle in the way of the Holy Spirit's goodness, nor to make any complaint against the way he works, for he gives his gifts where he will, and makes those who are unworthy worthy, and those that are sinful righteous. He is always ready with his mercy to help us, unless we ourselves are at fault, for he does not dwell in a body which is given over to sin. He shuns all falsehood and pretence and asks of us a lowly, meek and contrite heart, and a will disposed towards goodness.'** [Ch 18]

The fourth of the principal orders of friars were the Austin friars, or, to give them their official title, the Hermit Friars of St Augustine. These friars originated from a variety of semi-eremitical communities in Italy, the majority of them observing the Rule and teaching of St Augustine and having their headquarters in Rome. In England they flourished at the universities of Oxford and Cambridge and established their first friary in 1248 at Clare in Suffolk, of which considerable ruins survive to the present day.[9] The following episode again illustrates the popularity of the friars' preaching, which they were accustomed to undertake in their own churches.

During Lent a respected cleric, an Austin friar, preached in his religious house before a large audience, this creature being present too. By God's grace he was inspired to speak much of Christ's Passion, and his words were so devout and full of pity that she could not bear it, and fell down crying and weeping, which amazed the people. Then they cursed her and vehemently denounced her, thinking that she could have stopped if she had wished ... But this good friar said to the people, 'Friends, be quiet! You little know what she is feeling.' [Ch 68]

Annoying and disturbing though the people must have found Margery's crying, nevertheless worshippers in the Middle Ages were accustomed to constant disturbances during church services, where unruly behaviour was commonplace. Vergers fought a losing battle against noisy parishioners, who wandered in and out of church at will. Parish registers repeatedly record instances of roudy behaviour, chattering, laughing, joking 'jangling and japing', the playing of chess and gambling with dice during service and at sermon time.

Among the many books which Margery's confessors and scholarly friends read to her over a period of years, we can be almost certain that one of them would have been the well-known treatise by the Austin friar, William Flete, *Remedies Against Temptations*, which he wrote in c1359 and which survives in about fifty manuscripts. A particular passage in Margery Kempe's *BOOK* is strongly reminiscent of Flete's *Remedies*. She is describing how, on one occasion, a foolish young man made a lewd suggestion to her, with the consequence that she was severely tempted to dishonour her marriage vows. She reflects thus:

'Be sure of this our spiritual enemy does not sleep, but busily searches out our complexions and dispositions, and where he finds us most frail, there, by our Lord's permission, he lays his snare, from which no man may escape by his own power.' [Ch 4]

William Flete writes, 'The evil one explores each person's complexion or disposition and vexes, in a spiritual way, those who are prone to melancholy ... and so the devil assesses each man's weakness and tempts him accordingly'.[10]

An interesting character, though somewhat elusive and enigmatic, who does not figure much in religious text-books, William Flete was nevertheless a powerful spiritual influence in the later Middle Ages. He was a native of the small village of Fleet within the south eastern region of Lincolnshire, about twenty miles west of Lynn and on the direct route which Margery would have taken when travelling north to York. Born in about 1310, William Flete took the habit of an Austin friar in c1325, studying theology at the Lincoln friary, and from there he was sent to Cambridge. The earliest certain date of his career is 29 February 1352, when he was licensed for the diocese of Ely and lectured on the Bible. However, some time before 17 June 1358 he made it known that he did not intend to take his degree 'renouncing the coveted Magisterium'. Instead, in July 1359 he left England for Italy with two companions, resolving never to return to his homeland and severing all ties with family and friends. His destination was the famous monastery of his order, the Austin friars, in the hill country at Lecceto, four miles from Siena, where for thirty years he lived the true life of a hermit of St Augustine.

Flete soon attracted attention as a man of deep holiness, spiritual wisdom, severe mortification and great learning. A Florentine writer, recording impressions of him fifteen years after his arrival at Lecceto, states that he was 'a venerable man of great sanctity and solitude, living mostly in the woods in the cells that he has made ... there he brings with him his books in order to escape the conversation of people ... and to this place he goes, and comes from the church to the wood, and from the wood to the church ... a man of mature counsel, a friend of God, a man of great example; and he speaks little except when necessity obliges him'.

There, in the district of Lecceto, he met Catherine of Siena and became one of a circle of friars, priests and devoted female disciples, who gathered round this saintly woman and were profoundly influenced by her. She in turn was guided by Flete, a master of the spiritual life, though Raymond of Capua became her confessor in 1374. Flete also wrote letters of instruction to the brethren of the Austin friars in England, warning them to avoid always being about, 'as time and place allow, stay in your rooms as in a hermitage, in a solitary cell, and there apply yourself to study, contemplation and prayer'. He recommends reciting the Psalms and the reading of Scripture, especially the Prophets and the Gospels, but the brethren are also to undertake works of charity among the poor and in the hospitals.[11]

Beneficial and edifying as the friars were to medieval society as preachers, evangelists, educators, counsellors and confessors, it would be a mistake to suppose that all were true to the vision of their founders, living exemplary lives of apostolic fervour, virtue, poverty and simplicity, for, as Richard Southern points out 'the friars quickly developed the vices appropriate to their way of life ... the poverty and institutional begging of the friars led to a search for legacies and fees, and easily suggested a lenient treatment for penitents who were also benefactors'.[12]

The vocation of the friars was to a life of poverty and simplicity, to a reliance upon almsgiving for their sustenance, to preach the kingdom of God, to go about barefooted or in sandals if necessity required it, attired in coarse clothing, their dwellings simple huts. They were to be meek, peaceable, modest and mild. Francis had not intended his brothers to build themselves great convents and splendid churches, or to be possessors of property, for this would predispose them to pride, worldliness, materialism and a love of comfort, ease and luxury, stealing their hearts away from prayer and contemplation and the performance of good works. Neither had he intended them to possess books and become renowned for their learning, for this would lead to intellectual arrogance and involvement in philosophical and theological speculation and dispute. Francis had said 'a time of tribulation is to come, when books shall be useful for nothing and shall be thrown in windows and cupboards'.[13] He grieved if anyone neglected the practice of virtue and sought after science and knowledge 'which puffeth up'. To a novice who said to him, 'Father, it would be a great solice to me to have a psalter', Francis replied 'After you have a psalter, you will desire and wish to have a brevirary. Then you will sit in your chair, like a great prelate, and say to your brother, "Bring me the breviary".'[14]

But the intellectual life of man cannot be stifled and as the Franciscan and Dominican movements extended geographically and increased in numerical strength, they became more diverse and complex and attracted scholars and intellectuals, who wished to pursue their studies, to prepare sermons and combat heresy, and for this purpose books were necessary, and a place to house them and quietness to study them. The very ideals of poverty, simplicity and humility which characterised the mendicant orders in their beginning, attracted handsome donations and legacies from the wealthy, thus making the poor friars richer, and stimulating the building of larger and finer friaries and churches, which were often enriched by kings and princes, nobles and aristocrats, many of whom wished to be buried in them. 'Friars build many great churches, with cloisters like castles, and without need … for great houses do not make men holy and only by holiness is God well served' wrote John Wyclif.[15]

CHAPTER SEVEN

Vow of Chastity

Christianity, with its two virgin figures, Christ and our Lady, led to an exaltation of virginity above wedlock, a view given further impetus by St Paul whose opinions were profoundly influential in the formation of doctrine and religious practice in the early Church. On the question of marriage, widowhood and celibacy St Paul had expounded the view that it was good for unmarried people and widows to remain as they were, but if they lacked the gift of self-control it was better for them to marry. Each person must act according to his or her gift and calling. A Christian man, however, who was unmarried could give his undivided attention to the Lord's business, his aim being to please the Lord, while a married man's aim was to please his wife. The same applied to women regarding their married, single or widowed state (1 Cor. 7.25–34).

To both celibacy and marriage Jesus had given his positive approval. Celibacy was a special calling given to some, not everyone could accept it; but those who were called to it should accept it (Matt. 19.10–12). Marriage, he said, was a divine institution, ordained by God for the purpose of procreation and the help and affection which husband and wife should have for each other, the bond between them, designed by God from the beginning, to be of a permanent nature (Mark 10.1–2 & Gen. 2.24). He spoke too of the joy of motherhood, the blessedness of childhood and the reverence with which children were to be treated (John 16.21, Mark 10.13–16, Matt. 18.5–6).

But Jesus had also drawn a distinction between those who followed him and those who belonged to the pagan world, the Gentiles. People of the pagan world adopted a materialistic outlook on life and were anxious about earthly things, food and drink and clothes, wealth and possessions. His disciples, on the other hand, were enjoined not to be anxious about these things but to trust in God and to seek first his kingdom (Matt. 6.19–34). His disciples were *in* the world but not *of* the world. 'If you belonged to the world, the world would love its own; but you do not belong to the world, now that I have chosen you out of the world' (John 15.19). Similarly, St Paul enjoined Christians to 'conform no longer to the pattern of this present world, but be transformed by the renewal of your minds' (Rom 12.1–2). They were to walk no longer according to the flesh but according to the spirit, 'For the mind of the flesh is death; but the mind of the spirit is life and peace ... if by the spirit you mortify the deeds of the body, you shall live' (Rom. 8.5–14).

This notion of the other-worldliness of Christians and the necessity to detach themselves from worldly preoccupations applied to every aspect of life, the conflict between flesh and spirit being particularly marked in the realm of the appetites and desires. Ascetic practices chiefly concerned food and drink, sleep and sex. We have seen how Margery Kempe fasted, wore a hair-shirt, rose very early and spent many hours in prayer and vigils. This kind of asceticism, undertaken by Christian people, had a purpose beyond itself. The disciplining of the body and the curbing of the appetites and desires was practised in order that the body might be subjected to the mind and spirit, thus freeing the whole person for the purpose for which it was created, to love, serve and glorify the Creator.

The views of the world and of secular society were reversed by the Church. The world exalted the body, the Church the soul. The world deemed the marital state with its prestige and status to be at the summit of the hierarchy regarding state of life. This was followed by widowhood and, lowest in the hierarchy, the single state. The Church turned this hierarchy upside down, placing virginity or celibacy at the pinnacle, followed by widowhood and lastly marriage. Drawing on the doctrine of St Paul and the Church Fathers: Gregory of Nissa, John Chrystostom, Gregory of Nazianzus, Cyprian, Jerome, Augustine and others, all of whom took a somewhat jaundiced view of marriage, the Church formulated a doctrine of the Three States. Virginity, at the pinnacle of the hierarchy, was sometimes associated with the 'hundredfold' of the parable of the Sower, followed by widowhood, the 'sixtyfold' and lastly wedlock, the 'thirtyfold' of the parable.

Innumerable sermons were preached in the Middle Ages, and treatises composed, in praise of the Virgin Mary and the virgin saints, all of which enlarged on the excellence of virginity and its superiority to wedlock. Such lofty sentiments were expressed, for example, in the treatise *The Ancrene Riwle*, which asserted that 'No one can love Christ unless she preserves chaste cleanness; and this is possible in three states of life, in widowhood, in wifehood and at its highest in maidenhood'.[1] Maidenhood was nearest the life of the angels. 'The angels were free from earthly passions, and spent their time in uninterrupted contemplation of God. It was the object of the ascetic to imitate them as far as was humanly possible by mortification of the flesh and by constant prayer. Since there is no marrying and giving in marriage in heaven (Luke 30.35) consecrated virgins were seen as coming particularly close to the ideal of the "angelic life"'.[2]

But both in patristic and medieval literature, theologians stated emphatically that celibacy of itself could not be pleasing to God unless accompanied by other virtues: humility, charity, patience and the rest. What spiritual worth was there in a person, while being chaste in body, was guilty of the sins of pride, hatred, anger, avarice and other vices? 'Much better is humble married life than proud virginity' says Caesarius of Arles (470–543). Walter Hilton in his *Ladder of Perfection* enunciates a similar warning to the anchoress for whom he is writing. 'There may be many a wife and woman living in the world who will be nearer to God than you, and who will love Him more and know Him better than you, despite your way of life ... If you wish to grow in grace, forget your calling – for it is nothing in itself – and direct all your desires and efforts to acquiring charity, humility and other virtues'.[3]

Hali Meidhad, a treatise written to encourage women who had already taken a vow of virginity, or were considering such a vow, elaborate on the trials of marriage. 'You say that a wife has much comfort from her husband if the two are well suited, and each content with the other. But suppose it is so; in what is their comfort and delight but mostly in the filth of the flesh and worldly vanity, which turns everything to sorrow in the end ... Your husband chides and jaws you like a lecher does his whore; he beats you and mauls you ... Your bones ache and your flesh smarts, your heart swells with rage within you and your face burns with vexation'.[4]

Compare this with the beautiful description of married love in *The Book of Vices and Virtues*, a fourteenth century English version of a thirteenth century French work. 'The third branch of the tree of chastity is the state and the bond of marriage, for husband and wife should keep themselves for each other, cleanly and truly, without any wrongdoing by the one to the other ... For after they are knit together in the flesh, they are one body and one soul, as Holy Writ says, and therefore each of them should love the other as himself. For as they are one body, they should be of one heart by true love ... Marriage is a sacrament of holy church and betokens the marriage that is between Jesus Christ and holy church and between God and the soul'.[5]

For Margery Kempe however no amount of treatises on the value of the married state could deter her from lamenting the loss of her virginity. Her religious fervour brought her into contact with numerous men and women who belonged to the religious orders, and who were therefore dedicated to a celibate way of life, and as a married woman, with husband children claiming her time, attention and affection, she must often have eyed these with envy and nostalgia, since her love for Christ was so ardent that only the highest and the best would do for him. The smallest imperfection and failure in virtue irked her, for she feared above all to displease the one she loved most in all the world.

'Ah, Lord, how joyfully virgins must be dancing now in heaven! Shall I not dance with them too? Alas, I am no virgin, and my want of virginity is a great sorrow to me. Would that I had been killed as soon as I had been taken from the font, so that I should never have displeased you. Then, blessed Lord, you would have had my virginity for ever.' [Ch 22]

'Ah, daughter,' replied our Lord Jesus, 'how often have I told you that your sins are forgiven and we are united together for ever ... I have told you before that you are a special lover of God, and therefore you will have a special love in heaven, a special reward and a special honour. And because you are a virgin in your soul I will take you by one hand in heaven, and my Mother by the other, and so

you shall dance in heaven with other holy maidens and virgins, and I will call you dearly bought, and my own dearest darling. I shall say to you, my own blessed spouse, I welcome you with all manner of joy and gladness, to dwell with me here for ever, and never to depart from me.'

The idea of mystical or spiritual marriage between Christ and the soul received wide attention by the medieval saints and mystics, and, though the concept is firmly based on scripture, we must always regard it as essentially figurative and metaphorical. In the Old Testament God is depicted as the husband of Israel, his chosen people. 'For thy Maker is thine husband; the Lord of hosts is his name' (Is. 54.5). In the New Testament, in various verses and parables, Jesus, either explicitly or implicitly, refers to himself as 'bridegroom' (Matt. 9.15; 22.1–14; 25.1 and St Paul develops the idea of Christ as the bridegroom or husband of the Church (Eph. 5.22–33). The logical corollary of this collective piece of imagery of the Church as the bride of Christ, is that individual members of the Church can also be designated 'bride' or 'spouse' of Christ. Although the imagery is particularly appropriate to women, it is also applied to men, for as Bridget of Sweden says, 'The soul of a righteous man is my spouse, and I am his Maker and his Husband'.[6]

It would be a mistake to suppose that the divine discourses which Margery held with Christ, and her other mystical experiences, only dated from the time following her vow of chastity, as if there were some special connection between chastity and divine revelations. She was already being granted such visions and revelations and divine locutions while still a young woman and bearing children. She felt unworthy, she said, to be granted these holy visions from our Lord and to hear him speaking to her in so intimate and homely a manner while she was living with a husband and having sexual relations with him. To receive such holy revelations, she thought, was more suited to virgins. In his reply Jesus echoes the traditional teaching of the Church on the Three States.

'Yes, daughter, but be assured of this, that I love wives also, and specially those wives who would live chaste if they had their way and did all they could to please me as you do. For though the state of maidenhood is more [Ch 21]

> **perfect and more holy than the state of widowhood, and the state of widowhood more perfect than the state of wedlock, yet, daughter, I love you as much as any maiden in the world. No one may hinder me from loving whom I will, and as much as I will, for love, daughter, overcomes all sin. Therefore ask of me the gifts of love, for there is no gift so holy as the gift of love, nor is there anything to be desired as much as love.'**

Professor Meech, by piecing together a number of important contemporary events, such as the elevation of Philip Repingdon to the bishopric of Lincoln and the death of Thomas Arundel, has estimated that Margery and John Kempe made an agreement to live chastely on 23 June 1413, Margery being about forty years old and her husband probably somewhat older. She relates that for several years prior to the agreement, she had longed 'to live chaste' and had told her husband that although the law forbade her to withhold her body from him, all her love and affection were set primarily upon God.

> **Often she counselled her husband to live a chaste life and said that she knew very well that they had often displeased God by their inordinate love and the pleasure they had in using each other's bodies. But now it would be a good thing if, by mutual consent, they chastised and disciplined themselves by abstaining from the lust of their bodies. Her husband said that it would be a good thing to do, but not yet; he would when God willed. So he used her as he had done before and would not spare her. But she was for ever praying that she might live chastely, and after three or four years, when it pleased our Lord, her husband took an oath of chastity.** [Ch 3]

The first indication that matters were coming to a head in respect of their oath occurred on the Wednesday of Easter Week 1413, when her husband would have had intercourse with her, as he was accustomed to do, and she prayed 'Jesus, help me'. Then he suddenly had no power to touch her in this way, nor did he ever have intercourse with her again. But the question was not finally resolved until the June of that year, when they were travelling together on foot on Midsummer's Eve 'in ryght hoot wedyr' from York to Bridlington, carrying with them for their refreshment a bottle of beer and a cake. After prolonged discussion John Kempe finally consented to Margery's desire to take a vow of chastity, but on condition that she would pay his debts before she went on pilgrimage, that she would abandon her custom of fasting on Fridays and eat and drink with him as she used to do. To the latter request she was unwilling to comply, for Jesus himself had commanded her to observe a Friday fast.

> **'No, sir, I will never agree to break my Friday fast as long as I live' she said.** [Ch 11]
>
> **'Well then' he replied, 'I shall have intercourse with you again.'**

Very troubled and distressed by her husband's attitude, Margery left him for a while and wept and prayed by a wayside cross.

> **'Lord God, you know all things. You know with what sorrow I have desired to live in chastity of body for these last three years, and now it seems I could fulfill my desire if I would agree to break my Friday fast which you commanded me to observe. But I dare not do this for love of you, for you know, Blessed Lord, that I will not disobey your will ... Now Blessed Jesus, make your will known to me, unworthy creature though I am, that I may henceforth follow it, and fulfil it with all my strength.'** [Ch 11]

With great sweetness Jesus answered her that she may now relinquish her Friday fast and eat and drink with her husband, and so have her will to live in chastity of body. Thanking Jesus for his grace and goodness, Margery returned to her husband and told him she would agree to his requests if he, for his part, would not come into her bed, nor make any demands on her in respect of the debt of matrimony, to which John Kempe replied, 'Margery, may your body be as available to God as it has been to me'.

Margery's custom of wearing white clothes appears to date from the time when she took this vow of chastity and was a sign to the world that, though not a virgin, she was set on living a chaste and pure life from henceforth. Had not St John the Divine in the Book of Revelation stated that those who walked with Christ, the victorious ones, would be clothed in white? (Rev. 3.4–5).

But the idea of wearing white was not Margery's; it was the

Lord's. She must be clothed according to his will, he said, and he willed that she should be arrayed in white. To this command she at first objected.

> **'Ah, dear Lord, if I go about dressed differently from other chaste women, I am afraid that the people will slander me. They will say that I am a hypocrite and will be filled with wonder at my behaviour.'** [Ch 15
>
> **'Indeed, daughter, but the more ridicule you endure for love of me, the more you will please me.'**
>
> **So this woman dare not do otherwise than she was commanded in her soul.**

The vow, privately made, had now to receive the official recognition of the Church and the Church's representative, in this case the Bishop of Lincoln, for the Bishop of Norwich, in whose diocese Margery and John Kempe resided, had recently died, leaving the see vacant. Philip Repingdon had long wished to meet Margery and to speak with her, so he was pleased now to have the opportunity to do so and welcomed her heartily. After telling him of her manner of living and her mystical experiences she explained the real purpose of her visit.

> **'My lord, if you are pleased to do so, I have been commanded in my soul to ask you to bestow upon me the mantle and the ring, and to clothe me all in white clothes. It has been shown to me by revelation that if you clothe me on earth, our Lord Jesus Christ will clothe you in heaven.'** [Ch 15

Canon Law required that if one partner of a marriage wished to take a vow of celibacy, the other partner had to give consent also. The Bishop, therefore sent for John Kempe and addressed him thus:

> **'John, is it your wish that your wife take the mantle and the ring and live in chastity, and you also?'** [Ch 15
>
> **'Yes, my lord,' replied John, 'and as a sign that we both vow to live in chastity, I offer my hands into your hands.' And at that he placed his hands between the Bishop's hands.**

Profoundly serious as Margery is about her vow of chastity, yet there is something touchingly humorous about her and her husband's encounter with this eminent churchman. There stands John Kempe, something of a rustic figure, the father of fourteen children, his hands solemnly placed between the bishop's hands in the manner of taking a vow, swearing to keep his side of the bargain to live chaste. How precisely the vow affected him we cannot say, though his initial reluctance was categorical and had an Augustinian ring about it, 'Lord, make me chaste, but not yet'.

Philip Repingdon had qualms about bestowing the mantle and the ring upon Margery. Nuns, taking vows and entering the cloister were clothed in a religious habit and given the ring, and many pious widows who chose not to remarry, took formal vows of chastity before a bishop, and received the mantle and the ring. Such a woman was Lady Blanche, who in 1393, in the diocese of Ely, humbly asked the bishop to recognise her vow of chastity and to bestow upon her the mantle and the ring. 'Afterwards the said Lady Blanche, in the chapel of the Manor of Doddington, in the diocese of Ely, before the high altar, in the presence of the said reverend father ... solemnly made her vow of chastity.' Lady Blance was what was known as a 'mourning widow', her deceased husband having been Sir Nicholas de Styvede, Knight.[7]

But Margery Kempe was neither virgin-nun nor mourning widow, her husband being hale and hearty and probably still after fifty years old. Repingdon therefore delayed a decision for a few days while he pondered the matter and consulted his advisers. He prevaricated, since he doubted whether she officially qualified to receive the mantle and the ring. Moreover he had his reputation to consider, for Margery was under suspicion of being associated with the Lollards, and he himself had once supported John Wyclif, but had long since renounced heresy. It would be better not to get mixed up with a woman of dubious orthodoxy and of such unconventional behaviour. Caution would be the wisest policy.

Philip Repingdon, therefore, summoned Margery to appear before him so that he might give her his judgement on the subject.

'Margery, you and your husband spoke to me about giving you the mantle and the ring. I have consulted my counsellors on the question and they advise me not to profess you in this special clothing without higher authority. You tell me you intend to go to Jerusalem, God [Ch 15]

willing. I advise you therefore to pray to God about this matter and wait until you return from Jerusalem before taking a decision. This will give you time to put the matter to the test and help you to know your own mind.'

The Bishop further informed Margery that she did not come within his ecclesiastical jurisdiction, and that he had no final authority to give her the mantle and the ring. She must go to the Archbishop of Canterbury to obtain permission for him, Repingdon, to present her with the mantle and the ring. To this advice Margery retorted sharply that she would gladly go to the Archbishop, but that there were other questions of a quite separate nature which she wished to discuss with him. God did not wish her to consult the Archbishop on the subject of her vow of chastity and the conferring of the mantle and the ring upon her.

No further mention is made in Margery's *BOOK* of the mantle and the ring. It was sufficient for her that she had made her private vow to God and her formal vow before the Bishop of Lincoln, that she wore the white clothes which the Lord had commanded her to wear, and that she wore on her hand her 'marriage ring to Jesus' which was inscribed with the words 'Jesus est amor meus'.

Having secured her wish to live a celibate life, Margery now highly prized her chastity, and was in perpetual fear of being attacked and raped, especially when she was on pilgrimage, spending the nights in inns and hostels among throngs of jovial, drinking, wanton folk.

She was most afraid at night, fearing she might be assaulted or raped ... Whether her fear was justified or not, she dare not trust any man, but was always afraid, and dare not sleep at night for fear men might defile her. She was never happy on any night to go to bed, unless she had one or two women to sleep beside her. God was good to her in this respect, for wherever she went there were usually some girls who would cheerfully lie beside her, which was a great comfort to her. [Ch 7 [Bk II

In England while on trial for heresy at Leicester, the Steward of the town harassed her with his unwelcome attentions.

He took her by the hand and led her to his room and spoke many lewd and bawdy words to her, intending, [Ch 47

10. St Michael Weighing a Soul. Early 14th c. window, Eaton Bishop, Herefordshire.

11. Resurrection. Nave Clerestory window, York Minster.

so it seemed to her, to take her by force and to rape her. This caused her much fear and alarm, and she begged him for mercy. 'Sir, for the love of God, spare me, for I am a man's wife' she said.

Ordered by the Mayor of Leicester to be put in prison, she pleaded with him not to put her among the men, for she must keep her vow of chastity, she said, and her marriage bond to her husband. When on trial in All Hallows church, Leicester, she affirms her fidelity to her marriage vows and her obedience to the Two Great Commandments.

'I take my Lord Jesus Christ for my witness, whose Body is present here in the Sacrament of the Altar, that I have never sinned in body with any man in the world, and have only known my husband, to whom I am bound by the law of matrimony, and by whom I have borne fourteen children. For I would have you know, sir, that there is no man in this world whom I love as much as I love God, for I love God above all things, and I tell you the truth, sir, when I say that I love everyone in and for God.' [Ch 48]

CHAPTER EIGHT

Travels and Pilgrimages at Home and Abroad

The custom of going on pilgrimage was an integral part of pre-Reformation English life. Although comparatively few had the opportunity or financial means to make the three principal overseas pilgrimages to Jerusalem, Rome and St James Compostela, pilgrim sites abounded in England for the ordinary common folk to visit. There were famous shrines of national and international repute such as those of St Thomas Becket of Canterbury, Our Lady of Walsingham in Norfolk and the Holy Blood of Hailes in Gloucestershire, and if these were too distant there were innumerable local shrines to visit which marked the places where holy people lived and laboured, performed miracles and died.

The reasons for going on pilgrimage were manifold. Some went for purposes of devotion, others for adventure, or for relief from the tedium of life at home, some to enjoy the conviviality of the pilgrim band, to indulge in illicit pleasures, to atone for sins or to seek a miracle cure for sickness. Medieval folk had a powerful conviction that physical illnesses had spiritual causes. 'They were brought on by sin, from which it followed that penitence at the shrine of a saint effaced not only the sin, but the illness as well'.[1]

Pilgrimage undertaken for worthy motives could be meritorious, but preachers and writers of devotional treatises pronounced pilgrimage worthless, indeed positively evil, if embarked upon for unworthy and base motives. John Bromyard, a fifteenth century English Dominican states, 'There are some who keep their pilgrimages and festivals, not for God but for the devil. They who sin more freely when away from home, or who go on pilgrimage to succeed in inordinate and foolish love ... they make their pilgrimage away from God and to the devil'.[2] Thomas à Kempis likewise criticises the custom of going on pilgrimage. 'Many people go running off to various places to see the relics of the saints. They hear about the miracles they performed, and gaze in wonder at the great churches built over them. They feast their eyes on their holy bones wrapped up in silk and gold, and press their lips to them ... It is curiosity and love of novelty which takes them to see such things, and they return with little harvest in the way of improved lives'.[3]

Roman roads were still in use in the later Middle Ages, though many roads developed alongside them, travellers preferring the soft ground to hard surfaces. These alternative routes were no more than tracks trodden down by endless wayfarers, horse-riders, waggons, carriages, packhorses and carts making their way to market-towns, fairs, villages, hamlet, manors and churches.[4] Often the tracks were deeply rutted and dangerous to negotiate, making it necessary for the traveller to make lengthy detours. In 1406 the rainfall in England was particularly heavy, causing floods to inundate large areas of the countryside and bridges to break up. 'There were floods in the Waveney at Beccles, the bridge over the Nene at Thrapston was broken, the banks at the Humber were swamped from Hessle to the Derwent; and in the Isle of Ely around Cambridge in the marshland between Lynn and Wisbech, and in the Fen country ... roads, bridges and causeways were wrecked and washed away.'[5]

England was notorious for its thieves and robbers both in the countryside and in the towns. Wayfarers were in constant fear of attack by such people who lurked in woods, hedgerows and heaths, or of lawless gangs and armed bandits who rode on horseback, terrorising all who travelled the highways. Margery relates how, before setting off on her journey to Bristol in preparation for her pilgrimage to St James Compostela, citizens of Lynn were warning her of the many thieves she would encounter. This filled her with fear that her money, which she required for the voyage, might be stolen.

When Margery and her husband travelled from Bishop's Lynn to London or to Canterbury they would have followed the customary medieval route to Stoke Ferry, Brandon Ferry and from there to Thetford, Newmarket, Ware, Waltham Abbey and London, with numerous breaks for rest, refreshment and a night's sleep at inns, hostels, monastic guest-houses, or under the stars. Such a journey would probably have taken the wayfarers ten days or more to accomplish, depending on weather conditions and the health and vigour of the travellers. In summer, when the weather was warm and sunny, such an endeavour would have been a pleasant and enjoyable one, and it appears from the table of events covering Margery's life that the majority of her journeys were undertaken in spring or summer.

Just how circuitous, leisurely and protracted travel in medieval England could be is illustrated by Margery's account of her journey from Lynn to Ipswich in preparation for the voyage to Danzig with her daughter-in-law. The two women, and the hermit who accompanied them, had covered but five or six miles of their journey when they paused to hear Mass in a village church, after which instead of striking southwards and eastwards in the direction of Ipswich, as we would have expected them to do, they headed northwards, since Margery had decided to make her offerings at the shrine of Our Lady of Walsingham. On the way to Walsingham, however, people were saying that a certain friar was to preach at village church, which was too great an opportunity for Margery to miss, so the little band of travellers veered off course again and joined the large audience, eager to hear this eminent friar. This accomplished, they resumed their journey to Walsingham before turning south eastwards to Norwich where Margery encountered and conversed with an unidentified Grey friar, possibly John Brackley. Finally they proceeded southwards on the last lap of their journey to Ipswich, thus completing a trek of about 80 to 90 miles in all.

The shrine at Walsingham was second only to that of St Thomas of Canterbury in fame and popularity, even exceeding Canterbury at the end of the fifteenth century. All the kings and queens of England between and including Henry III and Henry VIII made the pilgrimage to Walsingham. It was here in 1051 that the young widow, Richeldis de Favaraches, lady of the manor of Little Walsingham, prayed that she might devote herself to some particular cause in honour of our Lady. In response to her prayers she was led in spirit to the house house of Nazareth, scene of the Annunciation and the upbringing of the child Jesus, and was instructed to build a replica of the house at Walsingham. Near to the springs that emerged on the spot where the vision appeared to Richeldis, she built the holy house in the form of a wooden hut surrounded by a flint and stone building.[6]

Within the chapel stood the celebrated image of the Virgin, adorned with jewels, around which incense burnt perpetually and the light of many candles flickered. All such shrines possessed what were claimed to be genuine relics, which were displayed to credulous pilgrims, Walsingham boasting a joint of St Peter's finger and a phial of the Virgin's milk, a relic which Erasmus (1460–1536) declared to resemble chalk mixed with egg-white.[7]

In about 1153 Richeldis' son Geoffrey, having visited the Holy Land himself, established a priory of Augustinian canons at Walsingham, the canons becoming guardians of the shrine, the holy wells and the relics. Franciscan friars came too to settle in Walsingham on the outskirts of the village, offering hospitality to pilgrims in their large and impressive guesthouse, considerable ruins of which survive today.

A shrine which Margery does not mention, but one which she can hardly have failed to visit, was that to the east of Walsingham, on the north Norfolk coast at Bacton. This was the famous shrine at Bromholm Priory, at one time equal in popularity to Walsingham itself. There in the Cluniac Priory was deposited what purported to be a true relic of the Saviour's Cross, a relic which attracted multitudes of pilgrims and brought wealth and fame to the priory. 'by the Holy Cross of Bromholm' became a binding oath in the Middle Ages. The miller's daughter of the Canterbury Tales calls upon the Cross to help her, and Piers Ploughman's avaricious tradesman swears to renounce his cheating ways. 'I'll make a pilgrimage to Walsingham … and pray to the Rood of Bromholm to get me out of debt'.[8] The priory at Bromholm figures prominently in the Paston Letters, since the Paston family lived in the adjoining parish of Paston, were on friendly terms with the prior and brethren and, were generous benefactors to the community.

Norwich, being the cathedral city of the diocese in which Margery resided, was a place of special importance to her and the home of several of her valued and influential clergy friends and

Norwich Cathedral, from a drawing by Mr S. K. Greenslade, 1891.

spiritual advisers. The town lay to the east of Lynn, a journey of some fifty miles or so. In the later Middle Ages Norwich had risen to become the second town in England, and chief market town in one of the country's most prosperous districts, the thriving market selling a variety of merchandise including wool, corn, cattle, pigs, sheep, poultry, vegetables, herbs and salt. So abundant were the commodities on sale that the principal market-place outgrew its capacity and spread to nearby localities, horses, for instance, being sold outside the churchyard of St Stephen's, the street name Rampant Horse Street reflecting this development. Over a hundred and thirty trades and occupants are recorded, and by the end of the fourteenth century, the town was the chief centre of worsted manufacture, the wealth produced resulting in the erection of numerous churches and municipal buildings.[9] Medieval churches numbered about fifty, of which over thirty remain, and all four mendicant orders of friars settled in the city where they built their friaries and fine churches.

Before departing from England on her pilgrimage to the Holy Land, and on her return, Margery Kempe visited Norwich Cathedral to offer her prayers and gifts in honour of the Holy Trinity, to whom the cathedral was dedicated, the income of the cathedral coming principally from the voluntary offerings of the faithful. To the north of the high altar stood the costly and magnificent patronal images of the Holy Trinity.[10] The most common form of imagery of the Trinity comprised representations of the Three Persons, the Father, the Son and the Holy Spirit, the Father being represented as a venerable, fatherly figure, crowned, sometimes with a triple papal tiara. Beneath was the Second Person of the Trinity, the Son, Jesus Christ on the cross, and somewhere in the group, usually above the head of Christ, was a dove, representing the Third Person of the Trinity, the Holy Spirit. This was most probably, the kind of representation of the Trinity which Margery would have witnessed in Norwich Cathedral at the time.

Although Margery makes no mention of a visit to the Shrine of St Thomas Becket in Canterbury Cathedral, it can be assumed that on the various occasions she visited the town she was among the throngs of pilgrims who flocked to this popular pilgrimage centre. Becket was murdered in 1170 and within a fortnight of his death his cult was established, but as with other saints, his cult was sporadic. 'Canterbury was a shrine of European importance, probably the most prosperous in Christendom, for about ten years after Becket's brutal death ... but in the early thirteenth century pilgrims who used to go regularly to Canterbury were reported to be abandoning it in favour of the holy rood, recently acquired by Bromholm priory ... The tendency of the laity was always to visit the saint whose cult had been recently established'.[11] On special occasions, however, such as the removal of a saint's body from one shrine to another, as in the case of St Thomas in 1220, when his body was translated from the crypt to the Trinity Chapel behind the High Altar, renewed enthusiasm occurred for pilgrimage to that particular shrine. 'The shrine of Canterbury was venerated by the whole medieval world ... kings and princes, barons and merchants, the poor and the oppressed, all found their way to Canterbury, "the holy blissful martyr for to seek".'[12]

Hailes Abbey in Gloucestershire, near the attractive little Cotswold town of Winchcombe, set in lush and beautiful countryside, was a favourite pilgrimage site for English folk in the Middle Ages. It was in mid-August 1417 when Margery Kempe made the fifty or so mile journey from Bristol to this great Cistercian abbey, a daughter house of Beaulieu in Hampshire, having recently returned to Bristol from her pilgrimage to St James Compostela in northern Spain.

The story goes that in 1245, Richard, Earl of Cornwall, brother of King Henry III, came into the possession of the manor of Hailes and the avowson of its parish church, and the following year, 1246, founded the Abbey, bringing to it ten monks and 20 lay brothers from Beaulieu. On Holy Rood Day (September 14) 1270, Richard's son, Edmund, presented the Abbey with a phial containing what was thought to be some drops of blood from Christ's holy body, guaranteed to be authentic by the Patriarch of Jerusalem, later Pope Urban IV. This phial, or glass bottle, containing the holy relic, was kept in a chapel behind the high altar of the Abbey church, and attracted throngs of pilgrims from all over England and Europe, swelling the monastic coffers.[13]

Margery did not remain long at Bristol, but went on to see the Blood of Hailes, and she made her confession [Ch 45]

there and received absolution ... Then the religious men took her in among them and made her very welcome, though when they swore blasphemous oaths, she rebuked them with words from the Gospel, which astonished them.

Of this visit to Hailes Abbey, and other similar visits to religious houses, David Knowles comments 'Trifling as these incidents are, they are precious vignettes of a passing moment in a monastery: the free conversation with women, the well-supplied board, the group of rustic Cistercians swearing and guffawing'.[14]

About a century after Margery's Kempe's time, Hugh Latimer, the Reformer, wrote to a friend from his rectory at West Kingston, near Chippenham in Wiltshire, on the topic of Hailes' Blood. 'I dwell within a mile of the Fosseway, and you would wonder to see how many come by flocks out of the west country to many images ... chiefly to the Blood of Hailes, which they believe to be the very blood of Christ, and that the sight of it will put them in a state of salvation'. In 1539 the Abbey and all its possessions were surrendered to the crown, Hugh Latimer heading a commission to investigate the supposed relic. The phial was declared to be filled with 'an unctuous gum, coloured and glistening red, resembling somewhat the colour of blood'. The contents of the phial were publicly destroyed by John Hilsey, Bishop of Rochester, who declared that it was 'not blood, but clarified honey and coloured with saffron'.[15]

In the autumn of 1417, having departed from Leicester after her trials for hersey in that city, Margery came to York, the chief reason for which, she declared, was to make her offerings at the shrine of St William. However, news of her supposed heretical views reached York and brought her into conflict with the ecclesiastical hierarchy, though some eminent clergy, we are told, befriended her and 'loved the said creature right well'.

The saint to whom Margery refers, William of York (d.1154), was a man of noble birth and royal lineage, treasurer of York and chaplain to King Stephen, and elected Archbishop of York in 1140. The election was challenged by the Cistercian monks, St Bernard in particular, who accused William of Simony and unchastity, though the pope allowed the consecretation to take place on condition that the dean of York could exonerate William of the charges. St Bernard's letters of protest to popes and legates continued until pope Eugenius III, a Cistercian himself, headed the protests and suspended and deposed William, who then retired to Winchester and lived a devout life as a monk until all his enemies and opponents had died. William was then restored to his see of York, 'mild and conciliatory towards his enemies' but within a few months of his triumphant return to the city he died suddenly, probably of poison. William was buried in his cathedral, miracles soon occuring at his tomb, testifying to his sanctity. He was well-favoured by the people, regarded as a victim of injustice, which together with his rumoured murder contributed to a popular demand for his canonisation. In 1421, the famous St William window depicting sixty two scenes from his life, death and miracles, was made and put in place in the Minster.[16]

Pilgrimage and travel overseas was an altogether more perilous adventure than travel at home in one's own country, since sailing ships in medieval times were fragile and unstable and conditions on board were atrocious, the lower deck being overcrowded and smouldering hot. Rats, mice, fleas, lice and other vermin made the voyage a misery for the passengers, and roudiness, fighting, drunkeness and thieving were commonplace, and many a woman lost her virtue, if not on board ship, then at some other stage of her pilgrimage. Not without cause did Margery fear for her chastity and pray, 'Lord, drive away my enemies and preserve my chastity'.

One of the most fascinating chroniclers of medieval pilgrimages is Brother Felix Fabri, a fifteenth century Dominican friar who asserts that sea-voyages 'strike terror into the soul, cause headaches, provoke vomiting and nausea, destroy appetite for food and drink, cause extreme and deadly perils, and often bring people to a cruel death'.[17] He describes how passengers, passed the time, playing games of cards or dice, singing songs, playing flutes, bagpipes, zithers and other musical instruments, reading books, discussing world affairs, praying, meditating, or sleeping the whole day on their berths.

Before departing from his native land a pilgrim was instructed to pay his debts, to make amends for any wrong he had done his neighbour, to take his leave of kith and kin, and to obtain the official blessing of his parish priest or some other devout cleric. With these regulations Margery faithfully complied before setting out on her pilgrimage to the Holy Land. She helped her husband with the payment of his debts and asked the parish priest, Master Robert, to announce from the pulpit her readiness to recompense anyone to whom she owed money. Then having bade farewell to her husband, the Dominican anchorite and Master Robert, she departed from Lynn with her fellow pilgrims and proceeded to Yarmouth, the port of embarkation.

From Yarmouth the pilgrim galley bound for the Holy Land sailed eastwards to Zierikzee, in Zealand in the Netherlands, a town belonging to the Hanseatic League, and from here the pilgrims set out on the long trek southwards through Europe to the German town of Constance, travelling chiefly on foot, with the occasional ride in wains, especially for those who fell sick on the journey or who were overcome by fatigue. At Constance an English friar, a doctor of divinity and the pope's legate, befriended Margery, heard her confession, comforted her and defended her against her hostile travelling companions who ostracized her because she wept so much, abstained from eating meat and spoke continually about God.

> **Her companions were very angry with her and handed her over to the legate and avowed that they would have nothing more to do with her. With great kindness and benevolence the legate took her to his heart, as though she had been his mother, and looked after her money, about twenty pounds, though one of her company wrongfully confiscated about sixteen pounds of it. And they also took her maidservant away, and would not allow her to accompany her mistress, even though she had vowed loyalty to her mistress, and assured her, that she would not for any reason desert her.** [Ch 27]

Here, too, at Constance Margery employed a guide, an old, white-haired, Devonshire man, to accompany her to Bologna and to Venice, and while travelling to Bologna she and her guide encountered many friendly people, who provided them with food and drink, none of them speaking sharply to her. At Bologna she and her guide met up again with the main party of pilgrims, who were amazed that she and William had reached Bologna before they had. From Bologna the pilgrim band proceeded to Venice, the principal port of embarkation for the Holy Land. The Venetians had monopolised the pilgrim traffic to Jerusalem and organised it with great thoroughness, accommodating pilgrims at inns, shepherding them about the strange city, providing them with guides and interpreters, and protecting them against potential exploiters and profiteers.[18] Felix Fabri relates that he and his companions purchased cushions, mattresses, pillows, sheets, coverlets, mats and jars for themselves in the markets of Venice to make their voyage more comfortable. The wise pilgrim would also purchase food for himself to augment the meagre and unsavoury diet provided on board, and good wine to supplant the sour wine supplied to passengers.

Pilgrims sailing from Venice reached Jaffa, the port of disembarkation for the Holy Land, in about a month. Records of other voyagers of approximately the same period of history as Margery confirm this, Felix Fabri making the voyage in 1483, leaving Venice on 1 June and arriving at Jaffa on 1 July. Professor Meech, by referring to specific dates, holy days of the Church's calendar, which Margery mentions, and other contemporary voyages, has estimated that Margery's whole trip to the Holy Land, Rome and Assisi, and the return journey took about a year and three quarters, that is from the Autumn of 1413 to the Spring of 1415.[19]

Margery relates that the party was delayed at Venice for thirteen weeks before sailing and that during that time she frequently visited the famous house of nuns in that city, probably the Abbey of Zacchariah, the most ancient religious community in Venice which possessed a large number of relics. There she was enthusiastically welcomed by the sisters, who marvelled at her copious tears and fervent devotion.

When Margery first set eyes on Jerusalem she offered her heartfelt thanks to God and prayed that, just as he had brought her to the earthly Jerusalem, so he would by his grace and mercy, bring her to the heavenly Jerusalem. So preoccupied was she with devout thoughts that she came near to falling from the ass on which she was riding, this being the chief means of transport for pilgrims to the Holy Land. Two German pilgrims came to her rescue and saved her from falling, gave her spices to eat, for they thought she was sick, and stayed by her to give her assistance.

In the church of the Holy Sepulchre the party was escorted round by a Grey friar who rehearsed the events which took place at each spot, the pilgrims being given a lighted candle to carry as they processed from place to place, Margery finding it difficult to hold her candle steady because of the powerful emotions she experienced.

The very same places in and around Jerusalem which the pilgrims viewed them are those which pilgrims view today: the room where Christ washed his disciples' feet and celebrated his last supper, the garden of Gethsemane where he prayed in agony and was arrested, the alleged sites of his crucifixion, burial and resurrection. The pilgrims visited the Church of the Holy Nativity too and the river Jordan where Christ was baptised.

Margery, probably older and feebler than the majority of the pilgrims and overcome by the fierce heat, experienced great difficulty making the ascent of the Mount of Temptation, near Jericho, where Jesus fasted and was tempted by Satan.

> **She asked some of the company to help her up the mountain, but they said 'no' for it was hard enough for them to climb up themselves. She was very upset that she was unable to ascend the hill, then it so happened that a muslim, a good looking man, came by and she put a groat (4d) in his hand, making a sign to him to assist her up the mountain, and at once he supported her with his arm and helped her up.** [Ch 30]

The tour or Jerusalem and all the holy places around had lasted for three weeks, after which the party returned to the port of Jaffa and sailed to Venice, where Margery's fellow countrymen forsook her and left her to fend for herself. Jesus, however, comforted her and promised to bring her safely to Rome and home again to England if she would continue to wear her white clothes as he had commanded her to do before she left England. No sooner had this promise been made to her than she saw a hunchback, a native of Ireland, a man of about fifty, whose name was Richard.

> **'Good Richard, escort me to Rome and you shall be rewarded for your labour' said Margery.** [Ch 30]
>
> **'No, woman, I cannot' he replied, 'for I know very**

well that your fellow-countrymen have deserted you, so it would be hard on me to have to accompany you. Your countrymen have got bows and arrows to defend themselves with, but I have no weapon except my cloak, which is full of patches. I fear that enemies might rob me, and perhaps take you away and rape you. Therefore I dare not be your guide; I wouldn't for a thousand pounds want any harm to come to you while you're with me.'

But the reluctant Richard was prevailed upon to accompany Margery to Rome when she offered him money and assured him that God would look after them. They set out, therefore, for Assisi, where, in the church of St Francis the veil of our Lady was on exhibit for pilgrims to see. It was here in Assisi that by chance Margery encountered the great lady, Margaret Florentine, who had come to Assisi on Lammas Day to purchase pardon and plenary remission of her sins. Being a lady of wealth and nobility she travelled in great splendour in a fine and well-equipped carriage, followed by a retinue of many knights and ladies in waiting.

Then Richard, the broken-backed man, went to her and enquired of her if Margery and he might travel with her to Rome, and so be protected from the danger of thieves. To this request the honourable lady agreed and allowed them to join her party and go with them to Rome. [Ch 31]

Because of Margery's acute poverty while in Rome, Christ promised to provide her with friends who would assist and cheer her, one of these being this same noble lady, Dame Margaret Florentyne.

Neither of them could understand very well what the other was saying, except by making signs and by a few words they had in common. Then the lady said to her, 'Margerya in poverte?' [Ch 38]

She, understanding what the lady meant, replied, 'Ya, grand poverte, Madam.'

Then the lady insisted that Margery eat with her every Sunday and she placed her at her own table, in a higher place than herself, and served her with food with her own hands.

Language was always a problem for the traveller abroad, since English was not the universal language that it is today. The pilgrim came across people of various races and nationalities who spoke French, German, Italian, Spanish, Basque, Greek, Turkish, Hebrew, Arabic and other languages. Margery, several times, speaks of the difficulties she faced in this respect. In Rome she was obliged to make a 'spiritual confession' to St John the Evangelist, since the local priest could not understand English. She was much saddened also that she was unable to understand the sermons of a particular German priest. In the church of St John Lateran she felt stirred to speak with the cleric who was celebrating Mass, but the priest understood no English and did not know what she was saying and therefore they spoke to each other through an interpreter.

One of the highlights of Margery's stay in Rome was her visit to the very room in which, in 1373, Bridget of Sweden, passed to heavenly glory, a room which had then been converted into a chapel. Margery was in the city in 1414, some forty years after Bridget's death, and while there the Council of Constance was in progress, considering the canonisation of Bridget and the authenticity of her visions and revelations. There were some who maintained that these were genuine and orthodox, and others that they were false and heretical. Margery would have known of the devoted admirer of the Swedish mystic, Adam Easton (born c1325) an Oxford scholar and a Benedictine monk of the Norwich priory, to which he bequeathed his large collection of books, and who in John Brunham's time aided the Benedictine cell at Lynn. While in the Roman Curia, Adam Easton, then a cardinal, may have known Bridget, at any rate he wrote and laboured for her canonisation.

He composed a treatise in which he refuted the criticisms which had been made against the Rule which Bridget drew up for her religious order, the Bridgettines. Objections had been made to a monastic Rule being produced by a woman, which Adam Easton defended. As W. A. Pantin points out St Bridget was the first woman to found a religious order, so an important principle was at stake. 'It was a true instinct that made him support St Bridget and her order, for the history of the 15th and 16th centuries was to show the Bridgettines, along with the Carthusians and Observant Friars, representing the most fervent and heroic element in monasticism'.[20]

In the Spring of 1415, following the Easter festival, Margery took leave of her friends in Rome, and with her fellow pilgrims travelled northwards to the seaport of Middleburg in Zealand, where they boarded a ship bound for England.

> **When they were in the little ship the sky began to grow ominously dark and the weather became fearfully stormy. Then they cried to God for grace and mercy and at once the storm abated, the skies cleared and the weather became fine. They sailed all that night and all the next day, and then landed at about the time of evensong.** [Ch 43]

Two years passed before Margery was off on pilgrimage again, this time to Santiago da Compostela on the Wednesday of Whitsun week in the year 1417. The ship was due to sail from Bristol, but when Margery and her company arrived there they were obliged to wait for six weeks before a ship could be found for the pilgrims, since every available ship had been requisitioned by Henry V for his second military expedition to France in 1417. A large number of ships had been assembled in the March of that year, but the great fleet of about fifteen hundred vessels, many of them Dutch and Italian as well as English, did not sail from the vicinity of Southampton until 30 July, arriving at the estuary of the Seine on 1 August. Margery relates very little of her pilgrimage to Santiago, which was a favourite pilgrimage for English people, over nine hundred people going there in the year 1428 and in 1434 well over two thousand.[21]

Margery never lost her fear of the sea. When therefore, at the age of sixty she was bidden by the Lord to accompany her daughter-in-law to Germany she protested, thinking it was hard on an old woman to have to undertake such an irksome endeavour. She attempted by every means to excuse herself from making the voyage: her confessor she said, had not given her permission to travel overseas and she was bound to obey him; she had insufficient money for the voyage; her daughter-in-law would prefer to travel alone; and perhaps the master of the ship would not allow her to sail with them on the vessel.

> **Then our Lord said, 'If I am with you, who shall be against you? I shall make provision for you and get friends to help you. Do as I command, and no one on the ship will oppose you.'** [Ch 2] [Bk II]

Margery thought therefore that she could do no other than obey the Lord's bidding, but her worst fears materialised when the ship ran into rough weather. Storms, high winds and mountainous seas rendered the ship ungovernable, so that the master and the crew were forced to abandon the craft to the mercy of God, allowing it to drift wherever it would. Fearing for their safety Margery cried to heaven for help.

> **Our Lord then answered her, 'Why are you so fearful? My power is manifest on the sea as on the land ... Everything I have promised you, I shall surely fulfil. Endure patiently for a while and trust in my mercy. Do not waver in your faith, for without faith you cannot please me. If you will wholly trust in me, and have no doubt, you will be comforted in your heart and you will be able to comfort your fellow-travellers who are so fearful.'** [Ch 3] [Bk II]

Soon afterwards the ship was driven onto the coast of Norway, after which the storm abated, so that they were able to land without mishap and to rest and refresh themselves before sailing on to Danzig in north Germany where Margery stayed awhile with her daughter-in-law. From Danzig the company sailed to Stralsund in Pomerania, a Hanse city, and made preparations to go on pilgrimage to Wilsnak, a small town near Wittenburg in Saxony, made famous, when in 1383 the church was burnt and from the ashes the parish priest discovered what he avowed were three consecrated Hosts, stained with the blood of Christ.[22] These three Hosts were put on display for the hordes of pilgrims to view and to venerate. Numerous centres, like Hailes in Gloucester, the basilica of Santa Maria Maggiore in Rome, and the abbey of Fécamp in Normandy, claimed to possess relics of Christ's blood. In the case of Wilsnak the Archbishop of Prague, in 1405, appointed a commission to consider the matter of the Holy Blood of Wilsnack, since he had heard of fraudulent claims of miracles having occurred in connection with the three Eucharistic Hosts. The commission, among whose members was John Hus, condemned such pilgrimages 'as the product of overripe imaginations and clerical avarice', and on examination the alleged miracles were found to be no miracles at all, a boy's deformed foot being worse than before, and those claiming to have had their sight restored never having been blind. In 1451, a new bull was issued by the papal legate, Nicholas de Cusa, 'forbidding the display of blood-stained Hosts and ordering the sanctuary of Wilsnak to be closed'.[23] When Margery Kempe made her arduous journey there in the summer of 1433 or 1434 the shrine was still open to pilgrims.

From Wilsnak Margery and her companions, travelling in wains, came to another great pilgrimage centre in Germany, that of Aachen, where four holy relics were displayed for the faithful and credulous to gaze upon and to pay the appropriate fee for the privilege. These were the supposed smock of our Lady worn at the time of Jesus' birth, the Lord's swaddling clothes, the loin cloth he wore on the cross, and the cloth that was wrapped around the severed head of John the Baptist.

Travelling now towards Calais, Margery endured many tribulations and hardships and was overcome with fatigue; but in the city she was welcomed royally by some kindly folk, who took her to their homes and gave her food and drink, one woman washing her clean from head to foot, dressing her in a new smock and comforting her in every way she could. Four days later Margery and the party boarded a ship for Dover, the crossing being so rough that the majority of the passengers were fearfully sick 'voiding and casting full boisterously and uncleanly' but she, in answer to her prayers, was spared this indignity and was able to help and cheer the others, much to the astonishment of her fellow travellers. And so to Dover, Canterbury and London.

Wherever she went in London she spoke boldly and vigorously against those who swore, cursed and lied, and against those guilty of other vices, and against the pompous manner in which men and women dressed. She did not spare them, nor flatter them, either because of the gifts they presented her with or the food and drink they gave her. Many people benefitted very much from the words she spoke. [Ch 9] [Bk II]

Therefore when she came into a church for her contemplation, our Lord blessed her with the gift of great devotion, thanking her for not being afraid to rebuke sin in his name, and for suffering scorn and reproach for his sake. He promised her an abundance of grace in this life, and after this life, eternal joy and bliss in heaven.

CHAPTER NINE

John Wyclif, The Lollards and Margery Kempe

John Wyclif (*c*1330–1384), fellow of Merton College, Oxford, Master of Balliol and holder of benefices at Fillingham in Lincolnshire and Ludgershall in Buckinghamshire, stands out on the pages of ecclesiastical history as the most celebrated English scholar and theologian of the fourteenth century, a man of unparalleled learning, well read in classical literature and the Church Fathers. First and foremost, however, he was a biblical scholar, intimately acquainted with the text of the Bible, which he contended was the ultimate standard of authority, against which tradition had no independent claim.

Wyclif expressed his opinions in an abundance of written works. 'He fought with tongue and pen to carry the vast, corrupt body of the Church, pope and all, back to first principles ... the important thing to look for in a man was not his rank or the splendour of his vestments, but the way he lived ... If one said that Christ's Church must have a head on earth, it was not the pope who ought to be its head, but Christ.'[1] Wyclif severely criticised the Church for its wealth, corruption and power, which contrasted sharply with the poverty, simplicity and virtue of the apostolic Church, the clergy in particular being denounced for their worldliness, avarice and immorality. He condemned the rule of compulsory celibacy for the clergy, advocating their freedom to marry if they wished, since God had allowed priests of the old law of Judaism to marry and there was nothing in the new law of Christ which forbade it.

Those clergy, declared Wyclif, who, because of their vicious lives, were not in a state of grace, forfeited their right to hold dominion and authority; their ministries were therefore invalid. A valid ministry depended on virtuous and righteous living according to the Gospel precepts. Wyclif placed great emphasis on the practice of virtue; the clergy especially were supposed to be imitators of Christ and an example to their flock. He himself was reported by Thomas Arundel to be a great cleric and a man of perfect life. The formal and outward observance of religion, to which the medieval Church attached so much importance, with its elaborate system of laws, ceremonies and rituals, did not in the opinion of Wyclif constitute the essence of religion, which for him resided rather in obedience to the Gospel teaching, faith in Christ and a right disposition of heart. 'The driving force of all his thought and preaching was his devotion to the incarnate Christ, his longing to bring men face to face with him as *verissima fratrem nostrum, homo cum alliis*. Almost everything in contemporary religious practice that offended him, from ecclesiastical endowments to the doctrine of transubstantiation, offended him because it seemed to blur or distort this vision of the human Jesus. More and more he himself found the Christ he was seeking in the Gospels, and missed him in the Church'.[2]

Wyclif's idea on the subject of dominion was not entirely original, but was a development of a theory promulgated by Richard Fitzralph, Archbishop of Armagh (1348–1360), that the lawful exercise of lordship was dependent upon Grace, a theory which applied at first to temporal lordship, but which soon extended to include spiritual lordship. Fitzralph, like Wyclif, was a prominent Oxford scholar and a fellow of Balliol, his views being expressed in a seminal work *On the Poverty of The Saviour*, a copy of which was presented to Merton College in the same year that Wyclif was made a fellow. 'How much the young scholar owed to it is abundantly proved by the close verbal correspondence between it and various passages in his own work'.[3]

Traditional sacramental doctrine came in for some severe criticism, in particular the doctrine of transubstantiation, which asserted that the sacramental elements of bread and wine, after consecration, were changed in substance and became the very body and blood of Christ. This change of substance Wyclif denied, although he acknowledged the mysterious presence of Christ in the sacrament. But in essence the bread remained bread and the wine wine; the senses bore testimony to this. In a lecture delivered in 1381, he declared that the doctrine of transubstantiation was without scriptural authority for 'the consecrated Host we see upon the altar is neither Christ, nor any part of him, but an effectual sign of him'.[4] This denial of the doctrine of transubstantiation, more than any of his teachings, earned Wyclif the title of heretic, and it was one which lost him the support of his most powerful patron and defender, John of Gaunt, Duke of Lancaster; it lost him too the support of the four orders of friars, who had hitherto been his enthusiastic disciples. It was the final act of heresy which resulted in his writings being denounced by Archbishop Courtenay in May 1382 as errors and heresies, Wyclif himself being banned from teaching.

The worship and adoration of the Eucharistic Host, which was a characteristic feature of medieval piety, was regarded by Wyclif as idolatrous and superstitious. For him, preaching took precedence over the celebration of the sacraments, and was the priest's primary work, in imitation of Christ, who preached and taught unceasingly, and exhorted his disciples to preach the Gospel to the whole creation. 'But it must be the Gospel message and solid instruction which the clergy were to deliver to their people and not mere rhetoric to dazzle and amuse.[5]

The sacrament of penance and compulsory confession before a priest was condemned by Wyclif. He conceded, however, that in some cases, confession before a priest could ease a troubled conscience, yet he contended that the soul had direct access to God through Christ without the necessity of a priestly mediator. True repentance of heart, confession before God and sorrow for sin were all that were required for forgiveness. Wyclif vigorously opposed the sale of Pardons and Indulgences, the purchase of which, it was claimed, ensured the sinner remission of his sins and deliverance from the pains of purgatory. The forgiveness of sins, said Wyclif, was a divine gift, freely given, and could not be purchased with money. So also was the sacred office of priesthood; Wyclif denounced the sin of simony, by which clerical office and preferment could be acquired by the payment of money.

Wyclif also attacked other important aspects of the Church's life and tradition, such as the popular devotion to images and relics, and the custom of going on pilgrimage. With respect to images the 'lewd' and uneducated laypeople did not always distinguish between the image itself and that which the image represented; they tended to pray to the image and worship the image instead of praying to that which the image represented – Christ, for instance, the Virgin Mary and the saints. The popular early fifteenth century treatise, *Dives and Pauper*, which sets out to expound the meaning of the Ten Commandments, but which incorporates a variety of other material, places 'images' in their proper perspective, explaining their true purpose, which is threefold: to direct the thoughts, to stir the emotions and to serve as a book or a medium of instruction for the common people. The people are exhorted to 'Worship God above all things, not the image, nor the stock, stone or tree, but him who died on the tree for your sin and for your sake … Kneel if you will *before* the image, not *to* the image. Do your worship *before* the image, not *to* the image, for the image sees you not, hears you not, understands you not. Make your offerings *before* the image, but not *to* the image. Make your pilgrimage, not *to* the image or *for* the image … but *to* him and *for* him that the image represents. For if you do it *for* the image and *to* the image, you commit idolatry.[6]

Wyclif's anti-clericalism encouraged a view of the laity which gave them an almost priestly status, the Church being a fellowship of believers rather than a clerical hierarchy. According to Wyclif the reading and studying of the Bible should be accessible to the laity, and not confined to the clergy, since all Christian people could, under the guidance and influence of the Holy Spirit, understand the Scriptures. To this end Wyclif, it is thought, instigated, supervised and inspired the translation of the Bible into English from the Vulgate, which was to give the laity a status, authority and independence, which they had never possessed before. To what extent Wyclif himself took part in the endeavour of translation it is impossible to ascertain, though in the trials of his Lollard followers, references are made to the accused possessing what were termed 'Wyclif's Gospels'. However, the principal translator is generally believed to be John Purvey, curate to Wyclif at Lutterworth, who describes himself as 'a simple creature' together with a group of Oxford scholars. The translation was widely copied in the fifteenth century, the Lollards having met a demand which extended far beyond the circle of their adherents.[7] It has rightly been said that Wyclif's production of the Bible in the vernacular marked a turning point in the religious development of this country. But one of its immediate effects was that it could lead to arrest and imprisonment, and for some, the actual penalty of death by burning, for infringing the Church's law, since Archbishop Thomas Arundel in his Constitutions of 1408 had forbidden the making or use of translations of the Bible, and the reading and preaching of Scripture by anyone without a license from the Bishop.

Many of Wyclif's opinions are echoed in the teachings of his followers, the Lollards, or wandering preachers. Initially Wyclif's supporters were his fellow intellectuals and members of the upper classes and nobility, though latterly, after his death, at the end of the fourteenth century, and in the first half of the fifteenth century, his disciples were drawn chiefly from the merchant and artisan class, and it is clear from the cross with which they signed their confessions that many were illiterate. They, and the unbeneficed clergy, poor priests and friars, toured the English countryside preaching in villages, hamlets and small market towns, disseminating Wyclif's doctrines, distributing religious tracts, pamphlets and extracts from Wyclif's Bible to lay supporters. Margery Kempe, in her travels through the towns and villages in England, in her encounters with a wide spectrum of society and in her life at home in Lynn, where William Sawtrey, a priest of St Margaret's had been condemned as a heretic, could not have been unaffected by this powerful religious movement.

Trials for heresy, like those recorded in the diocese of Norwich, concern such categories of people as artisans: glovers, skinners, shoemakers, carpenters, a parchment-maker, a tailor, a butcher, and four priests. Most come from a group of small towns and villages in the south east of Norfolk and the north east of Suffolk, though Norwich itself is conspicuous for its scarcity of Lollards and never seems to have been a centre of Lollardy as were London, Bristol, Coventry and some other cities.[8] The trials were held at the Bishop's Palace in Norwich or at his Manor at Thorpe, and on one occasion at Richard of Caister's church, St Stephen's, Norwich. These trials reveal the essential tenets of Lollard doctrine and in what manner the ecclesiastical authorities dealt with suspects, Bishop Alnwick himself conducting some of the trials and his Vicar-General others. The majority of those arrested and imprisoned pleaded guilty to all the charges brought against them, signed the document of confession and swore not to hold heretical beliefs again, nor to encourage others to do so. They promised also to perform the penances assigned to them and to inform the ecclesiastical authorities of any heretics known to them. They were then warned by the judge that if they relapsed into heresy they would be liable to be handed over to the secular arm and burnt at the stake. The records of the trials, however, indicate that the judges were painstaking and fair in their judgements and not eager to convict a person on mere suspicion, only convicting the stubbornly obdurate or relapsed heretics like William Sawtrey. In fact few met the ultimate fate of being consigned to the flames. 'The proportion of burnings to those prosecuted is very small. Among three to four hundred heretics in Buckinghamshire only four were executed'.[9]

Among the heresies commonly figuring in the Lollard trials, which at times display an element of rustic humour, was that of anti-clericalism, which claimed a belief in the priesthood of all believers, and that access to God by laypeople was available without the intermediary of priests. Confession to a priest was unnecessary, since God alone could forgive sins. Prayers, they said, should be directed to God or Christ and not to the saints who were 'man-made'. Priestly celibacy was attacked, the heretics claiming that it was more meritorious for priests to marry and 'to bring forth fruit of their bodies' than to remain celibate. Pilgrimage was denounced and ridiculed. Our Lady of Walsingham became 'the Lefdy of Falsingham' and Thomas of Canterbury became 'Thomme of Cankerbury'. Images were man-made, and honouring them was without any spiritual value. A certain William Colyn, when asked to assist with the painting of images stated that he would rather pay for them to be burnt.[10] It is noteworthy that the basic tenents of the Christian faith were never questioned, especially the death of Christ on the cross.

Confessions were sometimes made by heretics that they had attended 'schools of heresy' which were held in secret meeting-places, and that they had learned their heresies at such schools, where a number of priests were present. Flogging was the usual punishment for attending these schools and for propagating heresy, women being let off more lightly than men. Men could expect three to six floggings or more, and both men and women could be condemned to fasting on bread and water every Friday for a year. The floggings were inflicted in the parish church or in the cemetery, often during solemn processions on Sundays, the erstwhile heretic appearing bare-footed, bare-headed and stripped to his shirt and drawers, and women in similar discreet attire. Thus humiliated, they would walk in procession, carrying a candle which they would offer at the high altar when the flogging was over. In the case of William Smyth, who had taken an image of St Catherine from a church and burnt it to cook his vegetables, instructions were given that he should hold an image of St Catherine, kiss it, enter the church while Mass was being celebrated, stand before the crucifix, and on the following Saturday, wearing nothing except his underwear, stand in the market place of Leicester holding the image, and recite the Lord's Prayer and the Ave Maria.[11]

The matter of William Sawtrey's unorthodox teaching, his appearance before the Bishop of Norwich, his interrogation in St Paul's London, and his final condemnation by the Archbishop of Canterbury no doubt caused a considerable stir among the inhabitants of Lynn, Margery herself being about twenty eight years old when, in 1401, he was burnt at Smithfield in London. In 1399 Sawtrey was brought before the Bishop of Norwich, Henry Despenser, a committed enemy of Lollards, at his episcopal manor in South Emham, many distinguished persons being present, including John de Kinkingale, professor of divinity and Master of Gonville Hall Cambridge and later bishop of Chichester. For two days Sawtrey was questioned on the false doctrines he was said to have preached, opposing transubstantiation, image-worship, and pilgrimage, at the end of which time he was prevailed upon to repent of his errors and to recant. The public recantation took place on 25 May in the Churchyard of St James's Chapel of ease in the presence of the Bishop, the clergy and the inhabitants of Lynn, among whom, we may surmise, were John Brunham, his daughter

Margery and other members of his family. The following day in the Hospital of St John the Baptist in Damgate Sawtrey was required to swear on the Gospels that he would never again preach the doctrines he had disavowed, nor hear confessions without Bishop Despenser's license.

William Sawtrey's heretical beliefs persisted, however, and to escape the attention of the Bishop of Norwich he removed himself to London, where he was appointed parish priest of St Osyth's, Walbrook, and continued to preach his so-called heresies, which coincided with those preached by Wyclif, and which appear to many to be no heresies at all. Soon the Church authorities hunted Sawtrey out and on Saturday 12 February 1401 he was summoned to appear before a provincial council in the Chapter House of St Paul's, where the Archbishop of Canterbury, Thomas Arundel was presiding, and where after interrogation, Sawtrey was condemned as a lapsed and contumacious heretic.

On 23 February Thomas Arundel and six other bishops, before a large assembly, publicly condemned Sawtrey, the Archbishop taking advantage of the occasion to expound in English the story of Sawtrey's trials as an example to others not to follow the dreadful path that he had trodden. Sawtrey was then degraded of his orders and stripped of the various emblems of his office and pastoral authority: the chalice and paten and sacerdotal vestments, which deprived him of his power and authority to celebrate Mass; and the Gospels, which deprived him of the right to read and preach from them. He was further degraded of the minor orders of sub-deacon, acolyte, exorcist, reader, his clerical tonsure being shaved off and the woollen cap of a secular laymen being placed on his head. Sawtrey's appeal to the king availed nothing, and he was delivered as a layman to the secular arm, and on 26 February 1401, committed to the flames at Smithfield, a broad meadow beyond the boundary of the city where the inhabitants were accustomed to practise with their bows and arrows.[12]

In medieval times, as we have already stated, affairs of church and state were inextricably intertwined. Thus the Lollard heresy of the late fourteenth and early fifteenth centuries had repercussions for the state and crown, especially when Sir John Oldcastle, alias Lord Cobham, knight and property owner, turned traitor to his friend, King Henry V, a strong opponent of Lollardy, and staged a coup d'etat. Sir John was a renowned soldier, who fought in the wars of the Lancastrian Kings and had been active in the suppression of the Welsh rebellion, but when he came into contact with the Lollards, he was sympathetic to their doctrines and gave them his whole-hearted support. In January 1414 he led a rebellion against the king, intending to capture him and all the royal family and to seize political power by force of arms.

Oldcastle's fighting men, mostly craftsmen, weavers, shoemakers, tailors, carpenters and ploughmen, were no match for Henry's trained knights and men-at-arms and the rebellion failed miserably, the conspirators being rounded up and many of them hanged as traitors and burned as heretics. On 25 September 1413 Sir John himself was brought for trial before Thomas Arundel, who had been commanded by the king to proceed according to the law. Although Arundel was a determined foe of Lollardy, he was always reluctant to impose the extreme penalty of execution on any heretic, and provided them with every opportunity to repent and renounce their beliefs, and in Oldcastle's case he is reported to have shown particular patience and fair-mindedness. But Oldcastle remained unrepentant and stubborn, though very courageous. He refused to recant, and was therefore pronounced a heretic by Arundel, and handed over to the secular authorities who imprisoned him in the Tower. On the night of 19 October 1413, however, he escaped with the help of supporters and fled to Herefordshire, where he remained for four years. He was recaptured in 1417, brought to London on 14 December, condemned as an outlaw, traitor and heretic, drawn through the city on a hurdle, and hanged and burnt in the presence of the Duke of Bedford, third son of Henry IV and Lieutenant of the Kingdom.[13]

It was in the year 1417, probably in the late summer, while Sir John Oldcastle was still at large, that Margery Kempe, while in Beverley, was accused of being 'Cobham's daughter', that is, a spiritual daughter, or follower, of Lord Cobham, sharing in his heretical views. Her accusers were two of the Duke of Bedford's yeomen and they declared that she was considered to be the 'greatest Lollard in all this region of the country and around London too' (Ch 53). Furthermore the two yeomen, wishing her to be convicted of Lollardy, avowed that she had not been on pilgrimage as she claimed. Going on pilgrimage was a sign of orthodoxy, and if Margery had been a Lollard and follower of Wyclif's doctrines, she would not have participated in this custom, but would have disapproved of pilgrimage, as did Wyclif and his followers.

Why then was Margery Kempe suspected of Lollardy? We may conjecture that it was her familiarity with the Bible and her habit of quoting biblical texts on all kinds of occasions which provoked a suspicion of Lollardy, on the supposition that she had attended the forbidden Bible-Study circles, a characteristic feature of the Lollard movement.[14] Lay men and women, keen to read, study, discuss and understand the Scriptures for themselves, attended these Bible study groups, which was a violation of the traditional policy of the Church, the clergy being the only authorised students of the Bible and propounders of its message. Furthermore her propensity to cite scripture so readily seemed at times very much like 'preaching'. When tried for heresy at York, Archbishop Henry Bowet commanded her not to travel about his diocese teaching people and trying to win their support to her views, but Margery declined to make such a promise.

> **'No, sir, I shall not swear that, for I must speak about God wherever I go, and reprove those who swear blasphemous oaths ... Almighty God does not forbid us to speak about him, sir. The Gospel tells of a woman who, when she heard our Lord preach, came before him and exclaimed loudly, "Blessed is the womb that bore you, and the breasts which you have sucked." Then our Lord answered her, "Indeed, and so also are those blessed who hear the word of God and keep it." Therefore, sir, I think the Gospel gives me leave to speak about God.'** [Ch 52
>
> **'Ah, sir,' said the clerks, 'now we know for sure that she has a devil in her, for she speaks of the Gospel.' At once a great cleric brought out a book and quoted St Paul against her, citing his words that no woman should preach, to which she answered, 'I do not preach, sir; I enter no pulpit; I only speak of God in ordinary conversation and use edifying words, and this is what I mean to do as long as I live.'**

Margery, moreover, claims to have spoken with God's own authority, for never could she forget those words which Jesus had spoken to her regarding her fear of the sin of vainglory.

> **'Have no fear, daughter, for I will banish all vainglory from your heart. Those who honour you, honour me, and those who despise you, despise me, and I will rebuke them for this, for I am in you and you in me, and those who hear you, hear the voice of God.'** [Ch 10]

These words or words very similar, and with the same meaning, were originally spoken by Jesus to his chosen apostles, to the Twelve and Seventy Two (Matt. 10.40 and Luke 10.16), yet here is Margery Kempe, a laywoman, applying them to herself and claiming to speak in God's name and with apostolic authority. This was an astonishing claim for a layperson to make at a period of history when the clergy, and they alone, were authorised to preach and to teach about God, for as Edmund Colledge states 'For the laity to speak with any show of authority about religious matters was sufficient to brand them as false heretics'.[15]

Leicester, a stronghold of Lollardy, was the scene of Margery's first interrogation on the question of her religious beliefs. Where did she come from and whose daughter was she, demanded the mayor of the town, to which Margery replied that she came from Lynn in Norfolk, and was the daughter of a worthy man who had been mayor of the borough five times, and that she was married to a burgess of the same town of Lynn.

> **'Ah Ha!' retorted the mayor, 'St Catherine also declared what lineage she was of, but you are not like her: you are a dishonest, lying whore, a false Lollard, a deceiver of the people, and I shall have you put in prison.'** [Ch 46]

After a few days Margery was brought to All Hallows Church, now All Saints, in Leicester, where infront of the high altar, were assembled a number of eminent persons: The abbot of St Mary's Abbey, the dean of Leicester and many canons, priests and friars. Numerous laypeople too had assembled to hear the questioning, indeed so many that some stood on stools to obtain a better view of this woman and to hear what she would say. Having prayed for wisdom to answer her interrogators, Margery Kempe was made to swear on a holy book that she would answer honestly to all the questions that were addressed to her regarding the Articles of Faith. Then a priest led her by the hand to the abbot and his assessors at the high altar. First she was questioned as to her belief about the sacrament of the eucharist, to which she replied with a standard statement of belief in the validity of the sacrament, irrespective of the worthiness the celebrant.

> **'Sirs, this is what I believe about the sacrament of the altar, that if any man, who has taken priest's orders, even if he is a man of vicious life, says the words over the bread, which our Lord Jesus Christ said on Maunday Thursday at his Last Supper with his disciples, then that bread is his very flesh and blood, and no material bread, and once these words are said they cannot be unsaid.'** [Ch 4
>
> **She answered all the questions on the Articles of the Christian Faith, as many as they asked, and they were very pleased with her answers.**

Margery's most intimidating encounter and interrogation took place before the Archbishop of York, Henry Bowet, in the chapel attached to his residence at Caward, ten miles from the city. Unlike Thomas Arundel of Canterbury, who had treated her with admirable patience and tolerance, Henry Bowet was sharp and brusque with her and irritated at the conspicuous way she was dressed all in white from head to foot.

> **'Why do you go about in white clothes? Are you a virgin?' he demanded.** [Ch 5
>
> **'No, sir, I am not a virgin. I am a wife' she replied, kneeling before him.**

Then the Archbishop questioned her on the Articles of the Faith, to which she gave prompt and cogent replies, which elicited from the Archbishop a comment to his clergy and chaplains,

> **'She knows her faith well enough, but what shall I do with her?'** [Ch 5
>
> **'We know every well that she can say the Articles of the Faith' replied the clergy, 'but we will not allow her to stay here among us, for the people trust her and believe in what she says, and she might lead some of them astray.'**

The trial, however, ended on a conciliatory note, without any charge of heresy being brought against her. She then requested that the Archbishop should give her his blessing, which he did and he, in turn, asked her to pray for him. Then she left the district, accompanied by one of the Archbishop's men, and crossed the Humber and proceeded to Lincoln.

CHAPTER TEN

Margery Kempe and the Faith of the Church

The influence of the Church in medieval society was central, powerful and all-pervasive, its doctrines, beliefs, customs, rituals, ceremonies, guiding and shaping the day to day life, thought and behaviour of the majority of people. Despites its abuses, its authoritarian and dogmatic approach and the shortcomings of some of its clergy, it gave meaning, cohesion and stability to people's lives in an insecure and unstable world. Among all the uncertainties, hardships, tragedies and traumas of life, medieval folk had this steady, dependable and rock-like institution to which they could appeal, and which could assist them in all manner of situations and circumstances, providing them with a standard to live by and a set of beliefs to hold on to, and offering them hope, forgiveness and salvation.

Margery Kempe's *BOOK* furnishes us with a distillation of what the Christian faith is all about, for although she belongs to an age in the distant past, Christianity, we may claim, does not fundamentally change from one epoch of history to another, though the context in which it operates necessarily differs, and so of course does the manner in which it is expressed in the different denominations. But these differences are marginal compared to the essence of the faith and the eternal truths of the gospel.

Almost every facet of the Church's traditional teaching is touched upon in *THE BOOK OF MARGERY KEMPE*. Long before she could ever have heard of Richard Rolle and his *Incendium Amoris*, Walter Hilton and his *Ladder of Perfection* or any other of the great works of English devotional literature which so deeply affected her, she had the Church, in which she had been nurtured, to instruct and guide her, and a knowledge of its scriptures expounded in sermons, illustrated in ecclesiastical art and

The Sacrament of Baptism. Illustration from 'Parish Life in Medieval England'.

enshrined in Mystery and Miracle plays. As Edmund Colledge remarks, 'Her book stands as a remarkable and valuable witness to the degree of theological and scriptural knowledge to which an illiterate laywoman in the Middle Ages could attain'.[1]

Clergy were repeatedly exhorted to instruct their people in the essential tenets of the faith, and to teach them the Apostles' Creed, the Our Father, the Hail Mary, the Ten Commandments, the Seven Deadly Sins, the Seven Virtues and the Seven Sacraments. They were also enjoined to teach their flock the Seven Corporal Works of Mercy: to feed the hungry, give drink to the thirsty, hospitality to strangers, to clothe the naked, to visit the sick, and care for the prisoner (Matt 25.31–46), and the additional work of mercy, to bury the dead (Tobit. 1.17–18). Archbishop Peckham, at the Synod of Oxford in 1281, pronounced that every priest presiding over a flock must explain all these aspects of the Church's teaching four times a year, and he must do so in plain and simple language, so that all could understand. Handbooks were available for priests to assist them in their task of ministering to their flock and instructing them in the Christian faith, and as we have seen, of special importance was the ever popular manual of John Mirk, *Instructions for Parish Priests*, which gave the clergy guidance on what to teach, how to administer the sacraments, how to give spiritual counsel and so forth.[2]

The cardinal doctrines of the Christian faith figure throughout Margery Kempe's *BOOK*. The Incarnation, in which the Second Person of the Trinity took flesh and became man, is a repeated source of inspiration. Drawing on the Meditations of St Anselm on the Nativity, she imagines herself the handmaid of St Anne, mother of the Virgin. The popularity of the cult of the Virgin Mary in the twelfth century prompted an interest in her parents, traditionally known as Joachim and Anne, though neither figure in the Bible or in the annals of hagiography. Artistic representations of St Anne often depict her teaching the Virgin to read, a beautiful example of which exists in a 15th century stained glass window at All Saints church, North Street, York. In the Middle Ages St Anne was the patron of religious guilds, for instance in Bishop's Lynn, the Guild of St Anne was one of the seventy four or so guilds that existed at different times in the borough. Her feast day, on 26 July, was obligatory in England from 1382, when Margery Kempe was about nine or ten years old, so she was accustomed from childhood to observe this feast.[3]

The Virgin Mary, pre-eminent among the Christian saints, occupied a position of supreme importance in the Church's life and faith, her most important feast days being the Annunciation (25 March) the Nativity (8 September) and the Assumption (15 August), over two thousand churches in England being dedicated to her by the time of the Reformation. The Church Fathers Justin and Ireaneaus designated her 'the New Eve' whose obedience, in the new order of Christ, reversed the disobedience of Eve in the old order of Israel. Because of her motherhood of Christ, who was, according to tradition, both God and man, she earned the title of Theotokus, Mother of God, and was seen to have a vital role in the Incarnation and the Redemption. Marian devotion in England gained impetus in the twelfth century when William of Malmesbury made a collection of the Miracles of the Blessed Virgin Mary, which emphasised her intercessory power in helping sinners by appealing to her Son.[4] From the thirteenth century onwards devotion was paid to the humanity of Christ, particularly to his sufferings at the time of the crucifixion, which evoked an intensity of personal feelings and tenderness for Christ, as is vividly illustrated in *THE BOOK OF MARGERY KEMPE*. Intricately involved with Christ's sufferings were the sufferings of his Mother, the 'Lady of Pity' and a consequent devotion to 'the Seven Sorrows of the Blessed Virgin', which corresponded to the 'Seven Joys of Mary'. Medieval devotion to our Lady was lavishly expressed in literature and art, in the building of Lady Chapels in cathedrals and churches and the construction of shrines in her honour, such as that at Walsingham.

Margery Kempe progresses from her meditations on St Anne to a meditation on the Virgin Mary. She imagines herself accompanying Mary and Joseph to Bethlehem, where the child Jesus was born, and she takes the babe in her arms and wraps him in swathing bands, weeping with compassion at the thought of the death he would suffer for sinful humanity.

> **'I shall treat you kindly, Lord', she said, 'I will not bind you too tightly, so do not be displeased with me I pray you.'** [Ch 6]

Margery is not to be credited with originality when she meditates on St Anne, the birth of the Virgin Mary and infancy of Jesus, for she is drawing on a common store of medieval English tradition. Similarly when, in her imagination, she binds the Christ-child in swaddling clothes and weeps at the thought of his future suffering, she is echoing an idea which occurs in other works of medieval devotional literature. We discover, for instance, the very same idea occurring in *The Myroure of Our Ladye*, a text in daily use in the Bridgettine convent of Syon. 'When the Virgin bound him in the swaddling clothes, she saw in her mind how all his body would be torn by the sharp scourges. And as she gently wrapped the hands and feet of her little son, and placed them together in the bands, she thought of how they would be cruelly pierced through with iron nails on the cross'.[5]

Veneration for the Christ-child is expressed in medieval sermons, lyrics and religious treatises. There in the manger lay the helpless babe, 'born in winter, born at night in a stable to reprove the glory of the world and its vanity' says St Bernard in his nativity sermons. St Bridget of Sweden describes the beauty and tenderness of the holy nativity scene, the prayers of our Lady before the birth of her child, the delicacy and comeliness of the Virgin's body, the awe and wonder with which she held the child, and the manner in which she greeted him. 'Welcome, my God, my Lord and my little son! ... But the little child began to tremble and to weep with the cold of the hard ground where he lay, and he stretched out his little hands to his mother, as though he desired the comfort of her caresses'.[6] Apocryphal legends grew up around the Gospel narratives of the nativity, figuring in various devotional writings, for example they describe the ease of the birth. 'The Son of the eternal God came forth from the womb of his mother without a murmur or a lesion, in a moment. As he had been in the womb, so he was now outside on the hay at his mother's feet'.[7]

It was however, the doctrine of the Atonement, which was central to medieval piety, and upon this theme the mystics continually dwelt. 'Christ is truly our peace, for he suffered for our salvation. Gaze on him, and you will see that divine head crowned with thorns ... his venerable hands transfixed, his dear side pierced with the spear, his feet nailed through, and all that tender flesh marked with wounds'. So wrote Richard Rolle in his INCENDIUM AMORIS, encouraging his readers to contemplate Christ's Passion and so abandon sin. 'Leave then, leave your illicit lusts, and see what Christ suffered for you, so that your sins can clearly be cast away.'[8]

In a lady's private chapel in Norwich Margery Kempe was greatly moved by the sight of a 'pieta' – a representation of the dead Christ cradled in his mother's arms – and she became wholly absorbed in the contemplation of Christ's Passion and wept bitterly. Questioned by a priest as to why she wept so fervently, since Christ had died long since, Margery replied,

> **'Sir, his death is as fresh to me as if he had died this very day, and so I think it ought to be to you and to all Christian people. We ought always to have in mind his goodness and the sorrowful death he died for us.'** [Ch 60

Thus she sees the crucifixion of Christ as an event which took place in time, yet which is beyond time, and of eternal significance.

As with her meditations on the Nativity so also with her meditations on Christ's Passion, she draws on a common store of medieval artistic and literary tradition. She sees in her mind's eye how, when the soldiers nailed him to the cross, they stretched his limbs to make the nails fit the holes that had been prepared for them. In this aspect of the meditation she is echoing a detail commonly found in sermons, plays and artistic representations of the Passion.

> **She saw how his precious body shrank and drew together with all the sinews and veins, because of the pain he suffered ... and how they fastened ropes on the other hand, which, because of the shrinking of the sinews and veins, would not reach the hole they had bored for it, so they pulled on the rope to make it reach the hole.** [Ch 80

The same gruesome detail is depicted in a roof-boss in Norwich cathedral and occurs also in a fourteenth century French text, translated into English as *The Northern Passion*. It occurs too in the York Cycle of Miracle Plays, where the Third Soldier says, 'It fails a foot or more; the sinews are so gone in' and the First Soldier replies, 'Fast on a cord, and tug him to, by top and tail.'[9] Many other gory details of the Passion, such as the scourging, the tearing of the skin as the garments are stripped off, the fresh opening of the wounds, the searing pain felt as the cross jolts and falls sharply into the mortise prepared for it, occur repeatedly in art and Passion literature. 'This concentration on the suffering of Christ, at the expense of the Resurrection, has been regarded as excessively morbid and even spiritually unhealthy. In a world, however, in which agony was a common spectacle, in the form of painful disease, unrelieved by effective medicine, or of the dreadful executions inflicted on traitors and other felons, there must have been great comfort in the conviction that God had suffered with and for mankind.'[10]

Margery meditates on the subject of Christ's resurrection and ascension and relates how he appears to his mother and greets her. She feels his hands and his feet to discover if any soreness remains, but he assures her that all his pain has gone and that from henceforth he will live for evermore. Margery gives an accurate account of how Jesus appears to Mary Magdalene in the garden and sends her to Peter and the apostles with the message that he has risen. Margery meditates on his ascension with a mixture of joy and sadness.

She saw our Lord ascend up into heaven, and because she could not live without him on earth, therefore she desired to go with him to heaven, for all her joy and all her bliss resided in him, and she knew very well that she would never have any joy or bliss until she came to him. [Ch 73]

With the cathedral church in Norwich dedicated to the Holy Trinity, and the principal guild in Lynn also bearing the same dedication, it is not surprising that the doctrine of the Holy Trinity should feature conspicuously in Margery Kempe's prayers, meditations and writings. The mystery of the Trinity transcends the power of the human mind to comprehend; Margery therefore employs metaphor and imagery in an attempt to convey her ideas about the Trinity. In her imagination she envisages the Three Persons of the Trinity, each seated on a different coloured cushion. It is possible that she derived this imagery from depictions of the Trinity in paintings, or from the use of cushions in liturgical worship.

> **'Daughter, you sometimes imagine that you have a cushion of gold in your soul, and another of red, and a third of white silk. You think that my Father sits on the gold cushion, for to him belongs all power and majesty. And you think that I, the Second Person of the Trinity, your love and your joy, sit on the red cushion ... in remembrance of the red blood that I shed for you. Moreover, you think that the Holy Spirit sits on a white cushion, for he is all love and purity, and therefore it is appropriate that he should be seated on a white cushion, for he is the giver of all holy thoughts and chastity.'** [Ch 86

The notion of God sitting in man's soul is a favourite theme of the mystics. Dame Julian of Norwich writes, 'Most gloriously is he seated within the soul ... for man's soul is his dwelling ... the fact that I saw him *sitting* gave me particular happiness, for sitting means sure confidence and that in turn implies an eternal dwelling-place.'[11]

Could Margery have been drawing on the imagery employed by Bridget of Sweden in her meditations on the Trinity we may wonder, since there is an unmistakable similarity between them, though Margery's homespun imagery cannot match Bridget's beautiful description of the unity and diversity of the Trinity in the three colours, gold, red and white, each separate, yet each blending with the others.

Bridget writes, 'Each of the three colours was seen in the others. When I saw the gold colour I saw also within it the white and the red colours. And when I saw the white colour I saw also the other two colours within it. And when I saw the red colour I saw also the white and the gold. Each colour was seen in the others, yet each was distinct from the others and separate in itself. No colour took preference over the other colours, nor came after the others. And no colour was less than the others or more than the others. In all things they seemed equal ... That each of the three colours is seen in the others, yet each is perceived separately, betokens that God the Father is endlessly in the Son and in the Holy Spirit. And the Son is in the Father and the Holy Spirit. And the Holy Spirit is in them both. All three are of one nature, but distinct in their personhood.' (Revelations)

Margery concludes her meditations on the Trinity with an orthodox statement of Trinitarian doctrine, which she puts into the mouth of Jesus, but which she had doubtless committed to her memory.

> **'I know well, daughter, that you think you cannot worship the Father unless you worship the Son, and that you cannot worship the Son unless you worship the Holy Spirit. And sometimes you think, daughter, that the Father is Almighty and knows all, and is full of grace and goodness, and you think the same of the Son, that he is Almighty and knows all, and is all grace and goodness. And you think that the Holy Spirit has the same properties, equal with the Father and the Son, proceeding from them both ... Each knows what the others know, and each does what the others do, and each wills what the others will. This is the true faith, daughter, and the right faith, and you have this faith only because I have given it to you.'** [Ch 86]

Christianity may be said to be a sacramental religion, a religion of outward and visible signs of inward and spiritual graces, forming a framework of doctrine, faith and practice, beginning with baptism and followed by confirmation, eucharist, penance, marriage, orders and unction. To all these sacraments, except confirmation, Margery Kempe makes some reference and displays her orthodoxy in their regard.

Owing to the perils of child-birth in medieval times and the frequency of infant mortality, babies were baptised as soon as possible after delivery, so that they might die in a state of grace. One of the duties of the parish priest was to instruct parents and mid-wives on how to baptise babies. But anyone, a layman or woman, even a pagan or heretic, could baptise in an emergency and only two requisites were necessary: water and the invocation of the name of the Trinity. Baptism was only a beginning, a necessary condition of salvation, but insufficient in itself for the passage of the soul to heaven. Christians who lived unchristian lives and died out of charity, and in a state of unrepented sin, were destined

The Sacrament of Extreme Unction. Illustration from 'Parish Life in Medieval England'.

to hell.[12] All sins committed after baptism could be forgiven by repentance and confession in the sacrament of penance, as Walter Hilton explains, 'Two kinds of sin cause a soul to lose its likeness to God; the first is called original sin, being the first sin, and the other is called actual sin, being sin deliberately committed ... There are two remedies against these two sins, by means of which a deformed soul may be restored. The remedy against original sin is the sacrament of baptism, and that against actual sin is the sacrament of penance.'[13]

For about the first thousand years of the Church's history, baptism and confirmation were administered together, but in the Middle Ages the two sacraments were separated, though confirmation made little impression on the popular mind, and priests and people were indifferent to the sacrament of confirmation which was not regarded, like baptism, as necessary for salvation. Many people were never confirmed; conscientious and energetic bishops did confirm, though there is little, if any, reference to confirmation in episcopal registers. It was difficult for bishops to administer, for unlike the parish priest, who was on the spot, and easily accessible to his parishioners, the bishop could complete the circuit of his diocese only occasionally, dioceses often being vast and sparsely populated. The ceremony was often brief, the bishop stretching his hand over the candidate's head, praying that he might receive the gifts of the Spirit, signing him with holy oil and concluding with a few prayers. Accounts exist of bishops confirming children from horseback while riding through villages on their way to somewhere else. 'It was considered ideal to confer it as soon after baptism as possible. Some royal children were confirmed when only a few days old.'[14]

In 1215 the Fourth Lateran Council issued the injunction that all males aged fifteen or over and all females of twelve and over should make their confession and receive holy communion once a year at Easter, though devout Christian folk were recommended to come to confession three times a year, at Easter, Pentecost and Christmas. There were two main categories of sin to which the layperson's attention was drawn: venial sins which were less serious, not deliberate, arising from natural human weakness and not involving a loss of grace, nor excluding one from holy communion; and mortal sins which were serious offences, committed knowingly and intentionally against the commandments of God and only forgivable in the sacrament of penance. The condition of receiving absolution and forgiveness for sins was genuine repentance and confession before a priest, a determination to amend and the performance of the penance prescribed by the confessor, which for serious sins was always more severe than for venial sins.

The medieval church compiled exhaustive lists of venial and mortal sins to assist the priest in dealing with the penitent, and the penitent in examining his or her conscience. 'The sacrament if skilfully used enabled priests to give spiritual counsel to lay people about the practice of the Christian life, and in this way a rudimentary kind of spiritual direction was made available to all lay people.' [15] The psychology of the sinner was studied by the more able priests, who behaved with discretion, now gently, now sternly, according to the state of mind of the individual. The penitent was urged to keep to the point, to reveal only his own sins and not another's. The usual and best confessor was the sinner's parish priest, for he was the penitent's neighbour. He knew everyone's history and circumstances and sin seemed more shameful when told to a man one saw every day.[16]

Individual sins as well as being an offence against God and a marring of the divine image in oneself, were an offence against society. Strong emphasis was placed on the social group, the community, in the Middle Ages. There was no such thing as 'private sins' for all sins had repercussions in the lives of others and in the community, if not overtly, then in the diminishment of the individual's character and personality, which made them less edifying and beneficial to society at large. Hence the need for public penance and restitution, as John Bossy states, 'The granting of absolution was contingent on the penitent's performing visible acts of reparation for his sin … where the party offended was the neighbour, the reparatory act was that of restitution … without it, as without the laying aside of enmity, the process of reconciliation to God would not be achieved.[17]

Fervent souls like Margery Kempe made their confessions far more frequently than the prescribed annual confession or even the thrice annually for the more devout. She informs us that one of her initial acts of piety in her youth was to confess all the sins she had committed since childhood, so far as she could remember them, and that henceforward she was sometimes 'shriven' two or three times a day. By frequent confession she was perhaps seeking to emulate her spiritual mentors and heroines, Bridget of Sweden, Dorothea of Prussia, Marie d' Oignes, who exerted such a powerful influence on her by their writings. In her Revelations Bridget, for example, advised the earnest soul that 'the oftener and more fervently confession is made, for the smallest sins as for the greatest, so much the more is God pleased and draws the soul to himself'.[18] Margery's experience of forgiveness induced her to marvel at the graciousness of God and stimulated her to greater and more ardent love for him.

> **In process of time, her mind and her thoughts were so wrapped up in God that she never forgot him, but had him continually in mind and saw him in everyone. The more she increased in love and devotion, the more she increased in sorrow and repentance, in lowliness and humility, in holy fear of our Lord and in knowledge of her own frailty.** [Ch 72]

An aspect of Margery Kempe's religious life which distinguished her from the majority of ordinary layfolk was her custom of receiving weekly communion. The general rule for the laity was that they should 'be houselled' at least once a year, at Easter, but that they should be present at church to hear Mass every Sunday. The rule of annual communion is implied in Margaret Paston's comment on the small parish of Oxnede in Norfolk, of which she says 'It is an easy cure to keep, for there are not more than 20 persons to be houselled yearly'.[19] Devout people would have received communion more frequently, perhaps twelve times a year, or at all the major festivals and certain saint's days. The author of *The Ancrene Riwle* counselled the anchoresses to communicate 15 times a year. 'People think less of a thing which they have often, therefore you shall only receive communion 15 times a year as our lay brothers do ... before all these, be confessed and made clean.'[20]

But Margery had direct instructions from the Lord to receive weekly communion, a custom followed by her fellow-mystics Bridget of Sweden and Dorothea of Prussia.

> **'My dearly-esteemed daughter, you must forsake that which you love most in this world, and that is the eating of meat. Instead of meat you shall eat of my flesh and my blood, the very body of Christ, in the sacrament of the altar. This is my will, daughter, that you should receive my body every Sunday, and I will fill you with such an abundance of grace that all the world will marvel at it.'** [Ch

So Margery prays to approach the altar with tears of devotion.

> **'Lord, as surely as you are not angry with me, grant me a well of tears, so that I may receive your precious body with tears of devotion for your glory and the increase of my merit, for you, Lord, are my joy, my bliss, my comfort and all the treasure I have in this world.'** [Ch 3

The Mass was in Latin, which made it unintelligible to most worshippers and therefore promoted inattention and boredom. A famous Franciscan preacher, Berthold of Regensberg, states in one of his sermons that there are people who find it irksome to stand decently in church for one hour. 'They laugh and chatter as if they were at a fair' But the audience replies that they cannot understand the Mass, and this prevents them from praying as they ought and feeling the devotion that they ought. They can follow the sermon, they say, because it is in their native tongue, but not the Mass. 'We know not what is being sung or read, we cannot comprehend it.'[21] In the fifteenth century, however, the wealthy, as is witnessed in their wills, possessed 'prymers' and were able to follow the lessons in English as the priest read them in Latin. But the average illiterate worshipper would be content to repeat the Pater Noster or the Ave Maria many times during the service.

The elevation of the Host, the lifting up of the consecrated bread, or wafer, was a solemn and impressive part of the service, attention to which was drawn by the ringing of handbells, three times at each consecration. 'The choir had fallen silent, the congregation knelt in silence, and the whole church waited on God. until the chalice was elevated and the consecration complete.' This was followed by prayers for the living and the dead, the celebrant chanting the Our Father, and the choir singing the Agnus Dei while the celebrant and his assistants made their communion, followed by members of the congregation who wished to do so. 'Medieval church services were not designed to edify the congregation: their sole purpose was to offer worship to God, and lay people were encouraged to be present at mass in order to associate themselves with that worship.'[22]

Marriage was not strictly a ecclesiastical sacrament, and not until the eleventh century did matrimonial law come exclusively under the jurisdiction of the church courts. Theologians taught that marriage was the oldest of the sacraments, for it had been instituted from the beginning, when the world was created and when Adam and Eve were given to each other to be helpers, the one to the other, and to multiply and replenish the earth. This natural sacrament was endorsed, spiritualised and sanctified by Jesus in his lofty teaching on marriage, with an emphasis on its divine institution and the importance of fidelity and the permanence of the union. St Paul further spiritualised the idea of Christian marriage and bestowed upon it a mystical meaning in which husband and wife, in the married relationship, constituted an image of the union between Christ and his church, a union requiring love, sacrifice and endurance. But although marriage was extolled as a sacrament of the Church, it did not conform to the standard idea of what constituted a sacrament and to the three requisite conditions involved. These were First, the right matter or substance to be used. For instance water for baptism, and bread and wine for the eucharist; secondly, the correct form, for example the specific words used by Christ with regard to the institution of baptism and the eucharist; and thirdly the intention of carrying out the Church's design and purpose. So marriage was not an ecclesiastical sacrament which the Church could confer, since the ministers were the bride and bridegroom, the officiating priest being merely the chief witness of the couple's intention to become man and wife. The 'form' of the sacrament were the vows which they exchanged, and the sacrament operated through their love, the parties themselves being the only celebrants.

It was not essential to be married in church, except in the countries where it was required by civil law. The simple exchange of a verbal pledge 'I take thee to my wife' (or 'Husband'), followed by cohabitation, was a valid marriage, without a special ceremony or an officiating priest, though a priest could bless such a union. But

The Sacrament of Matrimony. Illustration from 'Parish Life in Medieval England'.

marriages of this sort were 'irregular' and were frowned upon by the Church, the parties being liable to severe punishment if the church courts decided to proceed against them.[23]

In church weddings the vows were taken at the church door, where the officiating priest would question the couple in a manner much as is done today.

Q. N hast thu wille to have this wommon to thi wedded wif.
A. Ye Syr.
Q. May thu well fynde at thi best to love hur and hold ye to hur and to no other to thi lives end.
A. Ye Syr.
Q. Then take hur by yor hande and say after me ...

And here follow the familiar marriage vows.

The author of *Dives and Pauper* exhorts the bride to be suitably arrayed. 'Three ornaments at marriage belongeth principally to the wyfe: a rynge on her finger, a broche on her breste, and a garland on her head. The rynge betokeneth true love; the broche betokeneth clenness of herte and chastity, which she ought to have; the garland betokeneth the gladness and dignity of the sacrament of wedlock.'[24]

We may be sure that Margery Kempe, because of her family's high standing in the town of Bishop's Lynn, and their prominence in church affairs, would have been married in the parish church of St Margaret's, and this probably followed by nuptial Mass, and therefore fully 'solemnised'.In her subsequent meditations she sees the sacrament of marriage as an image of the soul's union with Christ.

When she witnessed weddings, men and women being joined together according to the law of the Church, her mind at once turned to thoughts about our Lady and how she was joined to St Joseph, and how man's soul is spiritually joined to Christ. She prayed that her love and affection might be wholly united to him for ever and that she might be given grace to love and obey him, to be in awe of him, to worship and praise him; and that she might love nothing that he did not love, nor desire anything that he did not desire, and always to be ready, day and night, to fulfil his will without sorrow or complaint, but with gladness of spirit. [Ch 82]

The idea of mystical marriage between the human soul and God, its creator, occurs frequently in the writings of the saints and mystics, but Bernard of Clairvaux warns against applying a too literal interpretation of it. 'Take heed that you bring chaste ears to this discourse of love. When you think of these two lovers, remember always that not a man and a woman are to be thought of, but the Word of God and a soul. And if I speak of Christ and the Church, the sense is the same, except that under the name of the Church is specified, not one soul only, but the united souls of many.'[25]

Regarding the sacrament of Holy Orders, we have seen that Margery Kempe, in her reply to the Abbot's questioning in All Hallow's church Leicester, stated her belief in the validity of the sacrament of the eucharist irrespective of the virtue of the celebrant. This shows her familiarity with a controversy which exercised the minds of theologians as to whether the validity of the sacraments depended on the virtue of the priest who celebrated them, or were they, as Wyclif claimed, invalid if performed by a priest who was in a state of mortal sin. Reason prevailed and it was argued that only God could judge the state of a person's soul, and to some degree all clergy, being human, were sinners. 'It was decided that if the sacraments were performed using the right matter, the right form, and with the right intention, they were efficacious ex opere operato by virtue of their performance.'[26]

There were no such institutions as theological colleges for the training of secular priests, except for a few seminaries privately endowed. There were choir schools attached to some of the cathedrals, where able boys could receive a training and become highly qualified, though these did not normally undertake parish-work. Most ordinands before 1100 were trained by their parish priests, who taught them how to read the Latin service books, how to celebrate the sacraments and conduct public worship and exercise their pastoral duties towards their parishioners. But after 1200 the work of the mendicant orders greatly enhanced the standard of clerical learning, and in the later Middle Ages education was much more widely available, elementary schools being founded in most towns of moderate size, where boys could learn Latin and the rudiments of numeracy.[27]

The sacrament of Holy Unction possessed apostolic authority and was administered in cases of serious sickness, the patient being anointed with oil and prayers said for his recovery, if God so willed. 'Is one of you ill? Let him send for the elders of the church to pray over him and anoint him with oil in the name of the Lord; the prayer offered in faith will heal the sick man, the Lord will restore him to health, and if he has committed sins they will be forgiven' (James 5.14–15).

Every priest was expected to go at once on being called to a sick person at any time of the day or night, but the priest was not to wait for the call; he was to go immediately he heard of anyone's sickness. Before the sick person was anointed with the holy oil, he (or she) was to be questioned, if in a rational state of mind, as to whether he believed the Articles of the faith, whether he repented of his sins, whether he wished to amend and make satisfaction and whether he believed that Christ died for him. Clergy were ordered to avoid negligence in respect of this sacrament and never, without reasonable cause, to sleep outside their parish, and if obliged to do so, to find a suitable substitute, and they were never to ask for or expect any reward for this merciful service.

Margery Kempe recounts how she was anointed with holy oil while suffering from the acute attack of dysentery and not expected to live. She recovered, however, and relates how she witnessed other sick folk being anointed, some of whom died.

Many ill people wished this creature to be with them when they were dying and to pray for them. For although they disliked her weeping and sobbing while they were alive, they wished her to weep and sob when they were dying, and so she did. And when she saw sick folk being anointed, she experienced many holy thoughts and meditations, and if she saw them dying, she imagined she saw our Lord dying. [Ch 72]

Because of the precariousness of human life, the prevalence of disease and the recurrent outbreaks of plague in the fourteenth and fifteenth centuries,medieval folk were continually reminded of the imminence of death, the transience of earthly life and the vanity of riches and beauty. 'No other epoch has laid so much stress as the expiring Middle Ages on the thought of death ... Since the thirteenth century, the popular preaching of the mendicant orders had made the eternal admonition to remember death swell into a sombre chorus ringing throughout the world ... The endless complaint of the frailty of earthly glory was sung to various melodies.'[28] Frescoes adorned the walls of churches showing the Dance of Death in which grimacing skeletons danced with fair ladies, knights, popes, prelates and kings, reminding them of their mortality. Doom paintings depicted Christ in glory separating good souls from bad, angels bearing good souls aloft to the realms of heavenly bliss, demons hurling the wicked into the jaws of hell. From the late fourteenth century onwards cathedrals and churches contained two-tiered tombs, such as that of Archbishop Chichele in Canterbury, portraying on the upper tier a splendidly robed figure in cope and mitre, while underneath on the lower tier, was the shrouded corpse, or in some cases the naked, decomposed body. 'No one can get around it, dearly beloved, the true and eternal happiness of Christians is not here ... Our homeland is paradise, our city the heavenly Jerusalem. We should so strive to live by the spirit and to persist always in good works, so that the day of judgement may find us chaste, temperate merciful and holy,' says Caesarius, Archbishop of Arles.

For the medieval Church there was no clear dividing line between earth and heaven, the saints below and the saints above. The communion of saints covered the whole range of Christian souls on earth, in purgatory and in heaven. Prayers for the dead were a common feature of medieval piety, chantry chapels being built and money paid to priests for the purpose of saying prayers and offering masses for the souls of the departed. It was believed that there were souls so wicked that they went straight to hell, others so virtuous that they went direct to heaven, and between the two regions was the intermediate state of purgatory, where souls, ultimately destined for heaven, were purged of their sins with more or less severity, and for a longer or shorter duration, according to the number and severity of their sins while on earth. It was believed that prayers and masses offered for the souls in purgatory could assist them, and diminish the length of time they remained there and the severity of the pains they suffered. Thus Margery prays for all souls who are suffering pains in purgatory and who are awaiting the prayers of Holy Church and the mercy of God.

Margery herself, because of her holy life, her frequent confessions and penances and the sufferings she endured in this life, was one of those chosen souls who was to by-pass purgatory and go direct to heaven.

> **'I have promised you that you will suffer no other purgatory than the slander of the world ... I have tried you by many tribulations, great sorrows, many grievous sicknesses ... but I have delivered you from them all by my grace ... Daughter, you will be truly welcome to my Father, and my Mother, and to all the saints in heaven, for you have refreshed them many times with the tears of your eyes. Therefore all my holy saints will rejoice at your coming.'** [Ch 22]

The Sacrament of Penance. Illustration from 'Parish Life in Medieval England'.

Woodcut in Wynkyn de Worde's Booklet of Extracts from
THE BOOK OF MARGERY KEMPE.
Also used by William Caxton.

¶ Here begynneth a ſhorte treatyſe of contempla
cyon taught by our lorde Jheſu cryſte/or taken out
of the boke of Margerie kempe of lyn̄.

She deſyred many tymes that her he
de myght be ſmyten of with an axe
vpon a blocke for the loue of our lor
de Jheſu. Thenne ſayd oure lorde
Jheſu in her mynde. I thanke the
doughter that thou woldeſt dye for
my loue/for as often as thou thynkeſt ſo thou ſhalt
haue the ſame mede in heuen/as yf thou ſuffredeſt
the ſame dethe/& yet there ſhall no man ſlee the.
¶ I aſſure þ in thy mynde/yf it were poſſyble me
to ſuffre payne agayne/as I haue done afore/ me
were leuer to ſuffre as moche payne as euer I dyde
for thy ſoule alone/ rather than thou ſholdeſt de-
parte fro me euerlaſtynge.
¶ Doughter thou mayſt no better pleaſe god than
to thynke contynually in his loue. Than ſhe aſked
our lorde Jheſu cryſte/how ſhe ſholde beſt loue him
¶ And our lorde ſayd/haue mynde of thy wycked-
nes and thynke on my goodnes.
¶ Doughter yf thou were the haberyon/or þ here
faſtynge brede & water/& yf þ ſaydeſte euery day
a thouſande pater nr̄. thou ſholde not pleaſe me ſo
well as thou doſt whan þ art in ſcylence/ & ſuffreſt
me to ſpeke in thy ſoule
¶ Doughter for to byd many bedes/it is good to

Page from Wynkyn de Worde's printed Booklet of Extracts from THE BOOK OF MARGERY KEMPE. c1501

Postscript

MARGERY KEMPE'S AMANUENSIS

We have spoken at the end of chapter two of one of the last endeavours of Margery's life, namely the writing of her spiritual memoirs, for which endeavour she was assisted by a local priest. One tantalising question remains: who was this priest, whom Margery never names? She refers to him only as 'the priest who wrote this book'. Various people have been suggested as possible candidates, but to the present writer the most convincing of all is Master Robert Spryngolde, Margery's parish priest. To support this opinion I offer the following reasons.

First, we are told in Margery's *BOOK* that Spryngolde was a learned and well educated man, a bachelor of law and possessing a thorough knowledge of Scripture, and as such he would have been well equipped to undertake a literary work of this kind. His familiarity with Scripture would have enabled him to provide the reader with accurate biblical quotations and to correct or clarify any references to Scripture or to theological works which might have arisen as the work proceeded.

But secondly, not only a well educated man was required for the project, but one who knew Margery personally. This Spryngolde certainly did, for as her parish priest, confessor and counsellor, over a number of years, he would have acquired a keen knowledge of her character, temperament, trials, temptations, sins, weaknesses and, most important of all, her inner spiritual life and her claim to possess visionary and prophetic powers. He probably knew her better than anyone else in her life, and would therefore have been admirably suited to assist and guide her with the writing of her spiritual autobiography.

Thirdly, as a resident in Lynn, probably only a stone's throw from where Margery lived, Spryngolde would have been on the spot and readily available to visit, and spend time with Margery in her home where, we are told, the writing took place over a period of weeks and months. And it is of special importance to learn from the Lynn archives that Robert Spryngolde was still living at the time when Margery's *BOOK* was written.[1]

Who then was better qualified than he, as her parish priest and responsible for the pastoral care of his parishioners, to assist her in this religious and literary enterprise?

But the fourth, and perhaps the most convincing reason for believing that Robert Spryngolde was Margery's amanuensis, is that if we collect together all the references to 'the priest who wrote this book' and place them alongside the references to Spryngolde we shall find that there is a striking similarity between them. This is especially so with respect to their attitude to Margery, and their participation in various incidents which occur in her story. Indeed they are often phrased in precisely the same language, which leads to the conclusion that Margery's parish priest, Robert Springolde and 'the priest who wrote this book' are one and the same person. A few examples will make this clear.

We have seen how Margery complains to the Dominican friar that her confessor, parish priest of St Margaret's, is sharp with her and will not believe her revelations and feelings, but makes light of them. We read also of 'the priest who wrote this book' that he questions her about her feelings, prophecies and revelations and orders her to pray about certain matters, otherwise he will not write the book for her. So she complies with what he asks and 'yet he would not always give credence to her words' (ch 24). Both Spryngolde, then, and 'the priest who wrote this book' are doubtful as to the authenticity of Margery's revelations, strongly indicating that we may identify them as the same person.

Despite Spryngolde's reluctance to believe her feelings and revelations Margery several times expresses her great affection for him and says she tells us that she has a great affection for 'the priest who wrote this book' suggesting that Spryngolde is in fact 'the priest who wrote this book'.

In parenthesis we should note that, by various incidents that occur, and by various signs that testify to the fact, both Master Robert and 'the priest who wrote this book' are eventually convinced of the validity and authenticity of Margery's feelings and revelations and believe her to be the genuine recipient of divine disclosures. Indeed they grow to value her judgements, and ask her advice on various matters and regret the occasions when they fail to take her advice, again suggesting that the two men are one and the same person.

We have described in chapter three how the parishioners of St Nicholas' Chapel request a font to be installed in their place of worship and for permission to be granted for marriages and churchings to be conducted there. In this incident 'the priest who wrote this book' plays a vital role. He seeks the opinion of Margery as to whether the privileges which the parishioners desire will be granted to them. Margery replies that she knows by revelation that even if they pay 'a bushel of nobles' they will not obtain what they ask. Since this matter is of special importance and concern to the parish priest of St Margaret's church, the mother church of the group of three, we may reasonably conclude that 'the priest who wrote this book' is none other than Master Robert Spryngolde, the parish priest of St Margaret's Church in Lynn.

Notes

Introduction

1. *THE BOOK OF MARGERY KEMPE.* Introduction. Ed. S. B. Meech and H. E. Allen. Early English Text Society. No. 212. 1940/1982.
2. *Margery Kempe.* Edmund Colledge. Pre-Reformation English Spirituality. Ed. J. Walsh. London 1965.
3. *The Waning of the Middle Ages.* Ch 1. Johan Huizinga. London 1924/85.
4. *Margery Kempe.* Edmund Colledge. Op cit.
5. *The Ladder of Perfection.* Bk. I. Ch 49. Walter Hilton. Tr. Leo Sherley-Price. (London 1957/88).
6. Ibid. Ch 18.
7. *The Prickynge of Love.* Ed. H. Kane. P. 20. Salzburg 1983.
8. *The Cloud of Unknowing.* Ch 75. Tr. Clifton Wolters. 1963/71.
9. *The Middle English Mystics.* Ch 1. Wolfgang Riehle. London 1981. (present author's modernisation).
10. *The Ancrene Riwle.* Tr. Mary B. Salu. London 1955.
11. For a selection of the revelations see *The Revelations of St Birgitta.* W. P. Cumming. Early English Text Society. No. 178. Oxford 1929.
12. *Beguine Spirituality.* Fiona Bowie. London 1989. See also *The Book of Margery Kempe.* Introduction. Barry Windeatt. London 1985.
13. *Penguin Dictionary of Saints.* Donald Attwater. London 1965.
14. *The Book of Divine Consolations.* Angela of Foligno. Tr. Mary Steegman. London 1908, and *Angela of Foligno, Complete Works.* Tr. Paul Lachance. New Jersey. U.S.A. 1993.
15. *Beguine Spirituality.* Part II. Fiona Bowie. London 1989.
16. *The Life of the Servant.* Ch 33. Henry Suso. Tr. James M. Clark. Cambridge 1952/1982.
17. *The Life, Letters and Sermons of Bishop Herbert de Losinga.* Edward Gouldburn and Henry Symonds. Oxford 1878.

Chapter One

1. *The Ancrene Riwle.* Part I. Tr. Mary B. Salu. London 1955. See also *Ancrene Wisse.* Tr. Hugh White. Penguin. 1993.
2. *The Book of Divine Consolation* Trans. Mary Steegman (author's modernisation) Second Vision.
3. *Ancrene Wisse.* Part 1. Tr. Hugh White. Penguin 1993.
4. *Mystics of the Church.* Ch 4. Evelyn Underhill. Cambridge 1925/1975.
5. Ibid Ch 7.
6. *English Spirituality.* Margery Kempe. Martin Thornton. London 1963.
7. *Margery Kempe,* Ch 1. Martin Thornton. London 1960.
8. *The Revelations of St Birgitta.* Ch 4. Anthony Butkovich. California 1972.
9. *Little Flowers of St Francis.* Ch 2. London 1941.
10. *A History of the Franciscan Order.* Ch 39. John Moorman Oxford 1968.

11. *The Waning of the Middle Ages*. Ch 1. London 1924/85.
12. *The Life of the Servant*. Ch 20. Henry Suso. Tr. James M. Clark. Cambridge 1952/82.
13. *Life of St Francis*. Ch 2. St Bonaventure. Everyman's Library. 1941.
14. cf. 'I have inscribed you on the palms of my hands' (Isaiah 49.16). See also *Ancrene Wisse*. 'I have,' he says, 'painted you in my hands.' He does this with his red blood on the cross. Part 7. P. 182.
15. *The Ancrene Riwle*. Part 4. Tr. M. B. Salu. London 1955.
16. *The Goad of Love*. Ch 32. Clare Kirchberger. London 1952.
17. *The Revelations of St Birgitta*. Ed. W. P. Cumming. E.E.T.S. 1929.
18. *Medieval Women Writers*. Introduction. Katharina Wilson. Manchester 1984.
19. *The Fire of Love*. Ch 15. Richard Rolle. Penguin Classics 1971.
20. *The Fire of Love*. Richard Rolle. Ch 15 & Prologue Penguin Classics 1971.
21. Cf. the fire of Pentecost, 'there appeared to them flames like tongues of fire ... coming to rest on each one. They were all filled with the Holy Spirit.' Acts 2. 3–4.
22. 'Scripture speaks of things beyond our seeing, things beyond our hearing, things beyond our imagining, all prepared by God for those who love him.' 1 Cor. 2.9.

Chapter Two

1. *THE BOOK OF MARGERY KEMPE*. Ed. Sandford Brown Meech and Hope Emily Allen. Appendix III. (Early English Text Society. No 212. Oxford 1940/82).
2. Ibid.
3. *THE BOOK OF MARGERY KEMPE*. Introduction. Table of Events. (EETS).
4. *Women in Medieval Life*. Ch 2. Margaret Wade Labage. London 1986.
5. *Constitutions of Archbishop Reynold* (1322). Parish Life in Medieval England. Ch 9. F. A. Gasquet. London 1906.
6. *English Costume*. Ch 3. Doreen Yarwood. London 1952.
7. Ibid.
8. *Preaching in Medieval England*. Part Two. Ch 4. G. R. Owst. Cambrige 1926. (present author's translation).
9. *Fire Of Love*. Ch 39. Richard Rolle. Tran. Clifton Wolters. London 1972.
10. *The Treasure of the City of Ladies*. Part III. Ch 3. Christine de Pisan. Tr. Sarah Lawson. London 1985.
11. *Medieval Women*. Ch 3. Eileen Power. Ed. M. M. Postan. Cambridge 1975.
12. *Mystics of the Church*. Ch 5. Evelyn Underhill, Cambridge 1925/75.
13. *THE BOOK OF MARGERY KEMPE*. Introduction. Table of Events. (EETS).
14. *The English Medieval Town*. Ch 4. Colin Platt. London 1976.
15. *Angela of Foligno*. Book of Divine Revelations. First Treatise. Tr. Mary Steegman. London 1909.
16. *The Pastons and Their England*. Ch 6. H. S. Bennett. Cambridge 1922/1990.
17. *Medieval Women*. Ch 3. Eileen Power. Cambridge 1975.

18. *The Pastons and Their England.* Ch 6. H. S. Bennett.
19. *Margery Kempe and the English Devotional Tradition.* Susan Dickman. *The Medieval English Tradition.* Ed. Marion Glasscoe. Exeter 1980.
20. *THE BOOK OF MARGERY KEMPE.* Appendix III. (EETS).
21. *Margery Kempe and Wynkyn de Worde.* Sue Holbrook. *The Medieval Tradition in England.* Ed. Marion Glascoe. Cambridge 1987.
22. *THE BOOK OF MARGERY KEMPE.* Introduction. (EETS).

Chapter Three

1. *The Making of King's Lynn.* Introduction. Vanessa Parker. Phillimore 1977.
2. *Victoria County History.* Norfolk. Vol II and *The Making of King's Lynn.* Charter 2 Dorothy Owen. O.U.P. 1984.
3. *The Making of King's Lynn.* Introduction. Dorothy Owen.
4. *The Pastons and Their England.* Ch 5. H. S. Bennett. Cambridge 1922/1990.
5. *Thomas Arundel.* Ch 6 Margaret Aston, Oxford 1967.
6. Ibid.
7. *The Great Ouse.* Ch 2 Dorothy Summers. Newton Abbot 1973.
8. *History of the Borough of King's Lynn.* Ch 54. H. J. Hillen. Norwich 1907.
9. *Deeds and Records of King's Lynn.* p. 28 H. Harrod. King's Lynn 1874.
10. *The Making of King's Lynn.* Introduction. Dorothy Owen.
11. *The English Town.* Ch 3 Colin Platt. London 1976.
12. *The Medieval Town.* 1200–1540. Introduction. Ed. Richard Holt & Gervase Rosser. London 1990.
13. *The Pastons and Their England.* Ch 10. H. S. Bennett.
14. *Victoria County History.* Norfolk. Vol. II.
15. *Our Borough, Our Churches: King's Lynn.* p. 107 E. M. Beloe. Cambridge 1899.
16. *The Making of King's Lynn.* Document 109. Dorothy Owen.
17. *Parish Life in Medieval England.* Ch 3 F. A. Gasquet. London 1906.
18. *THE BOOK OF MARGERY KEMPE* (EETS) Appendix VII. and *Our borough, Our Churches: King's Lynn.* E. M. Beloe.
19. *Thomas Arundel* Ch 6 Margaret Aston. Oxford 1967.
20. *Anchorites and Their Patrons in Medieval England.* Ch 3. Ann Warren, California Press 1985.
21. Ibid. Ann Warren.
22. *English Wayfaring Life in the Middle Ages.* Ch 2. J. J. Jusserand. London 1889/1961.
23. *The Pastons and Their England.* Ch 10. H. S. Bennett.
24. *Deeds and Records of the Borough of King's Lynn.* p. 30 H. Harrod. King's Lynn 1874.
25. *The Making of King's Lynn.* Introduction. Dorothy Owen.

Chapter Four

1. *The Canterbury Tales.* Prologue. Geoffrey Chaucer. Tr. Nevill Coghill. London 1951.
2. See Matt. 10.28 & John 6.26–27.

3. *The Later Middle Ages.* Ch 3. George Holmes. London 1962/70.
4. *The English Church in the Fourteenth Century.* Ch 2. W. A. Pantin Cambridge 1955.
5. *English Life in the Later Middle Ages.* Annie Abram. London 1913.
6. See *The English Church in the Fourteenth Century.* Ch 2. W. A. Pantin; *The Later Middle Ages.* Ch 3. George Holmes. London 1962/70; *Religion in the West.* Ch 7. Bernard Hamilton. London 1990; *England in the Late Middle Ages.* Ch 4. A. R. Myers. London 1953.
7. Pantin. Op. Cit.
8. *The Church and Society in Late Medieval England.* R. N. Swanson. Oxford 1989.
9. *Medieval English Lyrics.* No. 61. Ed. R. T. Davies. London 1963.
10. *The Religious Orders in England.* Ch 10. Vol II. David Knowles.
11. *Thomas Arundel.* Margaret Aston. Oxford 1967.
12. Ibid.
13. *Six Medieval Men and Women.* H. S. Bennett. Cambridge 1955.
14. *Archbishop Henry Chichele.* Ch 2. E. F. Jacob. London 1967.
15. Ibid. Ch 8.
16. *The Religious Orders in England.* Vol II. Ch 10. Dom David Knowles.
17. *The Pre-Reformation Church in England.* Ch 7. C. Harper-Bill. London 1989/91.
18. Ibid.
19. *Parish Priests and Their People in the Middle Ages in England.* Ch 31. E. L. Cutts.
20. Ibid. E. L. Cutts.

Chapter Five

1. *Western Society and the Church in the Middle Ages.* Ch 6. R. W. Southern. London 1970/79.
2. Ibid.
3. *A Study of the Rule of St Augustine.* St Mary's Press. Wantage. 1952.
4. *Visitations of the Diocese of Norwich 1492–1532.* Edit. Augustus Jessopp. Camden Society. 1888.
5. *Medieval People.* Ch 4. Eileen Power. London 1924.
6. Ibid.
7. *England in the Late Middle Ages.* Ch 4. A. R. Myers.
8. *Five Centuries of Religion.* Vol I. G. G. Coulton C. U. P. 1923.
9. *Western Society and the Church in the Middle Ages.* Ch 6. R. W. Southern.
10. *Scenes and Characters of the Middle Ages.* E. L. Cutts. London 1922.
11. R. W. Southern. Op. Cit.
12. *The English Church in the Fourteenth and Fifteenth Centuries.* Ch 14. W. W. Capes. London 1900.
13. *Visitations of the Diocese of Norwich.* R. A. Jessopp.
14. R. W. Southern. Op. Cit.
15. *St John of Bridlington.* J. S. Purvis. Journal of the Bridlington Augustinian Society. 1924.
16. *The Medieval Monasteries of Great Britain.* Ch 7. Lionel Butler and Chris Given-Wilson. London 1979.

17. *Mirror of the Blessed Life of Jesus Christ*. Nicholas Love. Edit Laurence Powell. Oxford 1908.
18. *Mystic and Pilgrim*. Clarissa Atkinson. Ch 5. Cornell University Press 1983.
19. *Penguin Dictionary of Saints*. Donald Attwater. Penguin 1965 and *The Medieval Monasteries of Great Britain*. Butler & Given-Wilson.
20. *The Religious Orders in England*. Vol II. Ch 13. David Knowles. C.U.P. 1955.
21. *THE BOOK OF MARGERY KEMPE* (EETS) Note p. 245/31.
22. *The Myroure of Oure Ladye*. Edit J. H. Blunt. (EETS) 1923 (present author's translation).

Chapter Six

1. *The Franciscans in England*. Ch 3. J. R. H. Moorman. London 1974/1982.
2. *England in the Later Middle Ages*. Ch 4. A. R. Myers. London 1953.
3. *Western Society in the Middle Ages*. Ch 6. R. W. Southern. London 1970/79.
4. *Our Borough, Our Churches: King's Lynn*. E. M. Beloe. Cambridge 1899.
5. R. W. Southern. Ch 6. Op. cit.
6. Friar Brackley was an intimate friend, tutor, adviser and chaplain to the Paston family and was still writing letters in 1460.
7. *Revelations of Divine Love*. Ch 60. Julian of Norwich. London 1966.
8. *The Ancrene Riwle*. Part 4. Tr Mary. B. Salu. London 1955.
9. *The Religious Orders in England*. Vol II. Ch 10. David Knowles.
10. *William Flete*. Benedict Hackett, in Pre-Reformation English Spirituality. Ed. James Walsh. London 1965.
11. Ibid. Benedict Hackett. See also *William Flete and the De Remediis Contra Temptaciones in Medieval Studies* presented to Aubrey Gwynn SJ. Dublin 1961, and *The English Austin Friars in the Time of Wyclif*. Aubrey Gwynn SJ. Oxford 1940.
12. R. W. Southern. Ch 6. Op. cit.
13. *Mirror of Perfection*. Ch 69. Everyman Library. 1941.
14. Op. Cit. Ch 4.
15. *John Wyclif's Select English Works*. Ed. Thomas Arnold. Vol 111. 1869.

Chapter Seven

1. *The Ancrene Riwle*. Part VII. Tr Mary. B. Salu. London.
2. *Hali Meidhad*. Introduction. Bella Millett. (EETS No. 248) Oxford 1982.
3. *The Ladder of Perfection*. Ch 62. Bk I. Walter Hilton. London 1957/1988.
4. *Holy Maidenhood* adapted from *Hali Meidhad*. *Women's Lives in Medieval Europe*. Part II. Ed. Emilie Amt. London 1993.
5. *Women's Lives in Medieval Europe*. Part II Ed. Emilie Amt. London 1993.
6. *The Revelations of St Birgitta*. Ed. W. P. Cumming. (EETS No. 178) (present author's translation).
7. *Fenland Notes and Queries*. Vol I. 1889–1891. The 'mantle' was usually of a plain russet or grey colour, the colour of a poor labourer, denoting poverty and humility.

Chapter Eight

1. *Pilgrimage*. Ch 5. Jonathan Sumption. London 1975.
2. *Medieval Pilgrims*. Introduction. Alan Kendall 1965.
3. *Imitation of Christ*. Bk 4. Ch 1. tr. Betty Knott. London 1965.
4. *Medieval Roads*. Chs 1 & 5. Brian Hindle. Shire Publications. 1982.
5. *The Pastons and Their England*. Ch 10. H. S. Bennett.
6. *Relics and Shrines*. Ch 4. David Sox. London.
7. *The Folklore of East Anglia*. Ch 6. Enid Porter. London 1974. *Pilgrim Life in the Middle Ages*. Ch 6. Sydney Heath. Kennicat Press 1971.
8. *Canterbury Tales*. Chaucer. Tr. Nevill Coghill. Penguin 1971. *Piers the Ploughman*. Tr. J. F. Goodridge. Penguin 1959.
9. *The High Middle Ages*. Ch 7. Trevor Rowley. London 1986.
10. *Victoria County History*. Norfolk. Vol. II. p. 321–2.
11. *Pilgrimage*. Ch 10. Jonathan Sumption. London 1975.
12. *Thomas Becket*. Dorothy Mills. Friends of Canterbury. 1960.
13. *THE BOOK OF MARGERY KEMPE*. Note 110/33–4 (EETS); *Pilgrim Life in the Middle Ages*. Sydney Heath. Ch 6. Kennicat Press 1971; *Medieval Monasteries of Great Britain*. p. 258 Lionet Butler & Chris Given-Wilson. London 1979.
14. *The Religious Order in England*. Vol II. Ch 14. David Knowles.
15. Sydney Heath. Op. Cit.
16. *Oxford Dictionary of Saints*. David Hugh Farmer. Oxford 1980; *Penguin Dictionary of Saints*. Donald Attwater. London 1965.
17. *The Book of the Wanderings of Brother Felix Fabri*. Tr. A. Stewart. (Palestine Pilgrims Text Society. 1887–97).
18. *Jerusalem Journey*. Ch 2. H. F. M. Prescott. London 1954.
19. *THE BOOK OF MARGERY KEMPE*. (EETS) Note 60/18–19.
20. *The English Church in the Fourteenth Century*. Ch 8. W. A. Pantin. Cambridge 1955.
21. *Medieval Pilgrimage*. Ch 11. Alan Kendal. Wayland Press.
22. *THE BOOK OF MARGERY KEMPE*. Note 232/10–11 (EETS).
23. *Pilgrimage Jonathan Sumption*. Ch 15. London 1975; *Relics and Shrines*. Ch 4. David Sox. London 1985.

Chapter Nine

1. *England in the Age of Chaucer*. Ch 7. William Woods. London 1976.
2. *The Fourteenth Century*. Ch 16. May McKisack. Oxford 1957/76.
3. *John Wyclif and the Beginning of English Non-Conformity*. Ch. 3. K. B. McFarlane. London 1952/72; See also *The English Austin Friars in the Time of Wyclif*. Part II. Ch 4. Aubrey Gwynn. Oxford 1940.
4. *The Evangelical Doctor*. Ch 10. Douglas Wood. London 1984.
5. *The English Church in the Fourteenth and Fifteenth Centuries*. Ch 13. W. W. Capes. London 1900.
6. Quoted from *The People's Faith in the Time of Wyclif*. Ch 3. Bernard Manning. See also Margaret Aston's chapter on images. *Lollards and Reformers*. Ch 5. Hambledon Press 1984.
7. May McKisack. Ch 16.

8. *Heresy Trials in the Diocese of Norwich 1428–31.* Introduction. Norman Tanner. (R. H. S. London University. 1977).
9. *The Pre-Reformation Church in England.* Ch 7. Christopher Harper-Bill. London 1989/91.
10. Ibid.
11. *William Courtenay.* Ch 7. Joseph Dahmus.Pennsylvania 1966.
12. *History of the Borough of King's Lynn.* Ch 14. H. J. Hillen; *Foxe's Book of Martyres.* Ch 2. Ed. G. A. Williamson. London 1965; *John Wyclif and the Beginnings of English Non-Conformity.* Ch 5. McFarlane.
13. K. B. McFarlane. Ch 6.
14. 'As early as Alnwick's investigations, knowledge of the elements of religion, the Pater noster, Ave Maria, or creed in English, or the ability to recite from memory passages from the bible was regarded as evidence of heresy.' *The Premature Reformation.* Ch 3. Ann Hudson. Clarendon 1988.
15. *Margery Kempe.* Edmund Colledge, in Pre-Reformation English Spirituality. Ed. J. Walsh. London 1965.

Chapter Ten

1. *Margery Kempe.* Edmund Colledge. Pre-Reformation English Spirituality. Ed. J. Walsh.
2. *Instructions for Parish Priests.* John Mirk. Ed. E. Peacock. (EETS Ex Ser 19).
3. *Oxford Dictionary of Saints.* David Hugh Farmer. Oxford 1978/80.
4. Ibid.
5. *Myroure of Our Ladye.* Ed. J. Blunt. (EETS Ex Ser 19).
6. *Revelations of St Bridget of Sweden.* Part VIII. Ch 21.
7. *Meditations on the Life of Christ.* 14th cent Manuscript. Ed & Tr L. Ragusa & R. B. Green (Princeton 1961).
8. *The Fire of Love.* Ch 27. Richard Rolle.
9. *Everyman and Medieval Miracle Plays.* The Crucifixion. Ed. A. C. Cawley. London 1960.
10. *The Pre-Reformation English Church.* Ch 7. C. Harper-Bill. London 1989.
11. *Revelations of Divine Love.* Julian of Norwich. Ch 67.
12. *The People's Faith in the Time of Wyclif.* Ch 3. Bernard Manning, Cambridge. 1919/1975.
13. *Ladder of Perfection.* Bk. II. Ch 6. Walter Hilton. London 1955/1988.
14. *Religion in the Medieval West.* Ch 12. Bernard Hamilton. London 1986/90.
15. *Religion in the Medieval West.* Ch 12. Bernard Hamilton.
16. *The People's Faith in the Time of Wyclif.* Ch 3. Bernard Manning.
17. *Christianity in the West.* Ch 3. John Bossy. Oxford 1985.
18. *The Revelations of St Birgitta.* Ed. W. P. Cumming. (EETS O.S. 178).
19. *The Pastons and Their England.* Ch 15.
20. *The Ancrene Riwle.* Part 8. Tr. Mary. B. Salu.
21. *Medieval Panorama.* Ch 16. G. G. Coulton. Cambridge 1949.
22. *Religion in the Medieval West.* Ch 5. Bernard Hamilton. London 1986/1990.
23. *Medieval Panorama.* Ch 46. G. G. Coulton. Cambridge 1949; and *Religion in the Medieval West.* Ch 12. Bernard Hamilton. London 1986/1990.

24. Quoted in *Parish Life in Medieval England*. Ch 9. F. A. Gasquet. London 1906.
25. *Mysticism*. Ch 4. Michael Cox. London 1983.
26. *Religion in the Medieval West*. Ch 4. Bernard Hamilton.
27. Ibid. Ch 7.
28. *The Waning of the Middle Ages*. Ch 11. J. Huizinga. London 1924/1985.

Postscript

1. *THE BOOK OF MARGERY KEMPE*. Appendix IV. (EETS)

Further Reading

The Book of Margery Kempe

Butler-Bowden, W. *The Book of Margery Kempe.* (Oxford 1954).

Meech, S. B. & Allen, H. E. *The Book of Margery Kempe* (Early English Text Society. No. 212. 1940/1982).

Windeatt, W. *The Book of Margery Kempe.* (Penguin Classics 1985).

Margery Kempe – General

Atkinson, C. W. *Mystic and Pilgrim.* (Cornell 1983).

Colledge, E. *Margery Kempe.* Pre-Reformation English Spirituality. Ed. J. Walsh (London 1965).

Collis, L. *Apprentice Saint.* (London 1964).

Maisonneuve, R. *Margery Kempe and the Eastern and Western Tradition of the 'perfect fool'.* In the Medieval mystical Tradition in England. Ed. M. Glasscoe. (Exeter, 1982).

Thornton, M. *Margery Kempe: An Example in English Pastoral Tradition.* (London 1960).

Wilson, K. *Medieval Women Writers.* (Manchester 1984).

Medieval Mystics

Aelred of Rievaulx, *The Mirror of Charity.* Tr. G. Webb & A. Walker. (London 1962).

J. Ancelet-Hustache. *Elizabeth of Hungary.* (London 1963).

Angela of Foligno. *Complete Works.* Paul Lachance. (Paulist Press 1993); *Book of Divine Consolations.* Tr. Mary Steegman. (London 1909).

Bernard of Clairvaux. *On Loving God* (Cistercian Publications 1980); *On the Song of Songs.* (Cistercian Publications 1980).

Bowie, Fiona. *Beguine Spirituality.* (London 1989).

Francis of Assisi. *Life*; *Little Flowers*; *Mirror of Perfection.* Thomas Okey (London 1941).

Hilton, Walter. *Ladder of Perfection.* Tr. Leo Sherley-Price (London 1988).

J. Jorgensen. *Bridget of Sweden.* (London 1954); *Revelations.* W. P. Cumming. (E.E.T.S. No. 178. 1929).

Julian of Norwich. *Revelations of Divine Love.* Tr. C. Wolters. (London 1966).

Mechthild of Magdeburg. *Revelations.* Tr. Lucy Menzies. (London 1953).

Porete, Marguerite. *A Mirror for Simple Souls.* Tr. Charles Crawford. (Dublin 1981).

Rolle, Richard *Fire of Love.* Tr. C. Wolters. (London 1972).

Stimulus Amoris. *The Goad of Love.* C. Kirchberger. (London 1952); *The Prickynge of Love.* H. Kane (Salzburg 1983).

Wolters, C. (Tr). *Cloud of Unknowing, The.* (London 1973).

Mysticism and Spirituality

Dronke, P. *Women Writers of the Middle Ages.* (Cambridge 1984).

Jones, R. *Studies in Mystical Religion.* (London 1909).

Knowles, D. *The English Mystical Tradition.* (London 1961).

Matarasso, Pauline. *The Cistercian World.* (Penguin Classics 1993).

Northcott, H. *The Venture of Prayer.* (London 1951).

Petroff, E. A. *Medieval Women's Visionary Literature* (Oxford 1986).

Riehle, W. *The Middle English Mystics.* (London 1981).

Underhill, E. *Mysticism.* (London 1941/1993); *Mystics of the Church.* (Cambridge 1925/1975).

Walsh, J. (Ed). *Spirituality through the Centuries.* (London 1966); *Pre-Reformation English Spirituality.* (London 1965).

White, H. *The Ancrene Wisse – Guide for Anchoresses.* (Penguin Classics 1993).

Windeatt, B. *English Mystics of the Middle Ages.* (Cambridge 1994).

Ecclesiastical History

Aston, M. *Thomas Arundel.* (Oxford 1967); *Lollards and Reformers.* (Hambledon Press 1984).

Brooke, R&C. *Popular Religion in the Middle Ages.* (London 1984).

Cook. G. H. *English Monasteries in the Middle Ages.* (London 1961).

Dawson, C. *Medieval Religion.* (London 1935).

Deanesly, M. *The Lollard Bible.* (Cambridge 1920).

Gasquet, F. A. *Parish Life in Medieval England.* (London 1906).

Hamilton, B. *Religion in the Medieval West.* (London 1986).

Harper-Bill, C. *The Pre-Reformation English Church.* (London 1989).

Hudson, A. *The Premature Reformation.* (Oxford 1988).

Jacob, E. F. *Archbishop Chichele.* (London 1967).

Knowles, D. *The Religious Orders in England.* (Cambridge 1957).

Lambert, M. *Medieval Heresy.* (London 1977).

McFarlane, K. B. *John Wycliffe and the Beginnings of English Non-conformity.* (London 1952).

Moorman, J. *A History of the Franciscan Movement.* (Oxford 1968).

Owst, G. R. *Preaching in Medieval England.* (Cambridge 1926).

Pantin, W. A. *The English Church in the Fourteenth Century.* (Cambridge 1955).

Platt, C. *Abbeys and Priories in Medieval England.* (London 1984).

Southern, R. *Western Society and the Church in the Middle Ages.* (London 1970).

The Middle Ages – General

Anderson, M. D. *History and Imagery in British Churches.* (London 1971).

Bennett, H. S. *The Pastons and Their England.* (Cambridge 1922/1990).

Dyer, C. *Standards of Living in the Late Middle Ages.* (Cambridge 1989).

Holmes, G. *The Later Middle Ages.* (London 1962).

Holt, R. & Rosser, G. (Ed.) *The Medieval Town.* (London 1990).

Huizinga, J. *The Waning of the Middle Ages.* (London 1924/1985).

Jusserand, J. J. *English Wayfaring Life in the Middle Ages.* (London 1889/1961).

Lucus, A. M. *Women in the Middle Ages.* (Brighton 1983).

Platt, C. *The English Medieval Town.* (London 1976).

Sumption, J. *Pilgrimage.* (London 1975).

Westlake, H. F. *The Parish Guilds of Medieval England.* (London 1919).

Wood, M. *The English Medieval House.* (London 1965/1990).

Ziegler, P. *The Black Death.* (London 1969/1982).

Verse

Davies, R. T. *Medieval English Lyrics.* (London 1963).

Hartford, D. *Richard of Caister and his Metrical Prayer.* (Norfolk and Norwich Arch Soc. XVII 1908).

Stone, Brian. *Medieval English Verse.* (London 1964).

Woolf, R. *The English Religious Lyric in the Middle Ages.* (Oxford 1968).

King's Lynn

Beloe, E. M. *Our Borough, Our Churches: King's Lynn.* (Cambridge 1899).

Harrod, H. *Deeds and Records of the Borough of King's Lynn.* (King's Lynn 1874).

Hillen, H. J. *History of the Borough of King's Lynn.* (Norwich 1907).

Owen, D. *The Making of King's Lynn.* (Oxford 1984).

Parker, V. *The Making of King's Lynn.* (London 1977).

Richards, P. *King's Lynn.* (Phillimore 1990).

Index